ARGUMENTS IN HISTORY
Britain in the Nineteenth Century

By the same author

STUDIES IN BRITISH GOVERNMENT
(*Macmillan*)

With E. E. Reynolds

BRITAIN IN THE TWENTIETH CENTURY 1900–1964
(*Cambridge University Press*)

Arguments
IN HISTORY

Britain
in
the
Nineteenth
Century

N. H. Brasher

Senior History Master, Bexley Grammar School

MACMILLAN
London · Melbourne · Toronto
ST MARTIN'S PRESS
New York
1968

Published by
MACMILLAN & CO LTD
Little Essex Street London W C 2
and also at Bombay Calcutta and Madras
Macmillan South Africa (Publishers) Pty Ltd Johannesburg
The Macmillan Company of Australia Pty Ltd Melbourne
The Macmillan Company of Canada Ltd Toronto
St Martin's Press Inc New York

Library of Congress catalog card no. 68–10753

Printed in Great Britain by
Richard Clay (The Chaucer Press) Ltd, Bungay, Suffolk

CONTENTS

LIST OF PLATES

The painting of Queen Victoria and the Prince Consort by Landseer is reproduced by gracious permission of Her Majesty the Queen. The seven cartoons are reproduced by courtesy of the Trustees of the British Museum, and the seven portraits by courtesy of the Trustees of the National Portrait Gallery, London.

PREFACE

Professor C. H. Wilson in his inaugural lecture as Professor of Modern History at Cambridge University drew attention to the fact that modern historians are much less optimistic than their predecessors about the prospects of writing definitive history. Greater specialisation has created more, not less, uncertainty in our knowledge of the past. The definitive conception of history has emerged 'both bloody and bowed'.[1] Dr G. Kitson Clark in his admirable survey of Victorian England expresses a similar opinion. In a chapter significantly entitled 'The Task of Revision' he writes that, 'The account of the past which satisfies a particular generation must be regarded as a working hypothesis, no more'.[2] History must edge its way forward, footnote by footnote, towards greater accuracy of statement, or so it is hoped. It is a process of endless argument and it is upon this conviction that the present book is based. Some of the arguments spring from the opposing opinions of contemporaries; some from the conflicting judgments of historians; some, more fallibly, from my own judgment of the way in which strongly divergent impressions may be formed of the same characters and events; all are designed to involve the reader's judgment as closely as possible in the issues discussed.

Each chapter, therefore, is devoted to a single arguable theme. Each contains an introductory section designed to put into its context the character or problem being discussed. The remainder of the chapter is divided into two sections described simply as 'Attack' and 'Defence'; these contain opposing assessments of the policies, character, or theme under examination. These assessments are as strongly contrasted as possible

[1] C. H. Wilson, *History in Special and in General* (London: Cambridge University Press, 1964), p. 5.

[2] G. Kitson Clark, *The Making of Victorian England* (London: Methuen, 1962), p. 1.

in order to stimulate thought and argument. At the same time the aim has been to avoid advancing any opinion which cannot reasonably be deduced from the facts. No attempt has been made to sum up the arguments since this would have defeated the purpose of the book. The reader himself must be the judge, sifting the evidence, and adapting the arguments given in accordance with his own judgment. When the book is used for group work, in schools and elsewhere, it will be easy to use the individual chapters as a basis for discussion or debate. Once interest is aroused it is likely that the student will wish to consult the many excellent books there are on the subjects discussed; to assist him a bibliography is given at the end of the book. It will be evident to those already familiar with the books mentioned that the list serves also as the author's debt of gratitude for many of the ideas contained in the text.

It would be impossible to thank individually all those who in different ways have contributed to the writing and publication of this book, but this in no way diminishes my gratitude for a wealth of valuable advice and support. One debt of specific thanks must be paid, however. The cheerful skill with which my wife has managed home, children, and typewriter has been a constant help and has tremendously lightened the task of writing.

1. LORD LIVERPOOL
ARCH-MEDIOCRITY?

Prelude

Robert Banks Jenkinson, later to be second Earl of Liverpool and Prime Minister of Britain, was born on 7 June 1770. His father, Charles Jenkinson, was a well-known politician and a gifted administrator who held several governmental posts during his career, though he never attained Cabinet rank. Both Charles Jenkinson and his wife were members of younger branches of county families and lacked private fortunes of their own, but the circumstances of eighteenth-century political life made the holding of governmental posts a profitable business and the Jenkinson family was never hampered by lack of money. Charles, like his son, had an aptitude for winning the goodwill of those in authority, a characteristic which earned for him the liking of George III and a measure of dislike from less adaptable politicians.

Soon after Robert's birth his mother died, and though Charles Jenkinson later married again the strongest influence in Robert's upbringing was that of his father. Charles Jenkinson showed a kindliness towards his son which could not always be taken for granted in an age when fathers were apt to be more rumbustious and overbearing than is the fashion now. Even more exceptionally, Robert, as he grew up, showed no sign of any disagreement with his father's political outlook. It is natural enough for the young to challenge the attitudes of middle age, but this was not the feeling of Robert Jenkinson. The radicalism which influenced Canning and even Castlereagh in their youth made no impact on him. From his early days he was as staunch a Tory as his father.

His education was conventional. He attended Charterhouse from 1783 to 1787, and then proceeded to Christ Church, Oxford, where he was a close friend of Canning, and went down in 1789. He gave no evidence of academic brilliance but he did take a keen interest in political discussion, to such an extent that both he and his tutor began to feel that his studies were suffering as a result. His tour of Italy and France which followed his departure from Oxford coincided with the outbreak of the French Revolution. He witnessed the storming of the Bastille and acquired a marked contempt for the Revolutionary mob and for the weakness of a government which allowed such disorders to take place. Returning to England he became M.P. for Rye in 1790 and, not unexpectedly, a loyal supporter of Pitt. There was one matter, however, revealing a characteristic mental approach, on which he differed from his leader, namely the abolition of the slave trade. His opinion was that legislation was unnecessary. If slaves were treated with greater humanity they would eventually produce children in sufficient numbers to make it unnecessary to import slaves from elsewhere. It was an opinion which perhaps symbolises the thinking of Robert Jenkinson on social reforms. He was far from being an emotional Tory, incapable of justifying opposition to change with specific arguments. On the other hand his support of the existing order was exasperating to those who could see the immediate suffering which it was producing. R. J. White mentions the remark of a Frenchman who said of Lord Liverpool that if he had been present at the creation of the world he would have said, '*Conservons-nous le chaos.*'[1] The witticism is a fair comment on Liverpool's outlook. What it omits to add is that Liverpool would also have found compelling reasons for the continuance of chaos. His detached and, to his critics, irritating opposition to change was frequently evident in his career, notably on the issue of parliamentary reform.

Robert Jenkinson, as he was still called, made another visit to the Continent in 1792 and saw at close quarters the Austrian and Prussian armies mounting their disjointed and ultimately unsuccessful attack on the French Revolutionaries. Soon repercussions of the Revolution began to be felt in Britain. Tom Paine's *Rights of Man*, written in 1791, had made more coherent the latent resentment against political and social inequality in Britain. That 200,000 copies were estimated to have been sold in 1793 gives some indication of the intensity of interest in the fundamental issues raised by the Revolution. The growth of Corresponding Societies and of Radical clubs

[1] R. J. White, *Waterloo to Peterloo* (London: Mercury, 1963), p. 86.

helped to give purpose and organisation to unrest, though their members were relatively few in number. The mass of the people felt the same horror and contempt for the Revolutionaries which Jenkinson himself frequently expressed. Economic grievances, however, mingled confusingly with political demands. The war had raised food prices and at first was unpopular to such an extent that the royal carriage was stoned as George III went to open Parliament in 1795, and again on its return, though that redoubtable monarch seems to have been singularly unmoved by the whole episode. Rioting mobs in London were demanding parliamentary reform, the dismissal of Pitt, and the end of the war. Jenkinson, now in his twenties, was thus in the midst of scenes which reinforced his belief that the mood of mobs was folly laced with treason. Too irresponsible to share in government, they needed a firm hand, a need which Parliament had already recognised in a series of Acts against treasonable activities between 1793 and 1795, and in the suspension of the Habeas Corpus Act in 1794: later in 1799 and 1800 there followed the Combination Acts banning workers' trade associations.

Meanwhile Jenkinson was advancing in political experience and status. He became Master of the Mint in 1796, notoriously a profitable post, and possibly an opportune one since this was the year of his marriage. His wife was Lady Theodosia Hervey, daughter of the Earl of Bristol. Robert's father was now created first Earl of Liverpool and Robert adopted the courtesy title of Lord Hawkesbury, a title which had been granted to his father in 1786. By 1801, Hawkesbury, still only thirty, had achieved the transition from minor to major governmental rank. He accepted Addington's invitation in that year to become Foreign Secretary at the critical moment when the negotiations were taking place which led to the Treaty of Amiens. His experience was further extended in 1804 when, upon Pitt's return as Prime Minister, Hawkesbury became Home Secretary. He took energetic measures to organise local defence against the risk of French invasion, but of greater significance for his later career was the instrumental part he played in bridging the differences between Addington and his successor, Pitt. The latter had been largely responsible for the overthrow of the Addington ministry, but it was necessary in the national interests, as George III and Hawkesbury realised, that Addington and his colleagues should still co-operate actively with Pitt. It was Hawkesbury who brought the two men together at his house and secured a settlement of their differences. His talent for effective mediation between squabbling colleagues was of inestimable value both on this and later occasions, particularly at a time when political passions flared so strongly that politicians were capable of resorting to duelling pistols after they had exhausted the possibilities of abuse.

Pitt died in 1806 and it was not until 1809 that Hawkesbury, now Lord Liverpool after the death of his father in 1808, had any decisive opportunity to show his political abilities. Spencer Perceval, the new Prime Minister, appointed Lord Liverpool as Secretary of State for War and the Colonies in 1809.   To Lord Liverpool, therefore, went the vital duty of giving maximum support to Wellington in the conduct of the Peninsular Campaign, the 'Spanish ulcer' which was to drain away a great part of the French fighting effort. Liverpool showed outstanding singleness of mind in his refusal to be discouraged in this objective in spite of pressure to widen the campaign against France, and in spite of Wellington's bouts of gloom.

When Spencer Perceval was killed in the lobby of the House of Commons in 1812 by a mad merchant, Bellingham, who blamed the Government for his bankruptcy, it was obvious that Liverpool's experience, and possibly his character, gave him the best title to succeed. This was in fact the immediate intention, but there were the usual difficulties in securing any co-operation from the leading politicians before Liverpool was at last able to form a ministry on 8 June 1812. He was to be Prime Minister for fifteen years. This was the climax of his political career. His methods of government were to win him praise and blame to a confusing degree, and this is the period which now comes under review.

Attack

Of all the war-time Prime Ministers concerned in the struggle against Napoleon, Lord Liverpool was the most fortunate. He became Prime Minister on 8 June 1812. Sixteen days later

Napoleon's momentous invasion of Russia began. This was
the campaign which destroyed Napoleon's ambitions, eased
Britain's military task, and gave an auspicious start to the
Liverpool ministry. Important battles remained to be won in
Spain, at Leipzig, and at Waterloo, but the backbone of
French resistance had been broken on the desolate plains of
Russia. The new ministry in its first years was associated with
military victories and the rewards of a long-awaited peace.
Wellington, after temporary reverses, broke through into
France; Napoleon, elusive to the end, was driven back across
the Rhine by the European coalition; peace was signed in
Paris and, though the Hundred Days gave a rude shock to the
leisurely peacemaking, Napoleon was eventually safely isolated in St Helena. British soldiers had shown their worth in
Spain and at Waterloo. British seamen had shown their fighting supremacy throughout the whole length of the war.
Britain's prestige stood high. Alone of the peacemaking
powers no part of her homeland had been occupied, nor had
she had to endure the military and political humiliations
which Austria, Prussia, and Russia had experienced at the
hands of Napoleon. In the peace treaties of 1814–15 she
played a major role in the settlement of Europe, and her own
contributions to victory were rewarded with the cession to her
of a number of naval bases and trading posts strung across the
world: Heligoland, Malta, the Ionian Islands, Mauritius, the
Cape of Good Hope, Ceylon, Trinidad, St Lucia, and Tobago.

At home there was good reason to expect rapid increases in
productivity. Britain had been the pioneer of technical development in the textile industries, steam-power was being put
to greater industrial use, the war had encouraged advances in
the scale and techniques of iron production, and had likewise
shown the value of the slightly more scientific approach
adopted towards agriculture in the eighteenth century.
Property was unevenly distributed, but the encouraging fact
remained that the wealth was there, if only it could be tapped
and used. The organisation of banking and the provision of
credit for industrial development were still on a rudimentary
level compared with the advances to be made later in the
century, but in relation to our possible foreign competitors
the scale of British financial organisation was impressive.
Baring Brothers, the financial house, made a substantial

loan to the French Government to help pay off the indemnity imposed by the second Treaty of Paris, and rehabilitation loans were made to Prussia, Russia, and Austria. Potentially, Britain's economic position was very strong.

Before 1815 it can hardly be said that governments had social policies. Changes were slow to come except in dire emergencies, and when they did were apt to owe more to the consciences of individuals than to those of governments. Yet the French Revolution had provided a spectacular warning of the dangers of passivity in government, and in itself was an incitement to fundamental thought about the condition of the people, the more so because it is very plain from Liverpool's letters and speeches that he was fearful of revolution in this country. Moreover, coherent demands for a more humanitarian concern with the problems of the poor, the unfortunate, and the misfits of society had been growing for some time. Wilberforce and Buxton campaigned against the slave trade; Romilly campaigned against the harshness of the criminal law. Of greater significance still was Bentham's *Fragment on Government*, published in 1776; he and his followers based their philosophy on the principle that, 'It is the greatest happiness of the greatest number that is the measure of right and wrong.' It required no great intelligence for any politician to grasp that, whatever else Britain had achieved during the Napoleonic War, it had certainly not secured the greatest happiness of the greatest number; and yet, as has been pointed out, the means to advance that happiness were there: the ingenuity of her inventors, the energy of her industrialists, and the courage of her forces had given Britain unique trading advantages. The crucial matter now was whether the Government would show at least some grasp of the economic and social developments which had mostly been plain enough for the last twenty years. One of the strongest charges against Lord Liverpool is that in this changing situation he provided the country with government which was unimaginative and clumsy to an extraordinary degree. The major criticism of him is not that he was tyrannical, nor even that he was uninspired; he was merely uncomprehending: he was, as Disraeli said, 'the Arch-mediocrity'.

The tests of Liverpool's capacity to govern multiplied rapidly with the end of the war. Demobilisation was carried

out in an amateurish way which from the outset reflected little
credit on the Government's understanding. Three hundred
thousand men were released from the forces with a speed
which can only be regarded as irresponsible. Highland soldiers
landing at Dover after Waterloo were released from service,
and then faced the prospect of walking home. In England the
flood of untrained labour was of little service to industry as the
awkward transition was made from a war-time to a peace-
time economy. Working conditions and unemployment were
already urgent problems, whose remedy had been postponed
by war, but now it was folly to postpone reform. The advent
on the industrial scene of substantial groups of ex-soldiers,
used to the violence of war and disillusioned with the blessings
of peace, could only add to the bitterness of discontent. The
machine-breaking riots in Nottinghamshire and the north-west
in 1811 and 1812 had already given an indication, before the
war ended, of the strength of feeling among the workers. The
Liverpool Government had replied by introducing a Bill making machine-breaking punishable by death, an understandable
reaction at the time. After the war working-class discontent grew with alarming speed, and the Government put into
effect policies about which it can be said that, if they had been
the product of intelligent direction, they could be characterised as a calculated effort to intensify working-class discontent, to force it into the open, and to break it by repression.
The Government's use of W. J. Richards, known as Oliver the
Spy, and of a large number of similarly unsavoury informers
and *agents provocateurs*, gives a little support to the idea that
the Liverpool Government was following a calculated policy in
its treatment of the workers. But this would be an overesti-
mate of Liverpool and his colleagues. Isolated from the needs
of the community by their education, their rank, and their
invincible ignorance of the lives and feelings of the mass of
those whom they governed, the Liverpool Government had
neither the will nor the knowledge to produce a coherent
social policy of any kind whatsoever. It waited on events and,
when they came, handled them with clumsy inadequacy.

In 1815 the landowning classes in Parliament, the pre-
dominant class there, were able to secure the passage of the
Corn Law. Grain could not be imported until the home price
rose to 80s a quarter. This price had never been reached in

the eighteenth century, except in war-time, and gave British farmers a virtual monopoly which they retained until 1828, when a sliding scale of duty on grain was introduced during the Wellington ministry of 1828–30. For a variety of reasons wheat prices in most years took a downward trend between 1815 and 1827, in spite of the virtual exclusion of foreign competition; yet the Corn Law undoubtedly had the effect of making the price of bread higher than it otherwise would have been. Moreover, the law was difficult to operate in practice. The chief beneficiaries were not the British farmers but the corn merchants and speculators who made profits by hoarding corn when the duty was low. It was characteristic of Liverpool's outlook on these economic matters that he gave the Corn Law legislation no further attention until 1826, and was then only prompted to do so by riots in the north which were suppressed by the use of troops and artillery.

The repeal of the income tax in 1816 was even more short-sighted. If revenue needs could not be met by direct taxation they would have to be met by indirect taxation and, in proportion, the hardships of price increase would fall more heavily on the poor than on the rich. Liverpool and Vansittart, his Chancellor of the Exchequer, were well aware of this, and Liverpool was disappointed that many of his supporters placed their landed interests so flagrantly above national interests. The blame for the abandonment of income tax is generally ascribed exclusively to the selfishness of the landowning members of Parliament. Certainly the evidence points strongly in that direction, but it is reasonable also to consider whether Liverpool was as active in championing the principle of income tax as he might have been. Party loyalty in the nineteenth century was a very loosely applied idea. Often this was a handicap, and this particular issue of the repeal of income tax, where a government proposal was defeated by the opposition of some of its usual supporters, might be cited as an illustration of the point. But the looseness of party loyalties was not an unmitigated disadvantage. Given a leader of vision and strong character, like Pitt or Peel, it was possible, if the right mood was established, to induce a substantial number of independently-minded back-benchers to support policies which could be proved to be nationally beneficial. The retention of income tax was an issue of fundamental importance of this kind. Liverpool had neither the oratorical fire to make this plain, nor, failing that, the political wisdom to win support in advance. The latter would have seemed an ungentlemanly tactic to Liverpool; it was characteristic of the man thus to attach more importance to his minor prejudices than to the national interest. In an issue of primary importance to the nation he virtually abdicated his responsibility for leadership.

The consequences of these early misjudgments are well known. The grievances of the people festered in the iron-works of the Midlands, in the textile mills of Lancashire, in the coal-fields of the north-east, in the farming districts of East Anglia. Unrepresented in Parliament, unprotected by trade unions, and ruled by a government indifferent to their state, their only recourse in the end was violence. Demonstrations, such as that which preceded the march of the 'Blanketeers' from Manchester to London in 1817 to present their grievances to the Prince Regent, were apt to be broken up by troops, stationed by the Government in likely trouble areas. The Habeas Corpus Act was suspended from February 1817 to January 1818, and governmental repression produced desperation to such an extent that the 'revolution' which the Government feared broke out in Derbyshire in 1817. Jeremiah Brandreth led a small group of unemployed textile workers to capture Nottingham Castle. The rising was comically badly organised, but its end was tragic enough. The appearance of a group of Hussars was sufficient to disperse Brandreth's followers. He and three others were later found guilty of high treason. The life of one of the four was spared on account of his youth, but Brandeth and two others were hanged outside Derby Gaol.

The climax of this period of violence, 'Peterloo', was still to come, and it is significant that the violence here stemmed from the folly of the authorities and not from that of the crowd. The purpose of the crowd which met in St Peter's Fields on 16 August 1819 was to hear a speech by Henry Hunt on the subject of parliamentary reform. By the express wish of Hunt himself they carried no weapons. They came with their wives and children, dressed in their Sunday best. Hunt's presence to speak to so large a crowd was believed to threaten a breach of the peace, and the authorities already had a warrant to arrest him on that charge. Acting with reprehensible irresolution the Manchester magistrates failed to arrest Hunt before the meeting began, then, on a rash impulse, decided to order his arrest during the meeting. Military assistance was considered necessary to secure Hunt's arrest. The local Yeomanry, not very expert on their horses, attempted to make the arrest, but became wedged in the crowd. The Hussars, who were gathered in reserve, now charged in to support the Yeomanry. Many of the crowd were injured and eleven were killed. The blame for this gross mishandling of the situation rested immediately with the local authorities, the Manchester magistrates. The blame in a wider sense belongs to the whole Liverpool Government. This was the Government which had initiated and maintained the repressive approach which found such clumsy expression at Peterloo. Liverpool supported the conduct of the Manchester magistrates; he was aware that they had made misjudgments, but he believed that the root of the matter was that authority must be maintained against revolution. If there had been a danger of revolution, and if authority, represented by the Government, had exercised power in a responsible way, this would have been a tenable position. As it was, the Peterloo episode earned for the Government, then and later, the harsh criticism which it richly deserved. Peterloo was followed by the hasty passing of the Six Acts which clamped down on actions which could legitimately be accounted treasonable, but which also, and less legitimately, restricted the opportunities for distribution of Radical literature, and for public meeting. The subsequent madcap attempt by Arthur Thistlewood and his fellow conspirators to blow up the Cabinet, who were believed, wrongly, to be dining together at Lord Harrowby's house in Grosvenor Square, superficially gave the Government some justification for their policy. But the Thistlewood conspirators represented no one but themselves; one of the weaknesses of the Government was that it classified all its critics as irresponsible or treasonable. The Radicals, for instance, were putting forward claims for political and social reforms which were to receive and deserve serious political attention in a few years' time; yet almost throughout his ministry Liverpool remained wilfully deaf to the constructive suggestions being made for social reforms.

It was, after all, within the bounds of practical politics,

even in the early nineteenth century, to improve working conditions and to reduce some of the worst effects of unemployment. Sir Robert Peel, for instance, had sponsored the Health and Morals of Apprentices Act in 1802, and in 1819, through his influence and that of Robert Owen, an Act was passed for the further control of child labour in cotton mills. This Act proved ineffective, partly because of the lack of an inspectorate to enforce it, but more fundamentally because of the lukewarm support which was all that could be expected from Lord Liverpool in matters of this kind. This sprang from Liverpool's attitude, reminiscent of the eighteenth century, that the duty of governments in domestic affairs was to govern as little as possible. Like a police force its duty was to suppress disorder, not to remove its causes. Yet, even in the eighteenth century, when the need was less pressing, there had been at least one official attempt to mitigate the worst effects of working-class poverty. The Speenhamland System, introduced in 1795, was based on the principle of a minimum wage for agricultural workers, who in some areas were suffering acute hardship. The system was badly conceived in detail but at least marked a conscientious attempt to remove a social evil. An adaptation and extension of the scheme for the benefit of industrial workers, notably the hand-loom weavers, ought not to have been beyond the capacity of the Liverpool ministry: yet on this vital matter no remedial action was taken throughout the fifteen years of Liverpool's rule.

It may seem that the last years of the Liverpool ministry show glimpses of a more enlightened attitude on the part of the Prime Minister. Yet how far is this borne out by the facts? The initiative for the reforms which were effected came from individual ministers, not from Liverpool himself whose attitude to change varied between the apathetic and the obstructive. Such an outlook was totally unsuited to an age quickened by the driving force of the Industrial Revolution. In none of the major long-term economic decisions confronting the Government—the Corn Law, income tax, currency convertibility, and the relaxation of tariff rates—did Liverpool hold the initiative himself. The Corn Law and income tax abolition were foisted on him by landowning M.P.s; currency convertibility, admittedly controversial at the time but beneficial in the long run, was the work of Robert Peel; the relaxation of tariff rates owed far more to the enterprise of Huskisson at the Board of Trade than to Liverpool's direction. The latter was undoubtedly favourable to the movement towards Free Trade which suited well his *laissez-faire* philosophy. He had made his attitude plain by a series of public utterances from the very beginning of his ministry. Moreover, Free Trade obviously could not be adopted at once, partly because of the Government's dependence on import duties for revenue — a dependence which had been increased by the Government's inability to retain income tax in 1816. There were other difficulties, too. There was opposition from vested interests, and the difficulties imposed by post-war protectionist policies in other countries. Yet, when all this has been conceded, there remains the fact that Free Trade was the logical policy at a time of expanding industrial activity. The 1823–5 legislation brought in by Huskisson, involving a lowering of duties and reciprocal treaties with other countries, was eminently sensible, but it might well have been adopted before had Liverpool been capable of giving a constructive lead himself. In 1823 George IV commented that 'the misfortune of this Government is that it is a Government of departments'. It was a shrewd assessment.

The policy of drift was not confined to economic matters. The relaxation of the absurd harshness of the criminal law was achieved by Robert Peel during his tenure of the Home Office. The changes naturally required government support, yet the initial reaction of the Government, when an inquiry into the criminal laws had been proposed by Sir James Mackintosh in 1819, was to oppose that motion. In this the Government was defeated. The subsequent reversal of attitude by the Government may well have represented a change of head not heart, dictated by fear of the loss of political support.[1] Likewise the inability of Liverpool to grasp the implications of the repeal of the Combination Act in 1824 not only made a revision of the Act necessary in 1825 but also gives further insight into his ignorance of social problems.

There were in addition several issues in which action might have been expected but no action came. Parliamentary reform was not given serious consideration by the Government in

[1] See the comment in the *Edinburgh Review*, 1824, quoted in Asa Briggs, *The Age of Improvement* (London: Longmans, 1959), p. 217.

spite of Radical agitation over a period of some thirty years. Liverpool's witty half-truth that the important issue is not who elects but who is elected expresses his feelings on this matter. The creation of effective police forces, which might have moderated the violence of the 1815–20 period, did not occur until after Liverpool's death; nor did Catholic emancipation, though its merits had been aired for years before. The flurry of reforms after 1827 is in itself a commentary on Liverpool as an obstacle to progress.

The criticisms of Lord Liverpool are virtually confined to the Government's policies at home. His foreign policy, if it can be described in that way in view of his almost complete reliance on Castlereagh and Canning, is much less vulnerable to considered attack. France was treated with calculated generosity in the Treaties of Paris and subsequently, while at the same time the Quadruple Alliance of 1815 was in existence as an effective potential deterrent should the French trouble Europe again. The weaknesses of the so-called Congress System were recognised from the start,[1] but an open breach with the Congress powers was avoided until the post-war situation had clarified itself. These matters, after all, were the speciality of the British governing classes. They brought to them a professionalism which was markedly lacking in their domestic policies. Moreover, Liverpool was singularly fortunate to have in his service two of the strongest Foreign Secretaries of the century in Castlereagh and Canning. Yet the confident conduct of foreign policy merely serves to heighten the failure at home. It is one of the paradoxes of Liverpool's ministry that the predominantly liberal and flexible approach adopted in the handling of foreign affairs was the exact opposite of the reactionary and rigid policies adopted at home. It reinforces the view that Liverpool lacked the directive energy expected of a Prime Minister, and that his concept of leadership was to trail along lifelessly at the tailcoats of ministers whose minds were more agile and energetic than his own.

[1] See L. C. B. Seaman, *From Vienna to Versailles* (London: Methuen, 1955), p. 10.

Defence

No assessment of Lord Liverpool as a Prime Minister can be of
lasting value unless it takes into account the magnitude and
novelty of the problems with which he was confronted. There
was no precedent in British history to give Liverpool and his
colleagues any guidance in dealing with the complex political,
social, and economic effects which stemmed from Britain's
clash with Revolutionary France. The Revolution and the
dictatorship which followed it had an influence still visible
today on attitudes to political and social issues. If the impact
of the Revolution can still produce shock-waves one hundred
and fifty years later, it needs little imagination to visualise
the bewilderment and fear which the Revolution created for
those who had lived in close proximity to it. France was defeated in 1815 but not the Revolutionary spirit. This was the
inescapable fact which was to disturb the minds of politicians
for generations to come, and which would make the task of
government infinitely more difficult. It was the misfortune of
Lord Liverpool that he was the first British Prime Minister
called on to deal with the vast disruptive, material, moral,
and mental influence of the Revolution. In these circumstances it would be unrealistic to expect him or his colleagues
to slip on smoothly the attitudes of twentieth-century liberalism. Abbé Sieyès, when asked what he did during the French
Revolution, answered, 'I survived.' If the Liverpool Government in the aftermath of the Revolution likewise managed to
survive, as it notably did, that was as much as could be
expected by reasonable men. In fact it did more than this, as
the years of Liberal Toryism showed.

The least enduring but most immediately important consequence of the war was the economic distress it created, both
during its course and, more notably, in the awkward transition
from war-time to peace-time conditions after 1815. That
Britain was on the verge of a period of great industrial expansion was a fact available to later historians but not to the
Government of the time. That Britain had great potential
industrial strength brought no comfort to the unemployed
hand-loom weavers, to the workers in iron foundries and
textile mills whose employers were finding severe fluctuations

in demand for their products, to the workers in the ship-yards where ship-building, deprived of the stimulus of war, was in a state of decline, nor, most of all perhaps, to the agricultural labourers, by far the strongest numerical group, who found that the financial problems of the farmer were passed on to them. These were not matters for which the Government could be blamed. National economic planning is still in its infancy in modern Britain; in 1815 economic planning was the pipe-dream of isolated visionaries. Moreover, it would have needed international rather than national planning to achieve a satisfactory solution on the vexed question of the tariff war which developed between some of the nations after 1815, and which was the root cause of the slackening demand which be-devilled some of Britain's key industries.

The predicament of farming is an example of the practical difficulties which the Liverpool Government had to face. Byron had called Napoleon 'the patron saint of farmers'; certainly the need to produce wheat at home had added to the prosperity of farmers for much of the war. But in 1813 a good harvest led to falling prices and this process continued. Between 1812 and 1815 wheat prices fell by almost a half, from 126s 6d a quarter to 65s 7d a quarter. The incentive to increase the area of cultivated land disappeared, while the tithes and high rents, paid by farmers without difficulty while war-time prices were high, became a heavy burden in a period of falling prices. Seen against this background the Corn Law cannot be dismissed merely as a selfish manœuvre by land-owning M.P.s. Obviously their interests were closely involved in the change, but so too were those of the rent-paying farmers and those of the large numbers of farm labourers. The situation of farming in 1815 made it eminently reasonable to safeguard the interests of the most numerous occupational group in the country. Nor did the virtual monopoly of the nation's wheat supply by the British farmer lead to extor-tionate prices. With the exception of the occasional year such as 1817, when wheat prices rose to 96s 11d a quarter, the general price trend was downwards between 1815 and 1827.

The price of wheat was only one of several insistent eco-nomic problems. Industries such as the iron industry had profited from the needs of war. Peace-time brought with it sharp fluctuations in demand in which temporary booms were more than outweighed by periods of depression, until 1822 when recovery became steadier. The uncertainties of the situation discouraged industrial expansion and produced serious unemployment, particularly in the north and midlands. In addition, it was proving difficult to re-establish Britain's position in European trade. Countries occupied by Napoleon had been obliged to develop their own industries during the war, and consequently were much less dependent on British industries. Even where European demand for British goods survived, largely because of their quality, it was often artificially damped down by the use of protective tariffs. France, our nearest customer, provides a conspicuous example of this restrictive approach. These trading difficulties were not of a kind to be settled quickly or easily. It is scarcely reasonable to charge the Liverpool Government with inability to control the trading policies of other nations, nor with its powerlessness to control the economic forces set in motion by a long war; modern governments with more experience to guide them have shown themselves to be equally fallible in similar conditions. It is in fact very much to the credit of the Liverpool Government that so much progress was made in the mid 1820s in the relaxation of duties, both unilaterally and — in the reciprocal treaties — by mutual concessions by the countries concerned. The changes were brought about by Huskisson, but Liverpool's assistance should not be underestimated. There was strong political opposition to the changes. Had Liverpool himself not had a clear vision of the benefits which Huskisson's policy would give he, as an experienced politician, would scarcely have been likely to back a policy which was potentially politically damaging.

Liverpool also had to deal with another troublesome by-product of the war — inflation. Britain had abandoned the policy of currency convertibility in 1797. If this policy had been maintained indefinitely its effects would have been disastrous in an age when national and international methods of surviving a financial crisis were virtually non-existent. A feckless Government might have ignored its responsibility for the maintenance of a sound currency, but the Liverpool Government made determined and successful attempts to bring the situation under control. Amid a welter of opposition and conflicting advice the decision was made in 1819 to restore the convertibility of the currency, based on gold alone. The volume of notes under £5 in value was sharply reduced during the next two years, and by 1821 it was possible to put the Government's decision fully into effect. The Government's policy was held to be responsible for falling prices, though the evidence on this is uncertain; certainly farmers who had borrowed at high interest rates during the more prosperous war years now found it difficult to pay interest when the prices for their products were falling. On balance, however, the Government's decision was in the best interests of the nation; moreover, it illustrated that the Government was far more ready to take an initiative in economic matters than its critics are prepared to allow. The detailed work necessitated by the change was performed by Peel, but the decision was too important and too controversial to be left to one man: the Cabinet as a whole and Liverpool as its astute political manager were equally involved.

The difficulties imposed on the Government by the self-interest of its supposed supporters are well illustrated by the abolition of income tax in 1816. Financially and socially the need for retaining the tax was overwhelmingly obvious. The National Debt had almost quadrupled during the war and government payments to debt holders had risen accordingly. Income tax would provide much-needed revenue and would have the merit of bearing most hardly on those best able to pay it, a fact which those most affected were quick to appreciate, unfortunately. The House of Commons, that bastion of privilege in the nineteenth century, rejected by thirty-seven votes the proposal for the continuance of the tax. Liverpool and his colleagues were powerless to prevent this. They knew as well as their later critics that the rejection of the income tax proposal would be nationally harmful, but they had to face peculiar parliamentary difficulties at the time. When the tax had been imposed in 1797 Pitt had promised to remove it at the end of the war. It was a blind promise which weakened the position of the Liverpool Government. Even so common sense might have prevailed if party discipline had been of the least significance in early nineteenth-century Parliaments; but it was not. The House of Commons, so undemocratic in its electoral organisation, was in a sense alarmingly democratic in its conduct of business. The independently minded back-bencher enjoyed a pre-eminence greater even than he had had in the eighteenth century, when Governments could often manage the House of Commons by the use of influence and corruption. Pitt's reforms of the administrative system had greatly reduced a government's chances of winning support by the distribution of official posts. On the other hand the predictable party loyalties of twentieth-century politicians had not yet developed. Liverpool's political position was accordingly very difficult. The greatest parliamentary risk he had to face was not the declared opposition of the Whigs but the uncertain support of his own followers. A clear indication of his difficulties occurs in a letter which he wrote to the Prince Regent's private secretary in 1816, the year of the abolition of the income tax. 'The spirit of the House of Commons', he wrote, 'is as bad now as at any time within my recollection.'[1] This political uncertainty dogged the whole of his ministry: while it would be absurd to use this as an excuse for every governmental set-back it would be no less absurd to ignore the precariousness of Liverpool's political position on particular issues which might adversely affect the interests of his followers.

Critics of Liverpool may grant that he had difficulties of the kind indicated yet feel that his handling of the problems arising from the social distress of the period is indefensible. Demonstrations such as the attempted march by weavers from Manchester to London were broken up by troops, though the 'Blanketeers' merely had the intention of presenting a petition to the Prince Regent on the troubles of the cotton trade. Peterloo is looked on as a consequence of the Government's fear-ridden attitude towards radicals of all kinds. Habeas Corpus was suspended three times during the Liverpool ministry. Spies were used to foment violence in order to force the ringleaders out into the open. Cobbett felt obliged to flee to America in 1817 to avoid an arrest made probable by the reforming views he was advancing in *The Political Register*. The list of repressive actions could be extended, but there is one answer which holds good for them

[1] Quoted in Sir Charles Petrie, *Lord Liverpool and His Times* (London: Barrie, 1954), p. 231.

all. The first duty of a government is the maintenance of
public order. Without that assured basis reforms cannot be
put into effect. There was every justification for the Government to stand firm against reformers whose ideas were unrealistic and whose methods were suspect. 'Universal suffrage'
may have been an attractive slogan, but until there was universal education — and Britain still had to wait more than
fifty years for that — the demand was an act of deceit.
Liverpool and his colleagues described the demonstrating
mobs as 'deluded', and they were right.

Nor is that the only point which needs to be considered.
Peterloo is the best-known of the disturbances of the 1815–20
period, but it is not the most characteristic. Not all meetings
were so peaceful in intention. Illegal meetings of working-
class associations were given an edge of violence, not only by
industrial depression but also by the presence of ex-soldiers
released from the army at the end of the war. Violent conspiracies were matters of fact not fancy. The Derbyshire
rising and the Thistlewood conspiracy are not figments of the
imagination. Peaceful demonstrations were, in a way, more
troublesome still. The dividing line between demonstrations
and violence could easily be crossed, particularly when troops
had to perform the functions now carried out by the police
on these occasions. Even an apparently unprovocative march,
such as that by the 'Blanketeers', might easily swell into something much more violent and sinister as it moved south on
London. It is, after all, not so easy to distinguish between
rebels and reformers; they wear no labels. No Prime Minister
who had witnessed, as Liverpool had, the wild accumulation of
mob passions in France in the early days of the Revolution
could afford to hazard the nation's safety by tolerating disorder. Far too little credit has been given to Liverpool for
the steady firmness with which he brought a dangerous situation under control. That his merits were better recognised at
the time is shown in part by the localised nature of the disturbances; they sprang more from hopeless protest against
economic difficulties beyond the control of this or any other
government than from any widespread dissatisfaction with
the Government itself. It is significant that in spite of all the
troubles of the post-1815 period, Liverpool's tenure of the
office of Prime Minister for fifteen years is unmatched by any

of his successors, including Disraeli, who arrogantly labelled Liverpool as 'the Arch-mediocrity'.

To some extent this ability of the Tories to survive in office sprang from their moderation during the disturbances — a factor which it is easy to overlook. At a time when a low value was set on human life, as the penal code shows, very few rebels were executed; only three men, for instance, paid with their lives for their participation in the Derbyshire rising, which was after all a treasonable conspiracy. The suspension of Habeas Corpus is likewise seen in better perspective when it is realised that by the end of the critical year, 1817, only three people were left in custody as a result of the suspension of the Act. Again, no one who examines the terms of the Six Acts imposing restrictions on anti-governmental writings and meetings after the tragedy of Peterloo can seriously claim that the powers given are unreasonable or tyrannical in the context of the time. The most notorious abuse of basic rights during the period, Peterloo itself, was not the result of government action at all, but was produced by the ineptitude of the local magistrates and the Yeomanry. Liverpool's awareness of their blunder is abundantly plain from his correspondence, but it takes little imagination to see what the effect would have been on other magistrates about the country, faced with the possibility of similar awkward situations, if Liverpool had sought cheap popularity by disowning the action of the Manchester magistrates.

Having weathered the storm of the early post-war years, the Liverpool Government was able to enter on a more constructive and fortunate phase during the 1820s. The merits of Huskisson's relaxation of duties, and of Peel's reform of the criminal law, need no defence. Nor is it reasonable to belittle Liverpool's connection with their work. He was the man who recognised their promise and fostered it by appointing them to office during the reconstruction of the Cabinet in 1821-3, precisely at the time when disorder had been brought under control and reforms could be advanced from a firm basis of social order. Seen in retrospect the two phases of Liverpool's Premiership constitute a perfectly logical development, and are a tribute to the soundness of his political judgment; first came the maintenance of order, then came the steadily controlled movement towards reform. The reforms were in no way

out of harmony with Liverpool's own views. He had expressed
sympathy with the principle of Free Trade as early as 1812,
and his essential humanity of outlook is not only plain from
his excellent relations with his colleagues, but also from his
support of Sir Robert Peel's Cotton Mills Act in 1819, and
from his willingness to change his views on the slave trade.
He had the good sense to delegate the details of the changes to
the extremely capable hands of the ministers who piloted the
new legislation through Parliament, but this is a very different
matter from neglect of the responsibility of leadership. This
was the point which George IV missed when he described the
Government as 'government of departments'.

When, for instance, a financial crisis arose in 1825, Liverpool acted with a promptitude and leadership which gives the
lie to the representation of him as a mere lay figure propped
up by his brilliant colleagues. The rush on the banks which
followed a period of wild speculation led to the crisis. Parliament was in recess. Liverpool immediately summoned the
Cabinet, stopped the issue of small notes by the country
banks, increased the issue of small notes by the Bank of
England, since the resources of the latter would inspire much-
needed financial confidence, and introduced other measures to
help merchants who were in difficulties. A weaker man
would have waited for parliamentary approval; Liverpool
acted on his own. Furthermore it was enacted in 1826 that
the Bank of England should open branches in the larger
provincial towns, and that joint-stock banks, since they had
greater financial stability than the hotch-potch of minor banks
which existed before the crisis, might be established outside a
radius of sixty-five miles from London; the inner area remained the preserve of the Bank of England. The incident is
clearly worth attention for the light which it throws on
Liverpool's character. Equally revealing in this respect is the
high regard in which he was held by his Cabinet colleagues.
Personal loyalty to Liverpool reached a stage where it can be
said that some sense of collective responsibility was emerging
— a strong contrast with the unpleasant manœuvres among
ministers during the war-time years. Liverpool's gifts as a
reconciler of differences contributed much to the growing
sense of unity; no incident perhaps shows this more clearly
than his patient handling of the brilliant Canning, whose

capacity for annoying his colleagues and the King was almost as striking as his talent.

The foreign policy of the Liverpool Government is much less an object of attack than its domestic policy. The Treaty of Vienna is no longer regarded as an affront to nationalism as it once was, while Britain's skill in maintaining Austrian dominance in central Europe, as a barrier against Russian or French aggression, was shrewdly combined with support for liberal movements which seemed likely to prosper, and indifference to those which were not. The correspondence between Liverpool and his Foreign Secretaries, first Castlereagh and then Canning, makes it clear that these policies were not produced in isolation by the ministers concerned. The firm tone and good sense of Liverpool's directions are abundantly evident.[1]

These then are the points on which the defence of Liverpool's Premiership is based. Foreign and domestic policies alike were rooted in reality. Politics has been defined as the art of the possible and no one has known this better than Liverpool. Extravagant schemes for European co-operation by the Tsar, and, at home, violent pressures for parliamentary reform and Catholic emancipation left him equally unimpressed. Innovations not only had to be sound in principle: they also had to be well conceived in detail and assured of widespread political support before they deserved a place in the statute book. Liverpool's pre-eminent common sense made him well aware of these facts. If Liverpool was an 'Arch-mediocrity' then it is a pity that Britain has had so few of the breed since.

[1] Petrie, *Lord Liverpool and His Times*, contains a very useful selection of Liverpool's correspondence.

2. THE WHIGS 1830—41
REFORMERS OR REACTIONARIES?

Prelude

Party labels at any period in history are apt to be misleading. Even in modern times, when the political parties are more regimented than they once were, M.P.s from the same party may differ sharply from their colleagues on matters of detail, or emphasis, or even principle. If these differences exist today among members of the same party it is reasonable to expect party ties to have been much looser in the 1830s. Parliament was then dominated by men of independent mind and means, who had entered politics because it was the tradition of many of their class to do so. They did not fear responsibility though at times they were bored by it. Their attitude to the nation showed a marked resemblance to that of the squire to his village. They had a strong sense of duty, they were capable of benevolence, and even of sympathy to reform, so long as reform offered no challenge to their own supremacy in the structure of politics and society. Their lives were socially congenial, for their work at Westminster was performed in contact with their own kind. Among themselves they were tolerant of differences and eccentricities. They lacked the organisation to make party colleagues act as a disciplined political unit, nor did they greatly feel the need to do so, for they had little wish to impose party dogma by persuasion. Moreover, on fundamental matters there was a broad measure of agreement among all parties. The preservation of British influence in the colonies, the maintenance of a forceful foreign policy, the expansion of British trade overseas, except where this might be at the expense of our agricultural interest, and, at home, defence of the dominance of the ruling classes; these were matters on which there were no differences in principle and little in method.

This near identity of outlook brought with it advantages. Unity on fundamental issues made easier concessions on lesser ones. It was a situation, therefore, which was peculiarly favourable to determined reformers, men like Sadler, Chadwick, Wilberforce, Hobhouse, and W. Smith, so long as they confined themselves to proposals which did not impinge on the interests of the privileged classes. The miscellany of political groupings which made up the Whig Party was also conducive to a degree of flexibility in attitude. For some years before Lord Grey took office in 1830 the Whigs had been in a state of disorder. In the Commons the party had remained leaderless between 1821, when Tierney had withdrawn from the leadership following party disputes, and 1830, when the sluggish Lord Althorp reluctantly agreed to take over the leadership there. The Whigs during this period had an inclination towards reform but were unsure which direction to pursue. They shared a general belief in securing civil and religious liberty, but beyond that their reforming policies were at the mercy of the pressure groups whose support made possible the formation of a Whig ministry in 1830. These groups, the industrial interest, the Nonconformist interest, and the Benthamites, who were now devoted to the principle of State intervention in order to secure the greatest happiness of the greatest number, were to have a strong influence on the legislation of the 1830s. Nevertheless, policies never have been exclusively fashioned from below. The political attitudes and the personalities of the Whig Prime Ministers also deserve attention.

At first sight there seems little reason to expect that Lord Grey would be willing to give much impetus to the disjointed movements towards political and social reform of the 1830s. His career had followed closely the conventional pattern for the politicians of the time. He was educated at Eton and at King's College, Cambridge, and had become an M.P. at the age of twenty-two. Opportunities for achieving office were limited by the long dominance of the Tories, but he had become First Lord of the Admiralty in 1806 in the Grenville 'Ministry of All the Talents' and was Foreign Secretary for a brief period in the same ministry. Towards reform he maintained the equivocal attitude which was characteristic of the Whigs. In his younger days he had been a colleague of Fox and Sheridan and had a high respect for the limiting power of public opinion on government. In 1792, for instance, he had

been one of the founders of the Society of the Friends of the
People which aimed to secure fairer representation of the
people in the House of Commons. The membership of the
society, however, was more aristocratic than its name perhaps
suggests, and with the passage of time it began to look as if
Grey's reforming ardour had cooled. This is particularly evident in his attitude to the disorders of the 1815–20 period.
The violence and agitation of those years constituted a challenge to the established order and to the rights of property;
they were also a test of the strength and sincerity of the Whigs
as the party of reform. When this test came it was plain that,
at least at that particular point in time, the Whig leaders
were far more influenced by their aristocratic background
than by their reforming zeal. Grey was no exception. Yet by
the end of the 1820s it is possible to detect in Grey at least a
change in tactics on the issue of parliamentary reform, and
possibly a reversion to the principles of his earlier career,
when he regarded reform as desirable as well as expedient.
Whichever was the stronger motive it is a matter of fact that
he believed the refusal of Wellington to budge at all on the
matter of parliamentary representation was a mistake, and
that he himself in 1830 only took office on the understanding
that the Crown would support the introduction of a Bill on
parliamentary reform. Up to 1830, therefore, the evidence on
Grey's attitude to reform is mixed and possibly conflicting;
sometimes the reformer is uppermost, sometimes the reactionary.

The second Whig Prime Minister of the period, Lord Melbourne, was scarcely of the calibre to change the course of
history. Like Grey he was educated at Eton and Cambridge,
and like Grey also he showed tendencies in his youthful days
to deviate from orthodox thinking on political problems. At
Cambridge he even expressed disappointment over the failure
of Napoleon's Egyptian expedition, on the grounds that
England's defeat in the Napoleonic War would be greatly to
her advantage since it would lead to wholesale reform of the
English political and social system by that enlightened dic-
tator. It was a young man's fantasy but based fundamentally
on the admiration of the weak for dictatorship. Melbourne
was temperamentally incapable of effective leadership, as he
himself was aware; hence his reluctance to become Prime

B

Minister. He was too detached and negative to inspire confidence. Had he lived in the present day his objectivity and wit would have made him an admirable commentator on political events. He was in short a spectator, not a participant, and not of the stuff of which great Prime Ministers are made. Yet this does not indicate that reform would come to a standstill during his ministry. Unable himself to mould circumstances to his will, and for the most part unwilling to do so, he was not totally opposed to reform so long as others with more initiative than he possessed provided the necessary impetus. In 1819, for instance, he had been a supporter of Sir James Mackintosh's motion for an examination and reform of the penal code, at a time when sympathy for that idea was not widespread. One of the advantages of Melbourne's 'King Log' leadership when he became Prime Minister was that it did give scope for his Cabinet colleagues and for the various reforming groups in politics to press their views with more hope of acceptance than would have been possible under more autocratic leadership. Seen in this light Melbourne's apathetic leadership may have been an incentive to reform, not a restraint upon it.

Attack

When the Whigs came to power in 1830 it was the first time in the nineteenth century that they had had the opportunity to advance the reforms to which they were supposedly sympathetic; accordingly one would expect a great outburst of reforming activity. The Whigs paid lip-service to the principle of civil and religious liberty. If their championship of that principle had been honest the Whig ministries of the 1830s might have made a decisive contribution to social, economic, and political progress in Britain. Corrupt elections, the dominance of the landowners in Parliament, the power of vested interests in education and local government, the inequalities before the law of employers and employees, the exploitation of labour in factories and mines, and the persecution of trade unionism — these were all affronts to the idea of a justly organised society. A decade of Whig rule left these

injustices virtually untouched. In economic affairs the sluggishness of the Whigs in removing the obstacles to Free
Trade, in spite of the warning given by the difficulties of trade
in the 1836–41 period, was to delay by several years the great
trading expansion which Britain experienced as a result of
Peel's enlightened direction of affairs in the 1840s. In this
respect, at least, the Tories were more liberal than the Whigs.

Logically the first step for the Whigs in 1830.was to reform
the membership of the House of Commons. Once this was done
the new members would be able to perform their legislative
duties with the knowledge and sympathy which was so
markedly lacking in the unreformed House of Commons. The
result might have been a spate of reforms without precedent
in English history. Political reform had been far outstripped
by economic change; now was the time when they could be
brought into a closer relationship. This might well have been
the first stage in a Whig renaissance, much overdue, which
would ensure for them a long period of political dominance
comparable to that which they had enjoyed in the first half of
the eighteenth century. Yet, in practice, the opportunities
presented to Grey, Melbourne, and their colleagues were
almost totally ignored. Their timidity had the hall-mark of
the worst kind of conservatism; to describe them as reformers
is to misconceive completely their narrow and bigoted vision
of their responsibilities.

In simple outline it seems that the strategy of a legislative
programme beginning with a Reform Bill, broadening the
membership of the House of Commons, and followed by a
series of social reforms, was precisely that which the Whigs
followed. But this is a misleading simplification. What were
the motives for the Reform Bill? What changes did it make?
How far-reaching were the social reforms, and how much
do they owe to the Whigs? These are questions which need to
be considered in assessing the reforms of the 1830s. The
attitudes and motives of the Whigs need to be scrutinised
carefully, and the pressure of circumstances taken into
account, otherwise praise for the so-called Whig Reformers is
glib and undeserved.

The Reform Bill of 1832 was the only major Whig Bill
whose terms owed much directly to the initiative of the Whig
leaders themselves; and it was introduced not to open the

way to reform but to close it. Grey was a Whig and a conservative. There is no paradox here. Hazlitt compared the
two parties with rival stage-coaches proceeding along the
same road to the same destination. The ease with which
political groups transferred their allegiance from one party to
another during this period supports Hazlitt's comment.
Grey's social and educational experience had been identical
with that of his political opponents. His Cabinet, containing
only three commoners, was the most aristocratic of the century. He himself had the greatest respect for the fashionable
doctrine that a stake in the land was the best recommendation
for the exercise of political power; after all was he not a substantial landowner himself with a country estate in North-
umberland? On his own admission he had 'a predilection for
old institutions'. His motive in introducing the Reform Bill
was to make a limited political concession to the middle
classes, whose power was based on their economic usefulness
to the country. Grey had no great respect for them but plainly
they could not any longer be ignored; if they were they might
ally themselves with the working classes whose restiveness
was only too evident: the Reform Bill was the price to be
paid for internal peace. It was introduced by the Whig
Government not out of any love for reforming principles, but,
on the contrary, out of a wish to cling as far as possible to the
status quo. Like Guizot in France, Grey, in dealing with the
middle classes, saw the need for a government 'to be attentive
to the interests and desires of the class of the population
which has come attached to it'.[1]

Quite apart from his concern to maintain the advantage
of the class to which he belonged, Grey's desire to introduce a
Reform Bill was undoubtedly stimulated by the widespread
disorders of the time not only in England but in Europe
generally. The Bill was a product of fear as well as of political
opportunism. Grey formed his ministry in November 1830.
Four months previously the July Revolution had upset the
political regime of Britain's unpredictable neighbour, France,
and there were unsuccessful rebellions in Italy and Poland
during the course of the same year. In 1830 also there were
dangerous riots in the south of England by agricultural
labourers, which were firmly suppressed by Lord Melbourne,

[1] Letter by Guizot to Lord Palmerston, 1840.

then Home Secretary in the Grey administration. Nine
labourers were hanged and 457 were transported. The Government believed that the disturbances had a political origin, and
were so confident in this belief that Melbourne prosecuted
two journalists, Carlile and the more famous Cobbett, alleging
that they had incited the rioters to secure political change by
force. Carlile was imprisoned, but Cobbett defended himself so
ably that he was acquitted. The more important point, however, is that it was quite plain that the Whig Government was
extremely nervous that, unless the Reform Bill was forced
through Parliament at the earliest possible stage, the mass of
the people might become impossible to govern. The rioting
which broke out in Bristol, Nottingham, and other towns,
when the Lords rejected the Bill in 1831, gave added force to
these fears. So, too, did the formation by Francis Place of the
National Political Union, since this organisation, with its off-
shoots in some of the major cities, was dedicated to the cause
of parliamentary reform. Its widespread support and the fear
that it would give strength and coherence to demands for
reform, exceeding those the Government had in mind, disturbed Grey deeply.

The Government's fears of a political revolution were
greater than they need have been, though understandable in
the circumstances of the time. Nevertheless these fears were a
decisive factor in bolstering up Grey's determination to see the
Bill through Parliament, when he would have much preferred
to retire to the quiet of his Northumbrian estate. Therefore
he made use, a little reluctantly, of a threat to persuade the
King to create more Whig peers if the House of Lords persisted in rejecting the Bill: this threat was sufficient to secure
its passage through the Upper House.

The terms of the Bill make the intentions of Grey and his
colleagues perfectly plain, though at the time there was a
belief among the more politically naïve in the community that
the Reform Bill would be the prelude to an era of major social
reform; in this they were wildly mistaken. The Bill's main
object was to acknowledge the political existence of the
middle classes, though as voters rather than as M.P.s. The redistribution of seats which followed the disfranchisement of
the smaller boroughs made little difference to the social composition of the House of Commons itself. Sixty-five extra seats

were allocated to the counties, and in these the influence of the great landowning families was dominant. The over-representation of the agricultural southern counties was allowed to continue because of the Government's determination to uphold the privileges of the landed proprietors. The landowners' influence was still strong in the boroughs also, in spite of the acceptance of the right of some of the industrial towns to send M.P.s to Westminster. This was partly the result of the redrawing of borough constituency boundaries after 1832, so that the electoral boundaries of boroughs were widened to include rural areas, and partly also because of the continuance of the pernicious practice of open voting with its usual accompaniments of bribery and corruption.

The Bill thus made little difference to the membership of the House of Commons. On the other hand the clauses on voting rights had an important influence on the composition of the electorate. In the counties an amendment to the Bill extending the vote to the £50 tenants-at-will, who had been overlooked when the Bill was first drafted, conferred the vote on gentlemen-farmers whose interests could be assumed to be identical with those of the great landed families. More significant still was the clause which gave the vote to the £10 householder in the boroughs. The £10 standard was somewhat arbitrary since the level of rents naturally varied in different parts of the country, but there is no doubt that one of the effects of the clause was to deprive some of the poorer members of the community of the votes which they had possessed before the Bill as a result of the haphazard survival of ancient customs. The new electorate was thus less widely representative of the community than the old one had been. The 1832 Reform Bill was to acquire some importance historically as a precedent for later extensions of the franchise, but in the minds of its creators it had no connection whatsoever with a democratisation of government; such a concept was as repugnant to the Whig leaders as it was to their Tory opponents.

Apart from the Reform Bill itself the reforms which normally command most attention during the Whig ministries of the 1830s are the abolition of slavery in 1833, the Factory Act of the same year, the Poor Law Amendment Act of 1834, and the Municipal Corporations Act of 1835. The terms of some of these Acts undoubtedly represent an advance in matters where progress had been too long delayed, but they scarcely justify the praise which has sometimes been given to the Whig leaders. The impetus towards these reforms was largely provided by individuals and groups who were ready to make use of the Whigs but had little respect for them. Wilberforce, the central figure in the movement for the abolition of slavery, was far more influenced by his religious beliefs than by any sympathy for Whig ideals in pressing for that particular reform. The pressure for the introduction of a Factory Act came not from the Whigs themselves but from Oastler and Sadler who were Tories, from Lord Ashley who had been an anti-reform candidate in 1831, and from humanitarians such as Fielden. The Poor Law Amendment Act and the Municipal Corporations Act owed much more to the Benthamites, Chadwick and Parkes respectively, than they did to the Government itself.

The attitude of the Benthamites to the Government deserves particular attention. Bentham and his followers had been aware for some years that there was more hope of achieving social advance by co-operating with the Whigs rather than with the Tories. The Benthamites did not expect any positive lead on social legislation from the Whig leaders themselves; they knew their men too well to have any illusions on that score. But they did anticipate that the Whig Government, if only to preserve Benthamite political support, would not set its face against proposals for a more scientific approach towards social legislation. In this they were right. The Benthamites believed in detailed investigation of social conditions by commissions of experts as a necessary prelude to legislation; in central control of the agencies of reform, and enforcement of that control by means of inspection. It was difficult, even in nineteenth-century England, to challenge the usefulness of these methods, and they were accepted by the Whig Government; this is clear from the terms of the Factory Act and of the Poor Law Amendment Act. The criticism of the Whigs is that, having been presented by the Benthamites with an admirable system for securing social reform, they made such little use of it. If Grey and his colleagues had any zeal for reform the means to effect it now existed. A programme of reform far more extensive than that actually adopted could have been put into effect. In practice the Whig Governments proved to be at best somewhat passive supporters of progress, at worst active obstructionists. The way in which the intentions of the reformers of factory conditions were frustrated is one of the clearest indications of this latter point.

The two major Acts of 1833, the Abolition of Slavery and the Factory Act, both stemmed from the work of individuals and add little if anything to the prestige of the Whigs as reformers. Wilberforce had devoted his political career to the abolition of slavery. Abolition of slave trading by Britain in 1807 was insufficient since other countries accepted the idea more tardily, and even when they did so there was considerable illegal slave trading. Wilberforce realised that he must direct his efforts towards the abolition of the whole concept of slavery in colonial territories. From 1821 he was strongly reinforced by the help in Parliament of Thomas Fowell Buxton. The Tory Governments of the 1820s showed little sympathy for the cause of abolition. West Indian planter interests were strongly represented at Westminster, and M.P.s with financial interests in the sugar plantations feared for their money if slavery should be abolished. The issue was raised again by the reformers when the Whigs came to power, but, like their predecessors, they continued to prefer expediency to principle. The reform was eventually introduced not as a result of any change of heart by the Whig leaders but simply through the accident of personal circumstances. Lord Stanley, the new Colonial Secretary in that year, had previously held the post of Secretary of State for Ireland. It was a thankless position and Stanley's difficulties there inspired in him a determination to make a resounding and early success in his new post as Colonial Secretary. With the minimum of help from the Cabinet he introduced the Bill for the emancipation of slaves. The Bill itself was effective enough. Full emancipation was to be completed by 1840 and £20m was paid to the slave owners as compensation. Emancipation undoubtedly created economic difficulties for plantation owners in those islands of the West Indies where labour was scarce. On the other hand, the principle of slavery was pernicious, and its abolition was well worth the financial hardship it created for some plantation owners. It would have been more to the credit of the Whig leaders, the professed upholders of civil and religious liberty, had they recognised the need for abolition more quickly; after all, the demand for abolition was no novelty. The Bill deserved far more than the belated and tepid approval that the Government gave it.

Slavery abroad was matched by slavery at home. Factory workers in Britain were less likely to be the victims of flagrant cruelty than the Negroes in the West Indian plantations, but in other respects they were little better off. Hours were long; even children often had to work more than twelve hours a day. Working conditions were dangerous to health and even to life. Freedom to leave factory work was a meaningless right for most workers when the alternatives were either starvation or the humiliation and corruption of the system of Poor Relief. The need for reform had been abundantly obvious for years. The elder Peel had introduced Acts to regulate the use of child labour in 1802 and in 1819, but neither had proved effective. Radical politicians and pamphleteers had poured abuse throughout the 1820s on the exploitation of human labour in the factories. Robert Owen's conversion of a cotton mill at New Lanark into a model factory had been completed by 1826, and the humanity of the treatment given to his workers was in pointed contrast to the lack of it elsewhere. In short, no politician of any seniority could claim to be ignorant of the misuse of human beings which flourished under the English industrial system. The reaction of the Whigs to this problem when they came to power accordingly makes an interesting study. Together with the new Poor Law, the Factory Act provides an acid test of the right of the Whigs in the 1830s to be regarded as the party of reform.

Once more it is plain that the initiative for the reform came not from the Whigs themselves but from other sources. Richard Oastler's letters to the *Leeds Mercury* criticising the use of female and child labour in the Yorkshire woollen mills brought the issue into the forefront of attention in 1830. There then followed a persistent campaign by the reformers, headed in Parliament by the Tory, Sadler, for the introduction of a ten-hour day. By 1833 Sadler was no longer in Parliament, having lost his seat in the election following the Reform Bill, but Lord Ashley gave his formidable support to the cause; moreover, the pressure for reform had been strong enough to cause the Government to appoint first a parliamentary committee, and then, in 1833, a Royal Commission to investigate

*

factory conditions. Both the reformers and the manufacturers made use of every expedient they could devise to impress the investigators with the soundness of their respective views, but in the end the Commissioners' recommendations were much more in favour of the manufacturers than of the workers. If the working hours of children and young workers were much restricted it was apparent that the hours of adult workers would be shortened too, since manufacture was an integrated process. Adults and children both had their specialised tasks to perform and production depended on the presence of both. Manufacturers therefore feared a loss in production if the children's hours were reduced. There was no need for the Government to accept the Commissioners' recommendations, but they did so. The result was an Act whose terms were a bitter disappointment to the reformers; they are also a caustic commentary on any claim that the Whigs were reformers. The changes made were trivial compared with those which might have been made. The Act was limited to the use of juvenile labour in textile factories using power-driven machinery; lace mills were excluded. Children under 9 could not be employed; those between 9 and 13 were not to work more than nine hours a day; those between 13 and 18 were not to work more than twelve hours a day. When one considers the vast possibilities for reform which existed in other industries, the coal mines, the pottery industry, and the tailoring trade, for instance, the pettiness of the 1833 Factory Act is seen in its true proportions. Even the introduction of an inspectorate, which is considered as one of the virtues of the Bill, made little difference in practice. There were too few inspectors, evasion was easy, and made easier still by allowing factory owners to make use of a shift system so that supervision of the hours of individual workers became immeasurably difficult.

The reactionary harshness of the Whigs towards the poorer classes is exemplified equally well by the Poor Law reform of 1834. The motives for the reform were mixed. In many counties the Speenhamland System was in operation. This much-abused system was based fundamentally on the view, now generally accepted, that there is a general obligation to preserve at least a minimum living standard for all citizens. Unfortunately the administrative means of achieving this end were woefully inadequate. The result was that the system

at best encouraged idleness, since the poor were assured of
out-relief, and at its worst produced riots as in 1830, since
the parish was too small and sometimes too corrupt an administrative unit to perform its duties competently. The
parishes were under an additional handicap since, in the event
of unemployment in the towns, the Settlement Laws required
that the unemployed should be sent back to their own
parishes which had the sole duty of maintaining them. There
were workhouses in existence, but conditions in them were
appalling: entry into a workhouse was the final degradation of
the poor.

There were thus many eminently sound humanitarian
reasons for the reform of the Poor Law. The reason which
appealed most strongly to the Whigs was to save money on the
rates. Had they been influenced by other motives the new Poor
Law would have been much less vindictive in its operation
than it proved to be. The terms of the Bill make it evident
that, for the poor, the main difference made by this so-called
reform was to exchange the random harshness of the old
system for the organised harshness of the new one.

The administrative machinery set up by the Act was
partly in keeping with the ideas of the Benthamites. This is
entirely to be expected, since the most weighty influence in
securing a change in the administration of the Poor Law was
that of Edwin Chadwick, a leading Benthamite. It was his
report to the Commission of Inquiry into the state of the
Poor Law which became the basis of the changes embodied in
the 1834 Act. Some of these changes were desirable. Parishes
were grouped together into unions managed by Boards of
Guardians, since this would make easier the building of workhouses. Central control was established by the setting up of a
Poor Law department consisting of three Commissioners and a
secretary, all paid. These Commissioners had the right to
appoint Assistant Commissioners and clerical staff. Chadwick
was no doubt satisfied with his successful introduction of
Benthamite administrative methods, but even on that score
there was a serious omission. Bentham had strongly advocated
the scientific study of social conditions as a necessary prelude
to legislation; in 1834 this had not been done. No attempt had
been made to analyse the causes of poverty. No distinction
was made between the idle and those whose unemployment

was produced by economic movements far beyond their control.

This was a bad error of judgment but would have mattered less if the spirit infusing the Poor Law Act had been more charitable. In fact the deterrent principle was ruthlessly applied. A harsh system would cut the poor rate. Out-relief for the able-bodied was abolished, and every care was taken to make workhouse conditions as unpleasant as possible. Children were separated from parents, and husbands from wives, for the poor were already too numerous and should not be permitted to produce a new generation of paupers. Discipline was severe and food was sparse. The tyranny of the new arrangements did not even have the merit of efficiency. The Poor Law Commission Report had advocated that separate workhouses should be created for the different groups of paupers, the sick, the mad, the old, the young, the able-bodied. In practice this was ignored. The general mixed workhouse, with all the appalling degradation of its inmates, survived. The 1834 Act, in short, was one of the most lamentable pieces of social legislation devised in the nineteenth century. Fortunately, perhaps, a succession of good harvests from 1834-6, and the demand for labour created by the expansion of the railways, prevented the inadequacy of this petty inhuman measure from being fully exposed. Even so the resentment it created, particularly among the victims of structural and cyclical unemployment in the north, was one of the root causes of Chartism.

The last major legislative contribution of the Whigs, before they lapsed into somnolence for six years under Lord Melbourne's inert guidance, was the Municipal Corporations Act of 1835. The moving spirit behind the reform was a Radical, Joseph Parkes, secretary to the Commission set up to investigate municipal government in 1833. The methods of electing municipal councillors were almost as varied as those for the election of M.P.s before the Reform Bill. It was notorious that in some boroughs councillors appropriated for their own use money which had been left for charitable purposes, and that this dishonesty was particularly prevalent at election times when councillors used public money to support their own candidates. There was a political motive for the reform in that the unreformed boroughs were more sympathetic to the Tories than to the Whigs, but there was no doubt that the Whigs would be performing a valuable service to a large section of the community if, as well as securing a better political balance for themselves in the boroughs, they also used the reform as an opportunity to widen the administrative functions of the boroughs. Little attempt was made to do so. Street cleansing, the provision of a system of sanitation, and similar matters, had so far been the concern of Improvement Commissions. Their efforts had been inadequate as the prolonged outbreak of cholera from 1831–3 had shown. The Act, however, merely made it permissive for the municipal corporations to take over the work of the Improvement Commissions; few did so, and, once more, as in so much of Whig social legislation, an excellent opportunity to achieve a worthwhile advance was missed. In other respects the Act was an improvement on the former situation. The vote in local elections was extended to all ratepayers who had lived for three years in the towns concerned. The financial weaknesses of the old system were remedied by the creation of a borough fund into which all corporation income had to be paid, and, in addition, accounts were to be audited. It should be realised, however, that from the outset the Act, like the Factory Act of 1833, was narrowly limited in its range. Administration in the country districts remained unchanged, and towns of recent growth, where health problems in particular posed the greatest difficulties, were entirely unaffected. Manchester and Birmingham, for instance, since they had no charter, had no right to elect a municipal corporation at all.

Under close scrutiny these major reforms reflect little credit on the Whig Governments. The reforms which did come into being owed their origin either to men outside the Government, or to the pressure of circumstances which no government could resist. When the reforms were introduced the terms were generally botched, and characterised by a narrowness of vision which was the reverse of the reforming idea. The 1830s were thus a decade of lost opportunities. To describe the Whigs as reformers is a misuse of the word. The 'reforms' themselves give evidence of this, but if any more evidence is needed, it only needs to be remembered that it was Lord Melbourne's instructions to the magistrates to take every opportunity to suppress the trade union movement which led directly to the disgraceful sentence inflicted on the Tolpuddle Martyrs in 1834.[1] The party which was responsible for the Factory Act was also responsible for the transportation of six Tolpuddle labourers to Australia merely for the administration of illegal oaths to other members of their union. No one who has studied the attitude of the Whigs towards reform will feel the least surprise at what seems superficially to be contradictory behaviour. There is no contradiction. The Whig and Tory leaders were identical in their indifference and, at times, hostility towards the working classes.

Defence

The details of the Whig reforms provide an easy target for attack. It is true that the Reform Bill disappointed the hopes of those who had expected a dramatic widening of the franchise; that the Factory Act was very limited in its application, and unambitious in its restriction of the working hours of children and young people; that the new Poor Law was more methodically harsh than the old one; and that the Municipal Corporations Act was largely a political reform, which took little account of the part town councils could have played in improving the physical environment of their areas. All this is merely a smoke-screen of detail. To assess the merits of the Whig ministries of the 1830s, particularly that of Lord Grey, the first need is to see Whig policies in their historical context. Once this is done it becomes abundantly obvious that what was taking place was not merely the enactment of this or that reform, though some of these reforms deserve praise in their own right, but a legislative and administrative revolution. The means used by the Whigs to put into effect the social reforms of the decade marked the most important administrative advance since Domesday Book. The 1830s were, therefore, a watershed in English history. During the course of the five years from 1830 to 1835 the organisation of English society was projected out of the Middle Ages and into modern

[1] On this matter see Lord David Cecil, *Lord M.* (London: Constable, 1954), pp. 101–6.

times. If this was reactionary then words have lost their meaning.

The essence of the matter was the adoption of Benthamite methods of administration — the collection of facts by Commissions of experts as a prelude to legislation, central control, the use of inspectors, auditing of accounts, and the principle of utility.[1] These methods provided an admirable basis, notably lacking before, for the subsequent legislation in the nineteenth and twentieth centuries on factory conditions, public health, local government, the civil service, and all the measures which the State has taken to protect the community against exploitation and hardship. The Whig leaders did not invent these methods but they had the wisdom to give the Benthamites their head. The Factory Act, the new Poor Law, and the Municipal Corporations Act are outstanding examples of this new approach to social legislation. If the Whigs had contributed nothing else to history this would have been enough. Mistakes were made, but the fact remains that the Whigs were grappling with the realities of the Industrial Revolution in a way which by comparison makes the achievements of Tory social legislation in the 1820s seem insignificant, and even irrelevant. It is not too fanciful to see in the Whig reforms of the 1830s the origins of the Welfare State.

The determination of the Whigs to modernise the social and political system was evident from the outset. Grey refused to take office unless he were allowed to form an administration unanimously in favour of parliamentary reform; to this William IV agreed. Grey's demand was a bold one, since the Whigs themselves were far from united on the issue of rationalising the voting system. Nevertheless, in spite of the doubts of his supporters, the derision of his opponents, the obstructionism of the House of Lords, and the wavering of the King over the creation of enough peers to ensure the passage of the Bill through the House of Lords, the Reform Bill was passed. Grey's achievement was a triumph of determination. The anomalies of over-representation of the lesser boroughs and under-representation of the new industrial centres were to

[1] Historians differ on the importance of Benthamism. For two contrasting views see the articles by D. MacDonagh and H. Parris in the *Historical Journal* of 1958 and that of 1960 respectively (London: Cambridge University Press).

some extent removed.[1] The electorate was almost doubled. Broadly speaking the Bill extended the vote to the middle classes. Any further widening of the franchise at that stage would have been folly. Thirty years later a commission on education was to find that only one in five of the population could read. To have given the vote to the illiterate masses in 1832 would have been an act of irresponsibility. Grey was entirely right to steer a middle course between Wellington's obtuse defence of the old system and the wild demands of the radicals.

Admittedly the changes in the electoral system meant that some electors, previously enfranchised, now lost the vote, but the hotch-potch of medievalism and corruption which characterised the old system was of no use whatsoever for a society on the threshold of modern times. The Reform Bill, with its methodical approach, rationalised the voting system and, by doing so, made it easier for later reformers to extend the franchise by logical stages. Nor is it any criticism of Grey to point out that it was not his intention in 1832 to set the community on its way to becoming a parliamentary democracy. He was a statesman, not an astrologer. He was dealing with the problems of his own time, not with those of fifty or a hundred years hence. Moreover, his reform had the hallmark of courage. The idea of parliamentary reform was no novelty, but for years Tory Governments had ignored or resisted proposals for change. Grey, on the other hand, had taken action at the first opportunity. Extremists remained dissatisfied — this was one of the Bill's merits — but the concessions made were satisfactory enough to play a part in sparing Britain from the violent disorders which troubled many Continental countries in the years between 1830 and 1848. Admittedly abuses still remained, particularly in electioneering methods. The failure to adopt secret voting can be criticised. But it needs to be borne in mind that the abolition of influence would have been a gigantic task which would have diverted attention from other desirable legislative aims. Grey, heading an uneasy coalition of interests, could never have forced through Parliament a Bill which would have weakened still further the influence of the landed interests, already in a state of some concern over the changes made by

[1] N. Gash, *Politics in the Age of Peel* (London: Longmans, 1953), contains an outstandingly valuable analysis of the detailed provisions of the Act.

the Reform Bill. Finally, there was a feeling, however strange it now seems, that secret voting was underhand and unmanly. That Britain had to wait forty years for a Ballot Act is some indication of the pressures which existed in all parties against the idea of secret voting.

The major virtue of the Whigs' social legislation, namely the creation of an efficient administrative framework and method, has already been mentioned. Apart from this general consideration there are specific merits in Acts themselves. The 1833 Factory Act was the first stage in this new approach and, not surprisingly therefore, has its limitations. The system of inspection was at first inadequate. Only four inspectors were appointed and evasion of the regulations for the control of child labour was easy both for manufacturers and for parents, who, it should be noted, were often as hostile to an Act designed to protect the interests of their children as were the manufacturers themselves. The loopholes in the Act were steadily closed, however. The inspectors were allowed to appoint assistants, the procedure over the keeping of time books by employers became standardised, and the 1836 Act, by introducing a civil register of births, marriages, and deaths, made it difficult to practise deceit over the ages of children employed. The provision of the Act which required that children under the age of thirteen should receive two hours of schooling on each working day was too optimistic, and never worked well, but at least it is an indication of the reformers' benevolent intentions.

The major criticism of the Act, however, is that the reduction of children's working hours was much less far-reaching than might have been expected. The answer lies partly in the fact that this was merely a first stage reform, and did not preclude later improvements, but the more important point in defence of the Whigs' caution is that trading conditions were far from favourable. Britain's success in the export trade depended heavily at this stage on the cotton industry — hence the Act's preoccupation with the textile industry since this was the one in which hours and conditions were most likely to be abused. The volume of exports had increased but not the value because of a general fall in prices. The existence of tariff barriers in Europe and America added to the difficulties of the situation. It was in the interests of the country as a whole, as well as of the manufacturers, that there should be no reduction of output. There was a risk that this might happen if children's hours were reduced. Cobbett in attacking the Act remarked that the prosperity of England seemed to depend on the work of 30,000 little girls. It was meant as a gibe but it contained a grain of truth. The work of adults and children was interdependent, and a reduction in hours for children might well necessitate a reduction in hours for adults. If this were to happen it was feared that there would be a drop in output with serious effects on England's balance of trade. That shorter hours could lead to greater, not less, production was a view of a later period and found no support among the leading figures in the controversy. It was the fear of loss of production which led the Government to accept the manufacturers' right to make use of a shift system in their factories so that the reduction in children's hours made no difference to those of adults. In the context of the economic conditions of the times this is a less narrow-minded approach than it at first appears.

The Act for the abolition of slavery needs little comment. It was to the Whigs' credit that they gave the opportunity to reformers to turn years of campaigning into positive achievement. In this respect it resembles much of their other legislation which, though based on the ideas of individuals, was given practical effect by government action.

The reform which roused the most widespread hostility was the new Poor Law of 1834. The harshness of its terms is not in dispute, but this harshness had some justification; moreover, there were redeeming features about the Act which are too readily overlooked. In the first place the old Poor Law, administered by the Justices of the Peace and the parish officials, is recognised to have been corrupt and inadequate. Curiously enough the areas in the south of the country where the Speenhamland System was applied, a system which lent itself to exploitation by the lazy, able-bodied poor, were precisely those most troubled by agrarian rioting and disorders. The implication would seem to be that it was not the harshness of the Poor Law which aroused most resentment among workers of any self-respect, but corrupt and lax administration of out-relief. The administrative reorganisation of the Poor Law involved central control by paid officials, the Commissioners, and local control by elected officials, the

Boards of Guardians. The Justice of the Peace was thus stripped of much of his former responsibility for Poor Relief. This was a desirable change since those Justices of the Peace who were conscientious had been overburdened with work, and those who were not had been irresponsible or corrupt in their administration of the old Poor Law. For the labourer of integrity who could find work — and this became increasingly easy with the development of the railways and the approach of mid-century prosperity — the new Poor Law was distinctly preferable to the old. Admittedly in parts of the country willing workers could find no employment because of changes in economic demand, but in practice the Government moderated the strict terms of the 1834 Act, which had stipulated that out-relief for the able-bodied poor should be ended, and out-relief was granted. It is worthy of mention, too, that the Act, at State expense, provided that workhouse children be given education, a real concession at a time when universal education was still a very distant prospect.

The Act, therefore, introduced a note of realism and rationalisation into what had been a muddle-headed system. In the end the main virtue of the Act was the administrative method which it used. The principle of electing a local authority, the Board of Guardians, charged with the administration of a specific social function, was an anticipation of the wide range of functions now performed in local government. In one respect the Act was more boldly creative still. The Commissioners were given the power to arrange for the movement of labourers from areas where there was no employment to areas where their labour could be used. Until the recent attempts to secure redeployment of labour no British government of the twentieth century has dared to put into effect so revolutionary a proposal in peace-time. As an extension of this idea the Commissioners were also given the power to arrange for the emigration of labourers to the newly developing colonies. There is no escaping the fact that the 1834 Poor Law Act was a remarkably clear-sighted and comprehensive attempt at a much-needed reform.

The widening basis of the representative system created by the Whigs in local government is strongly evident also in the Municipal Corporations Act of 1835. A detailed defence of the Act is scarcely necessary for its merits are self-evident. The old method of election of municipal councils was subject to the same abuses of corruption and privilege as the election of M.P.s. Now this was largely ended. The Conservatives were able to introduce amendments which made the local franchise less wide than the Whigs would have liked, particularly by stipulating an income qualification for council members, but even so the composition of the new councils was markedly changed. Tradesmen and Nonconformists were much more strongly represented on the councils than ever before. In addition, the creation of a borough fund, the audit of accounts, the employment of paid officials, the power of councils to levy rates and to extend their administrative functions over social services marked in fact, and potentially, a tremendous advance. An enlightened approach to the administrative mechanism of local government had opened the way to the vast changes of later years.

It is patently absurd to belittle the achievements of the Whigs of the 1830s whose major reforms began with the 1832 Reform Bill and ended with the acceptance of Rowland Hill's idea of penny postage, while in between these two limits came a remarkable outburst of legislative activity which marked a revolution in administrative methods. Attention has been concentrated on the major reforms, but for a full defence of the Whigs the lesser reforms are significant too, in that they show the same willingness to examine afresh old institutions which had become overgrown with abuses. There are several examples, notably Hobhouse's Act of 1831 to provide for democratic election of vestries, which were then very important organisations in local government; the ending of the East India Company's monopoly of trade with China in 1833; the ending of the Bank of England's monopoly of banking activities in the London area by the Act of 1833; and the limitations imposed in 1836 on the right of clergymen to hold livings in plurality, a flagrant abuse which should have been rectified long before. There were many other reforms too, but the ones mentioned are particularly indicative of the attitude of mind of the Whigs. Many governments, fearful of being thought reactionary, yet also dreading action, have responded to reforming ideas with impotent sympathy. This was not the reaction of the Whigs: their legislative boldness has few parallels in our history.

3. PEEL AND THE TORIES
MARTYR OR RENEGADE?

Prelude

Robert Peel, the younger, was born on 5 February 1788. His father was a prosperous cotton-mill owner who had used his wealth to buy the position of a country gentleman and was the owner of a country estate near Tamworth in Staffordshire. His mother, sixteen years younger than her husband, conformed entirely to the pattern of behaviour expected of the ideal wife of the time. She was attractive in appearance, devoted to her husband, and attentive to his wishes. There was no doubt that the elder Robert Peel was the dominant partner in the marriage. He had a thrusting single-minded energy which had enabled him to advance from being a cotton spinner to a cotton magnate. This same energy would be used to carve out for his son, his first child, a political career which the nation would remember. The son would be given opportunities denied to the father, who would thus achieve political power by proxy. This unabashed middle-class obsession with achievement was as far removed from the gentlemanly indifference to power of Grey or Melbourne as it was possible to be.

Young Robert Peel was an apt and docile child. His career, apart from his unusual family background, followed closely the stereotyped pattern of the leading politicians of his time. He entered Harrow in 1801 and then proceeded to Christ Church, Oxford, in 1805, the year of Trafalgar. His agile brain and skill as a speaker had already been noticed at Harrow. In addition he had inherited his father's capacity for hard work, to such an extent that his tutor at Oxford was worried that Peel might drive himself too hard, an unusual fear in the Oxford of those days. Peel, however, duly showed his academic brilliance in the examinations. In 1809, at the age of twenty-one, Peel became the Tory M.P. for Cashel, an Irish constituency, and thus joined his proud father in the House of

Commons. The steps towards a career of political distinction
had been carefully followed. Moreover, the young Peel possessed in his own right the gifts which would enable him to
fulfil his father's hope of achieving national fame in politics.
Yet no man of Peel's intellectual calibre could be entirely
happy to have his career shaped for him by a father or anyone else, however well-meaning. There is an element of strain
in Peel's mind from an early stage and his early successes
heightened it. He felt the mental burden of a sensitive man of
whom much was expected. He did not differ from his father
in the latter's choice of a political career for him, but the level
of achievement expected of him was a daunting prospect.
The contradictory estimates of his character by his contemporaries lend some substance to the belief that throughout his
career he was troubled by internal mental conflicts. In later
years Gladstone was full of praise for him as a manager of men,
Palmerston detected 'a proud shyness', Carlyle talked of 'his
warm sense of fun', others noticed his hot temper, his frosty
silences, and his unease on social occasions. It is quite evident
that, except on rare occasions, he preserved the protective
covering of coldness and reserve characteristic of those primarily concerned in coming to terms with themselves rather
than with the outside world. His preoccupation with his own
thoughts, and his secretiveness, help to explain the bewilderment and annoyance of his political colleagues confronted, as
they were from time to time, by Peel's apparently inex-
haustible capacity for changing his mind on the major political
issues of his times. Yet it needs to be recognised too that,
apart from the influence on him of his father's expectations
and his own excessive conscientiousness, Peel was also troubled
by an antipathy, at times strongly marked, for the ruling
classes with whom he was required by political necessity to
work in close co-operation. With many of their aims he sympathised, notably in their opposition to parliamentary reform, but throughout his career there was a feeling of conflict
in Peel's mind between that part of him which remembered his
family origins and that part of him which was mindful of his
political future. The assumptions which the Tories were apt to
make, and the Whigs too for that matter, about the treatment
of the working classes were not fully shared by Peel. The twin
principles of Peel's conduct, his desire to fulfil his father's

ambition for him to make a mark in history, and his own feeling of special responsibility to the poor, are clearly marked in
his final speech as Prime Minister to the House of Commons
on 29 June 1846.

Meanwhile, for the young M.P. in 1809, this memorable
climax lay hidden far in the future. For the time being he commanded admiration on all sides. His maiden speech made as
strong an impression as Pitt's had done. Political office was
quickly attained. Having served briefly as Under-Secretary of
State for the Colonies in Spencer Perceval's Government, he
became Chief Secretary for Ireland when Lord Liverpool became Prime Minister in 1812. Peel was then aged twenty-
four. The Irish Catholics were violently hostile to the Act of
Union, which had put them under the rule of a Protestant
Parliament, and showed their feelings by mob violence. The
situation was a stern test for so young a man but Peel, at the
cost of nervous exhaustion which forced him to abandon the
appointment in 1818, was able to restore order, using a minimum of force. His experiences gave him an abiding dislike of
Catholics, and an almost obsessional belief that Catholicism
and treason were synonymous. In 1821, reinvigorated by his
eminently happy marriage in 1820 to Julia Floyd, a general's
daughter, Peel was glad to accept responsibility again and, as
Home Secretary, now brought to completion the reforms of
the penal code and of prison conditions for which Bentham,
Mackintosh, and Romilly had been pressing for some years.
It was congenial work, whose benefit to the working classes
was obvious. Nor was Peel blind to the fact that the reforms
were adding substantially to his political stature. These reforms he hoped would be remembered by posterity; the
Londoners' nickname ' Peelers ' for the police set up by Peel's
Metropolitan Police Act of 1829 was a slight but significant indication of the people's acceptance of Peel as a national figure.

Peel, in short, had now completed his political apprenticeship, and was ready for the highest office. By coincidence the
same year, 1829, witnessed his heart-searching on the issue of
Catholic emancipation, the first of the major conflicts of conscience with which Peel was to be confronted in the years between 1829 and his downfall in 1846. These seventeen years,
the focal point of his career, provided ample subject-matter for
his friends and his foes, and the debate is not finished yet.

Attack

Throughout his career up to 1829 Peel had been a consistently pugnacious opponent of Catholicism. His years as Secretary of State for Ireland had given him a profound distrust of Roman Catholics, founded not only on dislike of their religious practices but also on the belief that their religion made them potential traitors. It was a harsh view even in an age when men were more conscious of religious differences than they are now, but there was no doubt that Peel's attitude was based on very strong conviction. In 1819 he promised 'his sincere and uncompromising resistance' to Catholic emancipation, while in 1822, in a House of Commons debate on the same subject, he plaintively remarked in defence of his objections that it was the duty of M.P.s 'to maintain their opinions to the last' even though defeat was inevitable. This ostentatious high-mindedness was characteristic of Peel and makes his subsequent volte-face the more ironical. In 1827 the issue of Catholic emancipation was raised again in the House of Commons and once more Peel made a lengthy speech attacking the proposal. His principles were again put to the test when Canning, a sympathiser with Catholic emancipation, became Prime Minister in 1827. Peel refused to continue in office as Home Secretary since, if Canning pushed through an Emancipation Bill Peel, as Home Secretary, would have to enforce the Bill in Ireland, a duty which he would find repugnant. So far Peel had been entirely consistent. Nor was his political career much interrupted in practice since Canning died a few months after taking office and in 1828 Peel was restored to his position as Home Secretary under the more congenial leadership of the Duke of Wellington.

Among members of the Government, however, Peel was becoming increasingly isolated, and it was not a situation in which he took any pleasure. He was not a man who relished the challenge of opposition. From schooldays onwards his career had been buttressed by official approval. As a result he had become morbidly sensitive to criticism though, by the irony of history, Peel, who set so much store by the good opinion of others, earned more bitter enemies than any Prime Minister of the century. Now Catholic emancipation was to provide the first searching test of his political stamina. He had shown already some promise of greatness. He was an able speaker and an efficient administrator; but his capacity when confronted by more subtle difficulties remained untested.

The Irish situation had reached a stage where a clear-cut government decision on Catholic emancipation could no longer be avoided. Daniel O'Connell's victory in the County Clare election in 1829 made it certain that the next general election would see other Catholics winning constituencies in Ireland. If this were not legalised, political rioting there was certain. In a situation of this kind, when many in the Government itself favoured Catholic emancipation, the introduction of a Bill to that effect was plainly required. The major obstacle to such a Bill was the King. Peel, knowing that emancipation was imminent, wished to resign. Wellington was opposed to this. He wished Peel to stay in the Government on the grounds that the only hope of persuading the King to agree to the Bill was to show him that even Peel, the outspoken opponent of Catholic emancipation, was ready to accept it. With remarkably little protest Peel agreed not only to stay in office but also to introduce the Bill himself. It was an extraordinary reversal on a matter about which Peel had always felt most strongly. Even if Wellington's view is accepted, that Peel's continuance in office was necessary to prevent the King blocking the Bill, this still does not condone Peel's change of front on a matter of strongly held principle. Had he had the courage of his convictions there was no other course open to him but resignation. That his suspicions about the loyalty of the Irish Catholics remained as strong as ever is evident from a comment in his *Memoirs* written on 17 January 1829: 'It will remain to be considered what test of civil allegiance shall be administered to the Roman Catholics. I advise one which shall be a purely civil test but by which the Roman Catholic shall be compelled to abjure any principles or opinions that are dangerous to the State.' It might well be argued in addition, of course, that Peel's presence was not in fact a necessity for the Government. Wellington's political judgment was notoriously poor, and he may well have overestimated the importance of royal opposition. The King would certainly have opposed the Bill, but the Crown was far less strongly placed for effective action of this kind than it had been in the eighteenth century. The con-

clusion seems inescapable that Peel's attention in the whole
affair was directed towards his own political future. When the
test came his overwhelming ambition led him to sacrifice a
principle which he had been propounding for years. In 1829
he thus deluded himself into believing that he was abandoning
his principles for the sake of his party. In the debate on Corn
Law repeal in 1846 the same man was to declare that he was
abandoning his party for the sake of his principles. Peel's
principles were extraordinarily accommodating.

The 1830s were a frustrating decade for Peel. The future lay
with the reformers not with the defenders of privilege. Yet
Peel, in order to maintain his leading position in the Tory
Party, found himself obliged to strike attitudes which were
scarcely likely to earn him the national prestige which he so
much desired. The Whig Governments of the period were
stealing a long march on the Tories with a policy of reforms
which, though clumsily applied at times, did mark a new stage
in the relationship between the State and the citizen. Peel
found that it was politically expedient for the time being to be
the spokesman of reaction. He opposed the 1832 Reform Bill.
He opposed Roebuck's scheme of 1833 for State-controlled
primary education. He opposed the imposition of a graduated
income tax on the clergy in Ireland, though they could well
afford it. He supported the 1834 Poor Law though this was to
be expected from a Tory leader, since the Bill was welcomed
by the landowning interests who were naturally opposed to
the high rate of Poor Relief which existed under the old
system. In the same year Peel opposed a Bill to allow Dissenters to take degrees at Oxford or Cambridge. Had these
attitudes been a matter of deeply-held conviction Peel's
reputation would deserve more respect. There is a need for a
party of reaction as a check on indiscriminate and ill-considered
reform. Yet all the time there was the feeling about Peel,
evident among his fellow Tories, that this traditional Toryism
did not command his loyal support. The bitterness of the
Tories over Peel's betrayal of his party in 1846 was all the
greater because it was the product of long-accumulating suspicion; this was the penalty of Peel's opportunism.

Peel's Tamworth Manifesto, issued to the electorate in
1834, shows clearly why he was so little trusted. In the hope
of defeating the Whigs in the 1834 election he abandoned the

postures of conventional Toryism: he found them no longer convenient. His new approach has been described as Conservatism rather than Toryism, but Conservatism in the 1830s was a compromise, aimed, the cynic might say, at the electors. Peel therefore found it possible to give mild praise to the Reform Bill, to woo the Dissenters with suggestions for Church reform, and to commit his party to a policy of moderate reforms. His study of the events of the past few years had convinced him that there was no political future in adamant opposition to the reforming spirit of these years.

As a political gambit the move was successful. The Whig majority was greatly reduced in the 1834 election, partly by Tory gains but equally too by Radical gains — a fact which no doubt confirmed Peel's view that the new electorate was opposed to Toryism of the old stamp. Lord Melbourne's reluctance to take office led temporarily to a Tory Government under Peel. This was short-lived and might have been still-born altogether if Peel had made it plain to the King that there was not enough support in the House of Commons to justify a Tory Government. Nevertheless, once appointed, Peel clung stubbornly to office, but eventually resigned in 1835. He continued to lead his party in opposition. The next few years were unremarkable but not lacking in significance. Peel made a strong attack on the Anti-Corn Law League in a House of Commons debate in 1839, though the organisers of the League were unconvinced of the genuineness of his conviction. His shifts of policy in the past made him the obvious weak link in the Tory party; in the 1840s the Free Traders were to concentrate their pressure upon him, a policy whose success is self-evident in the events of 1846. A second point of significance was the growing feeling of estrangement between Peel and some sections of his party, as a result of his ambiguous leadership. A comment by Sir William Molesworth in a speech in the House of Commons in 1838 sums up this feeling clearly: 'I do not believe, Sir, that we shall ever again have a Government acting upon Tory principles. If the Tories were under the responsibility of office they would be as Liberal as the country.' Such had been the influence of Peel.

It was apparent in the 1840s, to Peel's friends and foes alike, that his ardour in defence of Protectionism was beginning to cool. It might be possible therefore to represent the aban-

donment of the Corn Laws as the entirely logical culmination
of a long period of thought brought to a climax by the tragic
situation produced in Ireland by the potato famine. This was
the impression which Peel, always with one eye on posterity,
was trying to create. Unqualified acceptance of this view is
difficult. There are clear indications in the 1841–6 period that
Peel's decision to repeal the Corn Laws was conditioned by
motives other than those which he advanced to justify himself in 1846. Peel's capacity for self-justification sprang from
long practice. Allied with a talent for oratory it enabled him
to put a gloss on his motives which has often deceived historians but which made little impression on his contemporaries.

In the first place Peel was clearly troubled throughout his
career by the strain between the memory of his family origins
and awareness of the company he had to keep as leader of the
Tory landowners. His self-consciousness in this respect was
unnecessary. Among those who had experienced public
school and university education, as Peel had, there was little
concern with family pedigrees. It was Peel's actions, not his
ancestry, which alienated him from so many in his party.
Nevertheless his morbid sensitivity on this totally irrelevant
social issue made up in emotional force what it lacked in
logic; it was a conditioning factor in his political behaviour
too important to be overlooked. Palmerston showed a half-
understanding of this aspect of Peel's character when he spoke
of the latter's 'proud shyness'. What he did not discern was
that this shyness was only partly adopted from a sense of
social inferiority; at a more fundamental level it sprang from
a bitter contempt for many of his colleagues in the Tory party.
The furtherance of his career made it necessary for him to
school his thoughts and conceal his hostility. Only at the end
of his career did his control break down when, in 1846, he
rounded on his opponents in the Tory Party and venomously
attacked what he chose to regard as their ignorance and frivo-
lity. Had this onslaught been made by an extreme radical it
would have occasioned no surprise; coming from the leader of
the Tory party it was extraordinary. For a man such as Peel,
bitterly resentful of criticism, the betrayal of the landowning
classes by the repeal of the Corn Laws would be a pleasure as
well as a duty.

Peel's tender-mindedness towards the manufacturers was increasingly evident as his career developed. The extensive cuts made in import duties in the 1842 budget are a clear sign that Peel was committing himself to the manufacturers' cause. Certainly he received much encouragement to that effect from Board of Trade officials and from Gladstone, though the latter asserted that Peel was far too strong a character to allow his actions to be guided by the advice of anyone else. There was little truth in this estimate. So far as Peel had strength of character it came from his ambition not from principle. He was the supreme opportunist.

The extent to which he could be influenced by others is plain enough from his conversion to Catholic emancipation in 1829 as well as by his reversal on Corn Law repeal. In respect of the latter the pressures so skilfully applied by the Anti-Corn Law League were an instrumental factor in changing Peel's mind. Peel had no relish for the role of reactionary defence against manufacturing progress. The efficiency of the Anti-Corn Law League, its brilliant propaganda, and the extreme lengths to which some of its supporters were prepared to go, were exactly calculated to play on Peel's fears and prejudices. In 1843 Peel's private secretary was shot by a man whose intention had been to murder Peel himself. Peel had no wish to achieve a short cut to immortality, particularly on behalf of a cause in which he had so little faith himself. Cobden and his colleagues had almost achieved their purpose. It only needed the accident of the Irish potato famine to push the hesitant Peel over the brink.

The difficulties in Ireland strengthened the case, at least temporarily, for repeal of the Corn Laws. Even so, Peel's Cabinet was much divided. Lord John Russell, the Whig leader, had written a letter from Edinburgh to his constituents on 22 November 1845, making plain his whole-hearted support for Free Trade. What was less plain, however, was whether he would be able to command majority support in the House of Commons for a Free Trade policy. Peel may well have had this difficulty in mind when he resigned on 6 December 1845. It was improbable that Russell would be able to form a government. Peel's resignation may therefore have been merely a tactical move, designed to end bickering among his own Cabinet. Brought to their senses by the shock of his resignation, they would not, he knew, be content to leave him sulking like Achilles in his tent once the Whigs had failed to form an administration. He would then be able to resume power, for which he had an extreme partiality, as Disraeli noticed,[1] and exercise his old dominance over a chastened and obedient Cabinet. How far Peel anticipated the exact course of events is necessarily uncertain, but Lord John Russell did fail to form a government and by 20 December Peel was back in office, more strongly placed than he had been before.

It could now scarcely be disputed that the Irish situation made repeal of the Corn Laws urgent. This urgency played into Peel's hands. His proposal was that the Corn Laws should be repealed not merely as a temporary expedient to save the Irish from famine, but as a permanent measure of wider significance. His defence of this action was that it was in the national interest to do so. His speech defending the change in 1846 is liberally sprinkled with self-righteous references to his duty to sacrifice party to national interests, a plea always a little suspect in political life. The economic merits of Peel's reasoning are very much in doubt. The landowners in the House of Commons did not merely represent themselves. Britain was predominantly rural. Agricultural activity provided a living for a very large section of the community. Falling wheat prices might lead to cheaper food for the industrial worker but they would not increase the prosperity of the tenant farmer nor of the agricultural labourer. Already between 1841 and 1845 wheat prices had been falling steadily, from 64s 4d in 1841 to 50s 10d in 1845. It was not surprising that a permanent abandonment of the Corn Laws caused such widespread disquiet. Although in the long run the repeal made remarkably little difference to wheat prices, the immediate effect of the change is quite clear and gives support to the fears of the Protectionists. Prices rose sharply in 1847 to 69s 9d a quarter but that was a result of bad harvests. When the normal pattern was resumed in 1848 the alarming downward trend continued from 50s 6d in 1848 to 38s 6d in 1851. It was not until the mid 1850s that prices rose above the 1841 level. The poor may have had cheaper bread but the change was no service to agriculture. The retention of a moderate duty, advocated by Palmerston, would have been

[1] See Disraeli's speech to the House of Commons, 15 May 1846.

far more in keeping with the needs of the situation. Nor is
there any indication that the repeal of the Corn Laws was
necessary for the attainment of industrial prosperity. There
is general agreement among economists of most shades of
opinion that wages and the standard of living were improving
for most industrial workers, including the unskilled, during the
1840s. This greater prosperity was the result of the completion
of the first, and at times socially painful, phase of the Industrial Revolution. By 1840 society had largely adjusted itself
to the vast changes brought about by the application to industry of the inventions of the eighteenth century. Compared
with this vast economic movement the influence of the repeal
of the Corn Laws on industrial opportunity is negligible. The
repeal made it possible for manufacturers to resist increases in
wages for their workers on the grounds that Peel had given
them cheap bread, but it had minimal significance in any
other respect.

If Peel had confined himself to saving the Irish from famine
his change of heart would merit respect. His motives for making certain that the Corn Laws would be totally abolished are
much more ambiguous. He was a man of high intelligence, with
a firm grasp of economic matters. It is highly unlikely that he
anticipated that the long-term benefits of repeal would be very
great for industry, while there were obvious risks for agriculture in the adoption of Free Trade. It was more obvious still
that the repeal would split the Tory party and ruin Peel's
career. Such a dramatic gesture of self-sacrifice seems entirely
out of keeping with the man's character. Why then did a man
of Peel's ambition jettison his political career, almost wantonly it seems, in support of a policy whose benefits he knew
to be uncertain? He himself warned M.P.s that the repeal of
the Corn Laws would not necessarily help industry. 'Your
precautions,' he said in the Corn Law debate of 1846, 'may
give no certain assurance that mercantile and manufacturing
prosperity will continue without interruption.'

No doubt, as in many important decisions, a number of
factors influenced him — the arguments and violence of the
Anti-Corn Law League, the persuasions of Gladstone and the
Board of Trade officials, and Peel's basic sympathy with the
manufacturing classes. Yet the violence of the attack on him,
not only by Disraeli whose motives were admittedly in-

fluenced by personal malice, but also by the large numbers of
Tory M.P.s who shortly secured Peel's resignation from the
Premiership, suggest that other factors, more discreditable to
Peel, were at work in his mind. Peel's attitude towards his
party had been causing unease for some time and he was unable at times to resist sharply-worded thrusts against his
critics within the party. His abandonment of the landowning
classes, in spite of the consequences, would cause him few
qualms for he had little sympathy with their outlook. The
repeal of the Corn Laws would mark a clean break with the
many Tories who roused Peel's antagonism. Peel belonged to
a class, the newly wealthy middle class, rather than to a
party. His membership of the Tory party had been a pretence
and now there would be a satisfaction in bringing the long
charade to an end. It is not without significance that those who
continued to support him were called Peelites. Their allegiance
was to the man, not to a party or group feeling, and Peel was
content that this should be so.

Yet beyond this there was another motive, strongly marked
in Peel from his early years, which influenced his behaviour in
1846. His father had always wanted Peel to make a name for
himself in history, and Peel had consciously designed his
career towards that purpose. The repeal of the Corn Laws was,
in itself, a measure of much less significance than his reform
of the penal code or the 1842 budget, but that is not how it
appeared at the time. Unlike these other matters, the repeal
had all the ingredients of high drama, with Peel as the lonely
heroic figure battling against the vested interests of the rich
to secure cheap bread for the poor. Peel's speeches of 1846
are heavily loaded with reminders of the benefit to the nation
of his spirit of self-sacrifice. 'It may be,' he said, in his speech
of resignation, 'that I shall leave a name sometimes remembered with expressions of goodwill in the abodes of those whose
lot it is to labour and to earn their daily bread by the sweat of
their brow.' Traditionally the British find irresistible a mixture of bathos, high-mindedness, and defeat. Peel's grand
gesture was exactly calculated to appeal to this sentiment:
exact calculation had always been one of Peel's talents.

Defence

Peel won his way to the forefront of politics as a result of intelligence and administrative ability of a very high order. These admirable qualities are apt to arouse respect rather than affection, particularly when exercised by a man of Peel's reserved and enigmatic character. Two later Conservative Prime Ministers, Balfour and Neville Chamberlain, had similar attributes and they became the victims of powerful critical elements within their parties. No doubt personal jealousies play their part in bringing down a leader of outstanding mental calibre, and this is evident, for instance, in Disraeli's excessively bitter attack on Peel in 1846; but of greater significance is the fact that intelligence is too fluid and exploratory a quality to be confined within the narrow bounds of party prejudices. The Marquis of Halifax in the seventeenth century expressed the point when he described party politics as 'a kind of conspiracy against the State'. The more able the politician the more likely he is to be aware of the conflict, always latent and sometimes blatant, between national and party interests.

It was impossible therefore for a man of Peel's ability to allow his mind to solidify into the prejudices of those Tories whose outlook had more kinship with the Middle Ages than with England of the late Industrial Revolution. Their limited mental growth had run its brief course by the end of their period of formal education, if not before. Age added to their emotional force but not to their intellects. They were the Peter Pans of politics, ideologically sterile, except in the House of Lords, where their spiritual descendants lingered on into the twentieth century. In the House of Commons, however, the 1832 Reform Act marked the beginning of the end of this reactionary Toryism. It was Peel's misfortune that his leadership of the party coincided with the period when it was appropriate for the whole Tory party to adapt itself to the world in which it lived. Peel, with his sensitive, alert, empirical approach to politics was eminently aware of this. He became the apostle of the new movement, Conservatism, far more adaptable than the old Tory movement, and far more able to come to terms with the changes which had taken place

c

during the previous seventy years. Misunderstood, distrusted, and at times hated, both as a man and as a political leader, he ushered modern Conservatism into the world, and his colleagues rewarded him by hounding him out of office.

Catholic emancipation was the first major test of Peel's statesmanship. Wellington was the Prime Minister, but circumstances had contrived to create a situation in which the future of Catholic emancipation lay in Peel's hands. Governmental support for the measure was assured, but the King's tetchy opposition to emancipation placed Wellington in a position of acute difficulty unless he could induce Peel, the foremost spokesman against Catholic emancipation, to forgo his strongly-held opinions and act in the national interest by supporting the Bill. Peel could have continued to brandish his principles by refusing to co-operate, and by leaving Wellington and his party to struggle on unaided. A weaker man might have done so. Fortunately Peel had the good sense to recognise that there are times when self-righteousness matters less than serving the best interests of the nation. To have refused Wellington's offer would have been irresponsible. Had he done so it would have provided precisely the encouragement which the obstinate old King required. Catholic emancipation would have been delayed at a critical juncture, with Ireland cock-a-hoop over O'Connell's victory in the County Clare election. Delay might well have produced mass violence in Ireland and disorders in England, where there were many Protestants and Nonconformists whose opposition to Catholic emancipation would have been dangerously intensified if Peel had become their spokesman.

Fortunately Peel was no demagogue. He had done his duty in making his protest against the Bill. Common sense and the acceptance of the majority opinion of his colleagues now combined to suggest that he would be doing a disservice to England, to Ireland, to his party, and to constitutional stability, if by continued opposition to the Bill he should reinforce the obstinacy of George IV. As it was, even after Peel's change of attitude, George hesitated right up to the moment the Bill was introduced whether to give it his approval or not. But now he had no Peel to turn to, and no other opponents of the measure capable of forming an alternative government.

Reluctantly George yielded. The wisdom of Peel's decision was plain enough to those who valued peace more highly than bigotry.

In 1830 Peel's father died. It was also the year of an election and of the formation of a Whig ministry. The Tory Party, troubled by divisions, and at the end of a long period in office, might very well have to act as the Opposition for some years to come. Leadership of the party in such circumstances was perhaps not inviting for a man who had just inherited his father's title and fortune. Peel could have led the life of a country gentleman, but it was not his practice to follow the line of least resistance. He had too much to contribute to political life to abandon it so easily. He not only became the leader of the Opposition but during the next years there crystallised in his mind a new concept of the role of the Tory Party in politics. Peel was not betraying Toryism but merely bringing it up to date. He retained a strong respect for the traditional methods of government. His opposition to Roebuck's Bill for the extension of education, his opposition to the admission of Dissenters to universities, and his support for the 1834 Poor Law Act, all sprang from a genuine conviction that it was to the benefit of the country as a whole that the privileges and interests of the upper classes should be safeguarded. At the same time he recognised that politics could not be quite the same after the 1832 Reform Act as they had been before. He saw that the new situation required a new approach by the Tory Party, taking much more fully into account the interests of the manufacturing classes and the need for a programme of moderate reform. No doubt his own origins and his singularly sound grasp of economic affairs predisposed him to believe that traditional Toryism must learn to come to terms with reality. If he succeeded in imbuing his party with his own views it would be a severe blow to the Whigs, among whose leaders the great landowners were so strongly represented that their reforming intentions were always suspect. Whig neglect of the country's manufacturing classes had become patently obvious by the end of Melbourne's ministry.

Since Peel had spent almost all the decade of the 1830s in opposition his chances of fostering the wider concept of Conservatism, rather than the narrower one of Toryism, were necessarily limited. Nevertheless the Tamworth Manifesto of 1834 expressed the readiness of Peel and his colleagues to examine existing institutions objectively and to engage in moderate reforms. The pamphlet was obviously designed to win votes, though it can hardly be criticised on that count for there were many less desirable methods of winning elections in the 1830s and later. It is also true that it represented no clarion call for the formation of a new party. Even so it has significance in showing the direction in which Peel's thoughts were tending. He envisaged a much more active constructive role for Conservatism than had been the practice in the past, and this became abundantly evident in the legislation which he introduced when he was Prime Minister between 1841 and 1846. Above all he had a clear vision of the Government's responsibility for securing the nation's prosperity. One aspect of this approach is shown in the firmness of the controls over note issue by banks in the Bank Charter Act of 1844. It is now recognised that the Act was an imperfect solution to the problem of controlling credit transactions, and it had to be suspended three times during the next twenty-two years. Nevertheless it illustrates Peel's belief that the State must give positive direction to the course of economic life.

This is seen more clearly still in his measures to promote Free Trade. The rapid expansion of Britain's economy as a result of the Industrial Revolution made a Protectionist policy obsolescent; she had nothing to lose by Free Trade. Yet the movement towards Free Trade had been painfully slow. Huskisson had reduced duties on imported raw materials, semi-manufactured and manufactured goods, in the early 1820s, together with a crop of other measures designed to speed up and widen the flow of trade. Since then the Whigs had allowed the movement towards Free Trade to lose its impetus, with consequences which are only too plain in the budget deficits in their last years of office. Peel, on becoming Prime Minister, immediately brought to an end this policy of drift. In the 1842 and 1845 budgets sharp reductions were made in import duties. The result was that most raw materials, with one or two exceptions, notably timber, were admitted duty free, as were many semi-manufactured goods also. Foodstuffs, such as butter, were also admitted at a reduced rate of duty in keeping with the Anti-Corn Law League's advocacy of the 'cheap breakfast table' policy. There was a basic fairness to the mass of the people in this policy which appealed to Peel's humanitarianism.

Peel has received less credit for this characteristic than he deserves, but it is important that credit should be so given since his humanity of outlook is a fundamental reason for his repeal of the Corn Laws. Superficially his opposition to Roebuck's scheme for elementary education and his support for the 1834 Poor Law suggest a stubbornly reactionary attitude, the very reverse of a humane concern for the needs of the people. Nor did Peel's coldness and reserve of manner make it easy to understand that he had a strong and genuine interest in the welfare of the people. Yet it was Peel who had swept away much of the harshness of the penal code in the 1820s, and in the 1840s he had in the very forefront of his mind the interests of the mass of the community, when he introduced the economic measures which he saw quite clearly would produce his own downfall. His outlook was essentially that of any strict but fair-minded employer of labour at the time, determined that his workers should know their station in life and be hard-working; in return the employer would take a paternalistic interest in their welfare. The restrictive side of the relationship had been uppermost in Peel's political activities in the 1830s; now in the 1840s his constructively-minded humanity was equally prominent. That he was prepared to take risks in defence of the workers' interests was shown, long before the Corn Law repeal, by his reintroduction in 1842 of the income tax, highly unpopular among those with whom Peel's political life brought him into contact.

It is indisputable that in repealing the Corn Laws Peel was reversing opinions which he had once held and strongly expressed. He knew that his decision would seem like treachery to many of his colleagues, and that he would be splitting his party by launching out into a course of action which many of them would regard as an inexcusable departure from the traditions of Toryism. Peel, for his part, considered that poverty and starvation were more cogent arguments than the maintenance of vested interests. His conversion to the idea of repeal was gradual and public between 1841 and 1846. Treachery is hardly an accurate description of a change of outlook which was apparent to all long before 1846. The Irish potato famine

merely gave an immediate opportunity to repeal the Corn
Laws; at a more fundamental level the repeal was the logical
culmination of policies which Peel had been introducing since
the beginning of his ministry in 1841.

The Protectionists could argue with some force that the removal of duties on corn would render no service to agriculture
in Ireland, and that by the time the duties had been completely
removed, in 1849, the Irish famine would be a thing of the past
anyway. But this ignored the fact that Peel's repeal of the
Corn Laws was part of a much broader policy to remove,
whenever possible, all impediments to Free Trade. The continuation of corn duties was out of keeping with the measures
by which he had swept away over a thousand duties between
1842 and 1845. If corn duties were retained they would keep
up the price of bread and reduce the buying capacity of the
British public, both for home products and for imported goods.
This reduction in imports would not be in Britain's interests.
Economists have demonstrated the close relationship between
import and export activity in the nineteenth century.[1] Reduction in imports would lead inevitably to falling demand from
foreign countries for British goods. Peel was convinced that
repeal of the Corn Laws would help to arrest this damaging
sequence of events. He may have overrated the importance of
his action, though a distinguished contemporary, Cavour,
believed that Peel's action marked a decisive economic turning
point. Even so, it may be that mid-Victorian prosperity owed
much more to the world-wide development of industrial
strength, to the vast improvements in railway communications, and to the gold discoveries in California and Ballarat
than to all the measures for freeing trade put together. But the
importance of Peel's decision on the Corn Laws is of less
consequence here than the reasons for it. Plainly he believed
that Britain now had the hope of achieving great material
prosperity. One great heave would make her advance certain.
He wished to see the vast strides made towards Free Trade
virtually completed by the removal of the last obstacle in the
path — the Corn Laws.

One other element in Peel's thinking deserves the closest

---

[1] See, for instance, A. H. Imlah, *Economic Elements in the Pax
Britannica* (Cambridge, Mass.: Harvard University Press, 1958).

consideration. This is his belief that the repeal of the Corn Laws would provide the strongest possible incentive towards more scientific farming.[1] 'High farming' is associated generally with the period after 1846, but the use of drainage schemes, new forms of crop rotation, and of fertilisers had been practised by the more enterprising farmers for many years before the repeal. Peel had personal knowledge as a landowner of the benefits this more scientific approach to farming might bring to agriculture if more widely diffused; the removal of the cushioning of Protection for arable farmers would be the quickest way of stimulating their enterprise; to give them an added incentive to improve the standard of their farming he outlined a scheme by which loans would be advanced to farmers for drainage schemes. It is more than a coincidence that the 'golden age' of British farming follows so closely after the Corn Law repeal.

But Peel was not merely a man of outstanding economic vision; he was also a humanitarian. Nothing makes this more clear than his speech defending the repeal of the Corn Laws in 1846. He attacked the absurdity and selfishness of retaining the Corn Laws when Ireland was in a state of acute distress. He was at least as much aware of the consequences for England also of the retention of the Corn Laws. He spoke of the hardships of the early 1840s and of the moral responsibility to avoid repetition. 'Gloomy winters, like those of 1841 and 1842, may again set in. Are those winters effaced from your memory? From mine they can never be.' He continued: 'Commune with your hearts and answer me this question: will your assurances of sympathy be less consolatory if, with your willing consent, the Corn Laws shall then have ceased to exist? Will it be no satisfaction to you to reflect, that by your own act, you have been relieved from the grievous responsibility of regulating the supply of food?'

These were powerful feelings and powerful arguments, the future prosperity of the nation and the welfare of the poor. There are times when set party attitudes lamentably fail to meet the needs of the nation: and this was one of them. Peel knew what the cost would be for the party and for himself of

---

[1] On this matter see D. C. Moore, 'The Corn Laws and High Farming', *Economic History Review*, 2nd Series, vol. xviii, no. 3 (1965).

the decision which he had taken. Fortunately for Britain he believed that these consequences were of smaller importance than what he himself described as 'urgent considerations of public duty.'

4. PALMERSTON AND FOREIGN POLICY GINGER BEER OR CHAMPAGNE?[1]

Prelude

In 1851, following Russell's dismissal of Palmerston from the position of Foreign Secretary, Queen Victoria, anxious to regain a degree of royal influence in foreign affairs, asked the Government for a statement of the general principles of British foreign policy. The Government complied, but their answer was unrevealing, not because of any particular wish to be unhelpful but because British foreign policy in the nineteenth century was a bundle of inconsistencies and improvisations from which it was quite impossible to disentangle any principles. Britain played a major role in the creation of the Congress System; and she played a major role in destroying it. She helped to devise the terms of the Treaty of Vienna and then frequently gave her aid to subverting it. She looked on foreign policy as an extension of her trading interests, yet devoted much of her energies in foreign affairs to antagonising her customers.

Her policies in Europe are supposed to be guided by the 'balance of power' concept. 'Half the wrong conclusions at which mankind arrive are reached by abuse of metaphors,' said Palmerston in 1839. The metaphor of a balance of power has had some validity at some stages in history. When Spain's interests were directed towards the New World, when Russia was merely Muscovy, when Prussia only existed in embryo, then France and Austria, the two great Catholic powers, could be regarded as equal weights in opposite scales. Yet what possible validity could the balance of power concept have in the totally different circumstances of the nineteenth century? If balance is to be achieved the forces need to be

[1] From Disraeli's description of Palmerston in 1855: 'An imposter utterly exhausted, at the best only ginger beer and not champagne.'

known, but where did power lie in nineteenth-century Europe? Did it lie in the uncertain strength of Russia, making occasional sorties into Europe to interfere in the affairs of her neighbours? Did it lie in the sprawling Austrian Empire which, with Russia, had been the most resilient of Napoleon's Continental opponents, and whose dominance of central Europe had been carefully fostered at the Congress of Vienna? Did it lie with France whose revolutionary past made her a permanent object of suspicion by the European powers? Did it lie with the fast-developing strength of Prussia? Or did it lie, not with nations as such at all, but with movements of like-minded people intent on constitutional liberalism? No one in Palmerston's lifetime could give any certain answers to these questions, yet unless they are answered the whole idea of Britain maintaining a balance of power loses reality. Power is dynamic, not static. In the nineteenth century, Britain and the other European powers were frequently in laborious pursuit of policies which the movement of events had made irrelevant. The young Queen might well ask her ministers for a statement of the principles of British foreign policy; unfortunately on this subject they were almost as bewildered as she was.

It is evident from the outset, therefore, that in assessing the foreign policy of Palmerston, or any other Foreign Secretary of the nineteenth century, too much should not be expected. There was no guiding principle of any consequence against which policies could be judged and described in terms of success or failure. The most which can be expected from the nation's leaders during this period, and subsequently, is a speedy grasp of what is immediately expedient for Britain in particular situations as they arise.

The policies of Palmerston's predecessors were not consistently based on either expediency or principle but wobbled uncertainly between the two. The desire to avoid involvement in any war which might arise in Europe was strongly marked, but alongside this there was the conflicting desire to give support to those groups in Spain, Italy, and elsewhere, who were trying to secure basic constitutional liberties. Yet the maintenance of peace would best be secured by co-operation with the established governments of the great powers who had enough armed strength to ensure the defeat of the weakly-led rebel movements of the post-war period. Britain's policy at the

Congress of Vienna and her participation in the Quadruple Alliance were both based on the assumption that the aim in foreign affairs was to achieve stability in Europe, and that the best means to do so would be by accepting the dominance there of authoritarian governments. Within a few years, however, Britain was showing a sympathy for liberal movements in Europe which her fellow Congress powers found disconcerting. On the other hand those attempting to organise these anti-authoritarian risings in Europe could place no reliance on British support. The British approved the suppression of the rebellions in Naples, Piedmont, and Spain in 1821. They encouraged the popular party in Spain to resist the French invasion in 1823 but gave no active support. The Spanish colonies secured their independence through British connivance, and the Portuguese constitutional party was given military and naval help by Britain. So too were the Greeks, though Canning until the very last moment was hesitant in his support. British intervention did not come until 1827 although the Greek rebellion had begun originally in 1821. Even when the Egyptians invaded Greece and Greek delegates pleaded for British help, Canning tersely refused.

Nevertheless Canning eventually took the decision to help the Greeks win their independence from the Turks. By the Treaty of London of 1827 he secured the support for this project of Russia and France, the two powers whose interests in the Mediterranean were most dangerous to Britain. This can be represented as a master stroke. Britain by allying herself with Russia and with France would be able to keep a better check on their ambitions in the Near East than by opposing them openly. Whether this policy was well advised in practice was another matter. There were doubts about its wisdom from the start among politicians and the press. Friendship with Turkey was the only logical policy for Britain, nor did this necessarily mean that the abuses of Turkish government had to be condoned. If it can be argued that Canning's policy of alliance with Russia and France gave the hope of moderating their ambitions in the Near East, it can be argued more conclusively that British support for Turkey could be used as an effective bargaining counter to persuade the Turks to reform their system of government and to grant virtual independence to the Greeks without the need for war at all. Had such a policy been adopted it is unlikely that Russia, and still less, France, could have found any excuse for military action against the Turks. Turkish forces would then have remained intact as a front line of defence for British interests in the Mediterranean. Canning's policy did admittedly secure the independence of Greece, but it also led to the destruction of the Turkish fleet off Navarino, to a dangerous southward advance by Russian troops, to French troops operating in the Morea against the Egyptian forces, and eventually in 1833 to the unnatural, desperate, and dangerous alliance of Unkiar Skelessi by which Turkey, deprived of the alternative of a British alliance, had to turn to her traditional enemy, Russia, for help against Mehemet Ali.

Canning's policy had been extraordinarily short-sighted and impulsive. 'Things are getting back to a wholesome state again. Every nation for itself and God for us all,' was his comment on developments in international affairs in the 1820s. It was a nonsensical and irresponsible remark. His handling of the Eastern Question had annoyed Austria whose support as a counterweight to French and Russian ambitions was essential. It led to no permanent improvement in relations with Russia and France who, on the contrary, were more tempted than ever to exploit Turkish difficulties in the Near East. Thus, when Palmerston became Foreign Secretary, relations with the European powers were ambiguous and confused. His responsibility was accordingly heavy, and was to be made heavier by the long duration of his management of foreign affairs, lasting with a few brief breaks until 1865. During these thirty-five years the great European powers were jockeying for supremacy in Europe itself, in the Middle East, and the Far East. They adopted menacing postures, backed increasingly with menacing actions. All of them at one time or another in this period were involved in wars. It was a period of unsettlement and danger which would test to the uttermost Palmerston's capacity to preserve Britain's status and interests in the world. He relished personal responsibility. Whether British foreign policy between 1830 and 1865 is regarded as successful or not depends very largely on the assessment of the decisions of this one man.

Attack

In 1848, midway through the period of Palmerston's long dominance of British foreign policy, he delivered himself of the pronouncement in the House of Commons that 'We have no eternal allies and no perpetual enemies. Our interests are eternal and those interests it is our duty to follow.' The word 'eternal' half suggested an identity of outlook between the Almighty and Palmerston which the latter may have been over-ready to assume, but the statement was also objectionable in its idea as well as in its wording. What Palmerston was saying, in effect, was that Britain could be counted on to pursue a policy of narrow self-interest, in the course of which she would freely abandon any allies if she found it convenient. Self-interest is admittedly not an unusual feature of national policies. Frederick the Great of Prussia had been the supreme exponent of the same outlook in the eighteenth century, but in general had the good sense to confide his intentions to his *Memoirs*. It was characteristic of Palmerston's clumsy arrogance that he should thus proclaim to the world in open debate in the House of Commons the assured unreliability of Britain as an ally. Had he been speaking from a position of strength, of unchallenged dominance of Europe, the statement would have been forgivable, if tactless. As it was, Britain's policies by 1848 had left her without a friend in Europe, nor had she the military strength to compensate for her blunders in diplomacy. By the 1860s this had become plain even to Palmerston, when the inability of Britain to influence the course of affairs in Europe was amply demonstrated during the Russian suppression of the Polish Revolution in 1863 and in the Austro-Prussian invasion of Schleswig and Holstein in 1864. These events were to show the hollowness of Palmerston's pretensions, but until that time Palmerston, to the detriment of British interests, was able to take refuge from reality in a smoke-screen of jingoist sentiment. He was not alone in that respect, though that in no way mitigates his own responsibility for the misdirection of British foreign affairs.

There is no doubt that Palmerston's actions were entirely consistent with his statement that alliances were less important than devotion to Britain's 'eternal interests'. More English than the English, this Irish peer had a rarely-concealed contempt for foreigners. He was as fickle in his policies as he was in his affections. By the end of his career he had befriended and antagonised every major power in Europe and for good measure left a legacy of distrust for Britain in China and America. These were the consequences of the policy of pursuing eternal interests. For the most part it is true that he had a clear vision of those interests. He wished to preserve the Turkish Empire as a bulwark against Russia, to maintain and extend British trading interests and to uphold British prestige. The fault lay not so much in these aims as in the means used to secure them. Wise, consistent statesmanship during these particularly formative years might have created a fund of goodwill for Britain which could have acted as a stabilising force for the whole of Europe. What was needed was a Gladstone, not a Palmerston. The latter had the misfortune to combine strength of character with weakness of perception, a dangerous combination much admired among those who suffer from it.

When Palmerston became Foreign Secretary in 1830 he was immediately confronted with the aftermath of the July Revolution in France, and of the Belgian rebellion to secure independence from the Dutch. Palmerston, in common with his Whig colleagues, approved of Louis-Philippe's seizure of power in France on the grounds that the Citizen King would be a more sober-minded and constitutional ruler than Charles X had been. On the other hand, when the risk arose that France might become dominant in Belgium, either through French military intervention to drive the Dutch out of Belgium or else through the establishment of the Duke of Nemours, Louis-Philippe's son, on the Belgian throne, Palmerston felt bound to oppose any extension of French influence. In general the wisdom of his policy is not in dispute but his own contribution to the settlement of the matter ought not to be overstated. He was given firm guidance by Lord Grey, and he was fortunate too in that the rapid defeat of the risings in Poland and Italy, by Russia and Austria respectively, released their forces to assist in driving the French forces out of Belgium, should Louis-Philippe adopt the dangerous policy of staying there. Fortunately Louis-Philippe was too peacefully inclined to be influenced overmuch by the hotheads in France, and the crisis subsided. Palmerston had not dominated the episode as he was to dominate later crises and this contributed to a peaceful solution. The politically inoffensive Leopold of Saxe-Coburg became the Belgian ruler, and Belgian neutrality was effectively guaranteed. The consequences of this episode were not wholly beneficial. The Tories were perturbed about the effects on trade of the worsening relations with Holland and, more seriously still, about the demolition by Leopold of the fortresses on the south Belgian frontier. The latter action was acceptable perhaps if French and British friendship were assured, but much would depend on the way in which relations between the two countries developed over the next few years.

It was in this respect that the first serious flaw in Palmerston's handling of foreign policy became apparent. The inability of the Turks, if unaided, to stem the advances of Mehemet Ali's Egyptian forces into the Turkish Empire was evident in 1831 and was to become so again in 1839. Palmerston was remarkably slow to arrest the anti-Turkish drift of British policy stemming from the Greek War of Independence. The Sultan, having appealed in vain for British help, turned as a last resort to Russia, forming with her the Treaty of Unkiar Skelessi. Apart from assuring Turkey of Russian support, the Russians also secured by a secret clause that the Dardanelles should be closed to foreign warships at the request of the Russian Government. The purpose was defensive, but Palmerston was uneasy, with some cause, that his delay in recognising the need to support the Turks might have led to clauses seriously harmful to British interests. The fact that this was not so in practice owed nothing to Palmerston's diplomacy.

Russia also consolidated her position a little in the same year by an agreement with Austria, the Treaty of Münchengrätz, by which they promised to assist each other against revolutionary movements, and to respect each other's interests in the Turkish Empire. The agreement was a product of Palmerston's obtuseness. Austria had as good reason as Britain to be suspicious about Russian intentions towards the Turkish Empire, but Palmerston could not reconcile himself to a policy of close co-operation with Austria. He resented Metternich's pretensions to be 'the coachman of Europe', and disliked the re-

strictions on freedom of thought in the Austrian Empire. In
practice these restrictions were irritating but not unduly
oppressive. Had Palmerston been able to master his prejudices
Russian power in the Near East might have been counter-
balanced by an Austria and Turkey friendly to Britain. As
events unfolded it became clear that Russia's interest in the
Turkish Empire was primarily defensive, but this was by no
means certain in 1833. Palmerston had allowed a situation to
develop in which there was a much stronger potential threat
to Britain's interests in the Near East than there need have
been.

Palmerston attempted to counter the Austro-Russian agreement by a Quadruple Alliance between Britain, France, Spain,
and Portugal. In the two latter countries the British and French
were giving somewhat variable support to liberal movements.
As an alliance of liberal Western powers against the authoritarian states of Austria and Russia it was a non-starter —
fortunately no doubt. Britain and France rapidly became
divided over their policies, particularly in Spain where the
extent of British aid for the Queen's party was the subject of
controversy. As the 1830s drew to their end it became increasingly difficult to maintain any firm friendship with
France, partly because of the suspicion that she was inciting
Mehemet Ali in Egypt to act against the Turkish Empire,
partly because of the ever-present possibility that Palmerston
would give vent to some tactless or offensive remark which
would exasperate even the placid Louis-Philippe. Relations
had become strained still further in the final settlement of the
dispute between Belgium and Holland in the years 1838–9.
Against French wishes the frontier between the two countries
was adjusted so that Catholics in Luxemburg and Limburg
were placed under Dutch rule. There was widespread hostility
to Catholicism in northern Europe. Palmerston's decision to
pander to this prejudice was of doubtful wisdom. Since Louis-
Philippe had come to the throne the general tendency had
been for Britain to aim at closer relations with France, but
Palmerston's policy in this respect shifted with every wind
which blew. Yet this was the man who in 1836, in urging one
of his envoys to strive hard for Anglo-French understanding,
reminded him that: 'England alone cannot carry her points
on the Continent; she must have allies as instruments to work

with.' Palmerston's flagrant disregard in later years for his own advice constitutes one of the most damning criticisms of his foreign policy.

Relations with France deteriorated to an alarming degree as a fresh crisis developed in the Near East. In 1839 the Turks launched an attack on Ibrahim Pasha's army in the hope of driving the Egyptians out of Syria. The defeat of the Turkish army and the desertion of the Turkish fleet to the Egyptians opened up possibilities of radical political changes in this strategically important area of the world. Russian and Austrian interests might be affected, while the French, already influential in Egypt, were delighted with the Egyptian successes and hoped for more. Fortunately the Russians did not intervene in the fighting. Instead they adopted the same defensive approach as they had at Unkiar Skelessi and were content with an agreement with Britain, Austria, and Prussia to preserve the neutrality of the Dardanelles. France might prove more difficult, but Palmerston was confident throughout the crisis that Louis-Philippe did not want a war against a coalition of European powers. The replacement of his chief minister, the volatile Thiers, by Guizot in 1840 was an indication of Louis-Philippe's support for moderate policies. Eventually the Egyptians under pressure from Britain, Prussia, Russia, and Austria, were compelled to withdraw from Syria. Palmerston toyed with the idea of forcing Mehemet Ali to abandon his governorship of Egypt but could not command sufficient support for this action among the other powers.

In some respects Palmerston's policy had been justified. The Turkish Empire had been maintained intact with a minimum of military effort but Palmerston's conduct of the crisis has often been praised by historians beyond its worth. Admittedly opposition to French support for Mehemet Ali was necessary, but it was easy to enrol the support of Russia, Austria, and Prussia for the expulsion of Egyptian troops from Syria; none of these powers wanted to see an extension of French influence any more than Britain did. Once general support had been secured for joint action against the Egyptians there could be no serious expectation of France engaging in a forlorn enterprise against the other powers. Palmerston knew this as well as Louis-Philippe. It was therefore all the more frustrating for the French to be subjected to the taunts of Palmerston who could never resist the temptation to exploit the difficulties of any of the great European powers. Palmerston's arrogance steadily drove Louis-Philippe into a state of exasperation which resulted in the rash French intervention in the Spanish marriages question in 1846 and to an open breach with Britain.

In 1841 the Tories won the election and Palmerston was therefore out of office. Shortly before this, however, he had been responsible for the outbreak of the Opium War with China which lasted until 1842. In part the war sprang out of disputes over the rights of Chinese courts to try British subjects and over the seizure in 1839 of all stocks of British-owned opium in Canton. By 1842 the Chinese had had enough. In the Treaty of Nanking they gave way on all the points in dispute and, in addition, had to open up five of their main ports to trade with other powers. Britain also gained the cession of the island of Hong Kong. It had been a successful exploitation of a power too weak as yet to resist British strength. Palmerston spoke of the action as a civilising mission. For the Chinese, Western civilisation had meant the large-scale importation of opium in opposition to the wishes of the Chinese Government, the bribery of Chinese officials to further the evil trade, the extortion of special trading privileges, and finally humiliating submission to armed force. Palmerston was supremely indifferent to the long-term consequences of his high-handed violence. The effect of his policy on China's relations with the West is plain enough now, but even in his own time the shortsightedness of securing commercial advantage by immoral means was pointed out by Gladstone.

Palmerston returned as Foreign Secretary in the Russell administration in 1846 and remained there until his dismissal in 1851. He had become increasingly vociferous against the French while in opposition between 1841 and 1846. It was no surprise therefore that his return to power made impossible a friendly settlement of the dispute with France over the Spanish marriages. Under Lord Aberdeen, the Tory Foreign Secretary, there had been a faint hope that an open breach between France and Britain on this issue might be avoided. Aberdeen and Guizot, the French minister, had shown that given good sense France and Britain could work together in harmony even in a tricky matter of this kind. The situation was the more delicate because it was one of a series of recent episodes, including the occupation of Tahiti and the methods of putting down the slave trade, in which British and French interests had clashed. Once Palmerston, the proverbial bull in the china shop, returned to office any hope of reconciliation or compromise instantly vanished. The mere fact of his return made Louis-Philippe and Guizot press on with their plan for betrothing Queen Isabella of Spain to the Duke of Cadiz, reputed to be impotent, and the Queen's sister to Louis's own son, the Duke of Montpensier. The expectation was that eventually the Duke of Montpensier would rule Spain through his wife and that French and Spanish interests would thus be permanently united. Louis-Philippe knew how unpopular this revival of the 'Family Compact' policy would be in Europe, and might well have been prepared to accept an alternative solution had he not been goaded past endurance by Palmerston's heavy-handed interference. Palmerston can hardly be said to have negotiated on this matter at all. He dictated his views with the utmost tactlessness to the French and Spanish Governments. He ignored completely the French marriage scheme, and indicated that husbands should be found for the Spanish Queen and her sister from three candidates, a Coburg prince and two Spanish cousins. This had the immediate effect of ensuring Spanish acceptance of the French marriage scheme. In addition the breach between Britain and France made it quite impossible for these two Western powers to bring any effective pressure to bear on behalf of the liberal movements in Europe in 1848, as they might have been able to do had it not been for Palmerston's consistent mishandling of relations with France.

The 1848 Revolutions gave Palmerston exactly the kind of opportunity for mischief-making which he found irresistible. In France he welcomed the fall of Louis-Philippe, then, out of contempt for the Second Republic, gave his approval to the *coup d'état* by Louis Napoleon in 1851. Events in the Austrian Empire and Germany posed a greater dilemma. The prospect of the Empire being splintered into small segments at the mercy of academic liberals and radical idealists would plainly be a menace to European peace. On the other hand Palmerston, like his predecessors, had a friendly regard for liberal movements in Europe, particularly as they showed a flattering wish to imitate the English parliamentary system. He half attempted to reconcile these conflicting attitudes by advising the Austrians that they would be strengthened, not weakened, by the loss of their Italian possessions. He was tartly told by the Austrians not to meddle in affairs which were not his concern. It was a well-deserved rebuke for a tactless remark. Moreover, there was no person or power in Italy at that stage capable of welding that country into a strong enough unit to ensure its safety from foreign intervention if Austrian power should be removed. Palmerston followed up this injudicious but characteristic interference by welcoming Kossuth, leader of the Hungarian nationalists, and by making clear his pleasure at the action of the London brewery men who attacked General Haynau, the Austrian general responsible for the harsh treatment of the Hungarian and Italian rebels. Palmerston could not resist the temptation of playing to the gallery of public opinion; Queen Victoria, however, insisted that he should send a letter of apology to the Austrian Government. Palmerston even contrived to make the letter of apology offensive, but was compelled to send a more satisfactory version. He knew that a strong and friendly Austria would be of great assistance to British policies in Europe, yet his habit of insulting foreign powers was too deep-rooted to be cured. It was not surprising that when Palmerston was dismissed in 1851 Schwarzenberg, the Austrian chief minister, gave a ball in honour of the occasion.

This undistinguished phase of Palmerston's career was rounded off by the Don Pacifico incident, and by his unconstitutional support for Louis Napoleon's seizure of power. Don Pacifico was a Portuguese money-lender, but nominally British because he had been born in Gibraltar. He was now living in Athens. Following a dispute with Greek citizens his house was burned down and he claimed compensation from the Greek Government. His claim was supported by British representatives in Greece. The Greeks were evasive. Palmerston without consulting France and Russia, the co-guarantors of Greek independence, ordered a blockade of the Greek coast in defence of Don Pacifico's claims. The move was successful in that the Greeks agreed to pay compensation, but Palmerston's methods were vehemently criticised in Britain. In defending his action in the Commons Palmerston used language as melodramatic as his actions had been. Just as a Roman subject in ancient days was protected wherever he was by his Roman citizenship, so too 'a British subject, in whatever land he may be, shall feel confident that the watchful eye and the strong arm of England will protect him against injustice and wrong'. Whether this admirable sentiment justified the clumsy arrogance of Palmerston's handling of the Don Pacifico incident is another matter, and this was recognised at the time.

On 3 December 1851, the day after Louis Napoleon's seizure of power in Paris, Palmerston, acting entirely on his own initiative, without any consultation with his Cabinet colleagues or the Queen, made known to the French ambassador his approval of Louis Napoleon's action. This was completely at variance with the policy of strict neutrality which both the Queen and the Cabinet supported. Queen Victoria was rightly indignant. Lord Russell, though sympathetic to Palmerston in general, had been placed in an impossible position and was obliged to ask Palmerston to resign his post as Foreign Secretary.

During Lord Aberdeen's ministry of 1852-5 Palmerston was Home Secretary and his influence on foreign affairs was confined to inflammatory comment. Public opinion for the most part was violently anti-Russian, a sentiment perfectly attuned to the striking of aggressive attitudes by Palmerston. Napoleon III's desire for prestige, and the blundering diplomacy of the Aberdeen Government and of Russia now combined to produce the Crimean War. Even as late as 1854 the war might have been avoided when Russia, under diplomatic pressure from Austria and Prussia, withdrew her forces which had invaded Moldavia and Wallachia. British and French troops, based on Varna on the Black Sea in readiness for action against the Russians in the Principalities,[1] now found themselves deprived of their purpose. Pressure, however, developed in Britain, with Palmerston as its foremost advocate, for an attack on Sevastopol, with the object of robbing the Russian fleet of its chief base on the Black Sea. The military commanders were doubtful of the wisdom of such an operation. Palmerston's recommendations were accepted, however, and by 1855 he was directing policy himself as Prime Minister. Peace was made after the fall of Sevastopol.

This peace, the Treaty of Paris of 1856, allowed the Princi-

[1] i.e. Moldavia and Wallachia.

palities a substantial degree of freedom from Turkish control; it prevented Russia from maintaining a fleet or naval arsenal in the Black Sea and closed the Dardanelles to foreign war-ships in time of peace; it deprived Russia of Southern Bess-arabia and provided for international control of the Danube; it insisted on the Tsar's abandonment of his claims to protect the Christian subjects of the Sultan. The most important part of the treaty was the restriction imposed on Russian use of the Black Sea. It proved quite impossible in practice to maintain this. The Russians took advantage of the Franco-Prussian War to break the treaty in 1870 by sending Russian warships into the Black Sea. Gladstone, then in power, had neither the means nor the wish, it seems, to oppose their action. It has been claimed, however, in defence of the Crimean War that it gave Britain the time and opportunity to stabilise the situa-tion in the Near East. If this was the intention then it proved a delusion. Far from solving the Eastern Question it made a solution more remote than ever. The major effect of the Crimean War was not to strengthen Britain's position in the Near East but to make it infinitely more vulnerable by the bitter resentment roused in Russia against the British and French. It is true that before the Crimean War Russia had toyed with a number of schemes to weaken Turkey and to keep it subordinate to her influence. Yet what is striking throughout the years before the Crimean War is the moderation in prac-tice of Russian demands on Turkey. This is evident at Unkiar Skelessi in 1833 and in the Straits Convention of 1841. It should be noted too that Russian participation in the Crimean War itself sprang in the first place from the threatening atti-tude of Napoleon III, backed up by demonstrations of French naval power in the Mediterranean. Anti-Russian feelings be-came obsessional in the West and blinded Britain in particular to the fact that Russian intentions in the Near East were de-fensive. Palmerston, though he talked of Britain pursuing her eternal interests, was incapable of deducing trends in policies from the course of events; his motives were a compound of bombast and prejudice.

Relations with China again became troublesome in 1856. The Chinese were doing their best to stamp out piracy, smug-gling, and the transporting of coolies by traders to the West Indies. It was a difficult task. Chinese officials at Canton boarded the *Arrow*, a lorcha, whose Chinese owner lived in Hong Kong. Twelve of the crew were arrested on the grounds that the Chinese believed there was a well-known pirate concealed on board. The ship had been flying a British flag, but so did many lorchas as a mask for illegal activities. The British consul at Canton demanded the return of the twelve men and an apology. The Chinese returned the men but refused to apologise. Events now followed their familiar course, beginning with a British bombardment of Chinese forts at Canton and culminating, during Palmerston's last ministry, in further trading concessions being wrung from the reluctant Chinese.

Palmerston was forced to resign in 1858 following one of the rare occasions, ironically, when he showed some moderation in his foreign policy. Orsini, an Italian patriot, had attempted to assassinate Napoleon III. He had organised the details of the plot in London. Palmerston introduced a Conspiracy to Murder Bill to make the plotting of assassinations by foreign refugees a felony, but anti-French feeling was strong, the Bill was defeated and Palmerston resigned.

In 1859 Palmerston came back to power for the last time following the defeat of the short-lived Tory ministry of Lord Derby. The futility of Palmerston's policy of 'meddle and muddle' became painfully clear between 1859 and 1865. Russell was at the Foreign Office, and he and Palmerston, 'those two dreadful old men' as Queen Victoria described them, were confronted with a swiftly changing pattern of events in Europe and America particularly.

In Piedmont Cavour was tortuously edging his way towards an open breach with Austria in collaboration with Napoleon III, whose mind was befuddled by the wish to imitate the deeds of the first Napoleon. Palmerston, as in 1848–9, sympathised with constitutional movements but had no wish to see Austrian power fundamentally weakened. He was therefore content that Britain should adopt a negative role for which she was admirably fitted. Italy's long coastline made her particularly vulnerable to British sea-power, but this did not lead to British naval action, except in the negative sense that Garibaldi was allowed to bring his troops from Sicily across to the Italian mainland without interference from Britain. Piedmont, with French help, went to war against Austria, but the French after victories at Magenta and Solferino withdrew from the war. The result was a compromise peace in which Piedmont received Lombardy but not Venetia. Austrian power was little diminished, and Napoleon was given the minor compensation of the addition to France of Savoy and Nice. As it happened an equilibrium of forces had thus been established in northern Italy. This owed much more to chance than to Palmerston; besides, it could not be expected to last for long. Palmerston's policy of limited support for the Piedmontese might very well be insufficient to gain their friendship but sufficient to break the remaining links with Austria.

Britain likewise avoided intervention in the American Civil War. This was a sound decision, but the *Trent* and the *Alabama* episodes were clumsily handled and cost Britain the goodwill of the subsequently victorious northern states. The *Trent*, a British ship carrying two envoys, Mason and Slidell, from the southern states to Britain was intercepted by a northern cruiser, and the two envoys were arrested. Palmerston, the more annoyed perhaps because he was now having his own high-handed methods used against him, sent a strongly-worded dispatch to the northern states. The protest was deserved but Palmerston had intended it to be even more forthright in tone than the version actually sent. Fortunately Prince Albert was able to persuade him to modify the wording of the first draft.

Palmerston and Russell were even more blatantly at fault over the escape of the *Alabama* from Liverpool to join the southern states as a sea-raider. The ship, built at the request of the southern states, was not launched until 1862. There was little doubt that Britain would be infringing her neutral status if she allowed the *Alabama* to sail to join the South. Legal technicalities might be used in defence of such an action but they became irrelevant anyway when slack supervision enabled the ship to be put to sea while investigations over her right to sail were taking place. The immediate responsibility was Russell's but Palmerston was clearly involved too, particularly when the Federal states later raised the issue of compensation for the large amount of tonnage sunk by the *Alabama* before her capture in 1864. Palmerston refused to pay. Fortunately Gladstone, in 1872, took a larger view of Britain's responsibilities and £3¼m was paid to the United States.

Palmerston, now in his late seventies, was increasingly a

liability to Britain in every aspect of policy. At home his presence blocked any hope of reform. In foreign policy he lived in a world of illusion and was quite incapable of grasping the implications of political developments, particularly in central Europe. Two episodes illustrate the weakness of his judgment at this stage — the Polish rebellion and the question of the duchies of Schleswig and Holstein. The Poles rebelled against the Russians in 1863. Their defeat was certain and made doubly so by Prussian help for Russia. Military intervention by Britain was quite impracticable. It is therefore very much open to question whether Palmerston's tirades against Russian action were worth while. One of the most unfortunate effects of this policy of bluster from weakness was that the Poles were encouraged to continue their revolt in the faint, though useless, hope that the Western powers would intervene to save them.

That Palmerston had not yet learned his lesson was now decisively demonstrated in the Schleswig-Holstein crisis. When the Danish King, Frederick VII, announced his intention to incorporate Schleswig in the Danish Kingdom, German opinion was outraged. Palmerston believed that a strong Denmark would be a useful agent of British influence in northern Europe; the recent marriage of the Prince of Wales to Princess Alexandra of Denmark had also strengthened friendship between the two countries. Moreover, Palmerston had a contempt for the German states. He underestimated the strength of the Prussian army and believed that Bismarck's policy was merely bluff. The only danger he visualised was that Bismarck's threatening attitude might give an excuse for French intervention which, so Palmerston believed, would lead to the destruction of Prussia. He therefore decided to give firmly-worded support to Denmark in the hope that this would deter the Prussians from action. In the event of any infringement of Danish independence those concerned would find that 'it would not be Denmark alone with which they would have to contend'. Napoleon III angled for co-operation with Britain, but Palmerston, suspicious of his intentions, would have none of it. Bismarck, assured of Austrian support, now launched an attack on the Duchies during which Prussian troops occupied Schleswig and Austrian troops were established in Holstein. The Danes appealed for help to Britain. Palmers-

ton replied that 'to enter into a military conflict with all
Germany on continental ground would be a serious under-
taking'. The Danes had wanted a squadron of British ships;
instead Palmerston sent them Britain's 'honourable sympathies'. It was a fitting end to a blustering foreign policy
which had alienated every major power with whom Palmerston had come into contact, and many of the lesser powers too.
Later generations have been left to foot the bill for Palmerston's blunders.

Defence

The influence which one man can bring to bear on the course
of foreign policy is necessarily very limited. There have been
exceptional situations when one power, or grouping of powers,
has been strong enough to dominate much of the European
continent by force; then it is possible for a Napoleon or a
Hitler to exert a powerful influence on European affairs. But
this was not the situation during Palmerston's long management of foreign affairs. No power, acting alone, was strong
enough to impose its will by force, nor was there any firm
alliance among the European powers to achieve the same
effect by co-operation. The grouping together of the Congress
powers had broken down completely before Palmerston became Foreign Secretary and nothing had taken its place.
Crises were therefore solved by hastily improvised collective
action in which it was almost impossible to forecast in advance
which powers would take part and what the extent of their
aid would be. Moreover, the ally of today could become the
enemy of tomorrow with disconcerting speed; no wonder
Palmerston concentrated on Britain's 'eternal interests', and
rejected the idea that Britain should have 'eternal allies' or
'perpetual enemies': any other policy would have been totally
unrealistic. Naturally his policy led to difficulties and to
errors of judgment at times. Any man who had the invidious
task of anticipating the probable course of conduct of the
other European powers in the middle years of the nineteenth
century would have made mistakes. The most a Foreign
Secretary could do was to direct the foreign policy of his own

country; he could not direct the foreign policies of other
countries too. The briefest study of the tortuous foreign
policies of France and Russia, for instance, between 1830 and
1865, would show the impossibility of anticipating their
reactions, still less of influencing or controlling them for any
considerable length of time.

Any assessment of Palmerston's foreign policy which dis-
counts the enormous difficulties he thus had to face is unfair.
Nor is it reasonable to overlook the tremendous burden of
work and responsibility which Palmerston shouldered for the
best part of thirty-five years. He had to cope with the steadily
accumulating strain imposed by one crisis after another as the
powers jockeyed with each other for commercial and strategic
advantage, and all the time nationalism and liberalism,
tremors from the earthquake of the French Revolution,
threatened to destroy the fabric of society from below. To be
Foreign Secretary at such a time demanded sound judgment
and a capacity for hard work which Palmerston retained to
the end. He attended to the rapidly multiplying paper-work
at the Foreign Office with a directness and energy that impressed and, at times, alarmed the officials there. In 1851 he
informed Earl Granville, who was then succeeding him at the
Foreign Office, that routine Foreign Office business would
require seven or eight hours work a day from him, quite apart
from parliamentary duties and the extra work imposed by the
onset of crises. To perform this work Palmerston was given a
ludicrously inadequate staff of clerks. The meanness of governmental expenditure on administration at this stage of Britain's
history is pointedly shown in a letter by Palmerston to Russell
in 1850. Queen Victoria had complained that Palmerston had
not been sending her Foreign Office dispatches. Palmerston
pointed out to Russell the difficulties imposed on him by the
great pressure of business, and that as business had increased
the old practice of making copies of dispatches sent to the
Queen had had to be abandoned. It had become difficult
therefore to keep the Queen in close touch with affairs without
delaying Foreign Office business to do so. However, Palmerston said he would go back to the old practice, '*and if it shall
require an additional clerk or two you must be liberal and allow
me that assistance*'. Perhaps only in nineteenth-century Britain
would it be possible to find such a cheese-paring attitude to

necessary administrative assistance. The general and personal difficulties under which Palmerston thus laboured need to be borne strongly in mind in judging his policies; they make the considerable achievements of his foreign policy all the more remarkable.

Palmerston had no opportunity to accustom himself gradually to the demands of Foreign Office work in 1830. The July Revolution had taken place a few months previously in France and events there needed to be kept under close observation; simultaneously a tricky situation had developed as a result of the Belgian seizure of independence and the risk of the French gaining control of that country by one means or another. British reactions to this threat were firm and wisely calculated. The pressure for aggressive action in France was strong. An eastward extension of the French frontier had been a traditional objective of that country for centuries, and a situation even arose, as a result of the Dutch attack on the Belgians, in which a French army was established on Belgian soil. Nevertheless, Palmerston was able to persuade the French to withdraw after the Dutch had been ousted from Belgium, and was also able, without losing the goodwill of Louis-Philippe, to establish Leopold of Saxe-Coburg on the Belgian throne in preference to Louis-Philippe's son, the Duke of Nemours. Grey, a former Foreign Secretary himself, played his part in this, but his role should not be overestimated. He was primarily occupied with pushing the Reform Bill through Parliament and, as time went on, he became increasingly impatient with the negotiations over the Belgian question. The handling of the affair gradually became Palmerston's sole responsibility, particularly in Melbourne's ministry during which Palmerston was able to persuade the French to join with Britain in guaranteeing Belgian neutrality. This was a very successful solution to a vexed issue. It saved Belgium from war in 1870-1 when the Prussians defeated France, and it served as an effective barrier against the possibility of an attack on Belgium until the Germans infringed Belgian neutrality, to their own disadvantage ultimately, in 1914.

During the early stages of the Belgian question the harassed Palmerston was confronted in 1831 with the dangerous threat of Mehemet Ali's advance into the lands of the Turkish Empire. The extent of practical help which could be given at this stage, in view of the delicate situation in Europe, was necessarily limited. Geographical and military considerations alike hampered prompt intervention, and Palmerston had no option but to allow events to run their course. He did know, however, that France, preoccupied with the Belgian question, was unlikely to intervene on behalf of Mehemet Ali. It was reasonable to assume, too, that if Russia took the opportunity presented by this situation of striking at Turkey she would have to reckon with the opposition of Austria, always sensitive to the effects of political change in the Balkans. Although the Austrians made the Treaty of Münchengrätz with Russia in 1833, this treaty in no way marked any fundamental departure from the Austrian policy of keeping a wary eye on Russian ambitions in the Near East. Austria, as Palmerston was well aware, was too anxious to keep control of her main line of communication, the Danube, to remain passive if the Russians made any advance into Turkish territory; it was precisely to guard against this risk that the Treaty of Münchengrätz was made. The Unkiar Skelessi treaty between Russia and Turkey was an unexpected and unwelcome turn of events, but hardly one for which Palmerston could reasonably be blamed. Moreover, Palmerston's sturdy self-confidence made him less fearful than some of his colleagues of the actual or potential dangers of Russian policy in the Near East. The ineptitude of the Russian army in the Crimean War was even greater than that of their opponents, and later gave some justification to Palmerston's refusal to be alarmed by the ponderous diplomatic activities of the Russian leaders.

Relations with France, which had improved at the accession of Louis-Philippe, steadily deteriorated. The fault lay partly with Palmerston's exuberant tongue but other factors played their part too. Friendship with France was difficult. It was too much to expect France to co-exist peacefully with the remaining European powers while she still hankered after recreating the excitements of the Revolution and of Napoleonic rule. The instability of her parliamentary system increased her unreliability — there were sixteen governments in ten years in France in the 1830s. Attempted assassinations of Louis-Philippe became a national pastime in which, fortunately, no one developed very much skill. The excitable Thiers had twice been in and out of office by 1840, and his policies in Spain and elsewhere caused almost as much consternation in France as they did in Britain. Finally, relations with Britain were understandably troubled by Palmerston's doubts of French intentions in the Near East inspired by French backing for Mehemet Ali. The *entente* between Britain and France in the 1830s thus rested on a very slender basis. Complete fusion of interests was lacking, and Palmerston was right to retain reservations about too close a relationship with France.

This was clearly shown in the crisis in the Near East in 1839–41. The Sultan, acting against British advice, initiated this crisis by attacking the Egyptian forces in Syria. Palmerston secured the approval of Austria, Prussia, and Russia to drive the Egyptians out of Syria and to bring the fighting to an end. He half-hoped that it might be possible to remove Mehemet Ali from his governorship of Egypt. In this he was disappointed, but it was not an unreasonable plan in view of the difficulties Mehemet Ali had been creating, with French connivance, in the Near East. Palmerston was unable therefore to carry out his intentions to the full, but Mehemet Ali and Louis-Philippe were obliged to accept the check to their interests involved in the episode. Had Palmerston been influenced by a sentimental attachment to France based on the flimsy structure of their rather closer relationship in the 1830s, a major war might have developed which could easily have led to the destruction of British influence in the eastern Mediterranean. Palmerston rightly valued British interests more highly than the uneasy friendship with France and deftly disposed of the threat from Mehemet Ali. The Straits convention which followed closed the Dardanelles and the Bosphorus to foreign warships when Turkey was not at war. This was not a new principle but it was given more formal approval than ever before; it helped to moderate the extreme sensitivity of the great powers on the risk of warships passing through the Straits whether from the Black Sea or the Mediterranean side. France also accepted the convention, though admittedly this was on the prompting of Metternich rather than of Palmerston.

During the 1840s relations with France continued to worsen, but it would be crude simplification to regard this merely as a consequence of the strains which developed be-

tween Britain and France over the 1839–41 crisis. There had
been strains before this crisis developed, particularly over the
extent of help to be given by the two countries to the constitutional movements in Portugal and Spain. Moreover,
Palmerston was rightly suspicious of those groups in France
who were pressing for a more dramatic foreign policy. It was
this pressure, much more than any words or actions uttered or
performed by Palmerston, which prompted Louis-Philippe to
make his impulsive acceptance of the scheme for a French
marriage alliance with the Queen of Spain and her sister. If
Spain and France thus became linked it seemed likely that it
would give the latter country undue influence in Western
Europe, even if the risks were less than they had been when
Spain possessed a great Empire. Aberdeen's dithering easy-
going approach when he was Foreign Secretary had been
making it far too simple for the French to achieve their ambition. Palmerston's blunt rejection of the scheme was naturally
irritating to the French but this was not a time for tact.
In practice Louis-Philippe had gone too far to draw back, but
within the context of what was possible Palmerston took the
most sensible course. Had he been in Aberdeen's place a little
earlier his quick recognition of the undesirability of the
marriage alliance might well have scotched the scheme at
birth.

Palmerston was forced to resign in 1851 as a result of ex-
pressing premature approval of Louis Napoleon's *coup d'état*.
His offence was slight. An unguarded comment to the French
ambassador showing satisfaction that the disorders in French
domestic politics would now be brought under firm control was
used as an excuse by the Court to hound him from office. He
still retained the confidence of Russell, the Prime Minister,
and, as Palmerston pointed out in the House of Commons
when defending his actions, all the ministers in the Cabinet
had subsequently expressed the same point of view about
developments in France as he had himself. He was guilty of
no more than a technical breach of protocol. It is easy to feel
sympathy for Palmerston's opinion in 1851 when, after the
erratic wobbling of French ministries, it seemed at last that
firm unified direction was to be given to her affairs.

If Palmerston had been the fire-eating diplomat which his
critics represent him to be, the 1848 Revolutions, with the

whole of Europe in a state of flux, would have given him an irresistible temptation to intervene on the Continent. In fact he handled all the major issues arising from the disturbances with consummate skill. It was particularly to his credit that he did not allow himself to be carried away by his sympathies for liberal movements, nor was he influenced, as a man of lesser judgment might have been, by their early successes. British troops and ships gave no help to the revolutionary movements though they could have done so, particularly in Italy. But Palmerston was not convinced that Austria was a spent force yet. He judged that, in spite of the bravery of Mazzini, Manin, and Garibaldi, the time for action had not come. In central Europe there was no hope of influencing the course of events, but it was eminently right to protest against the ferocity of the suppression of the rebels in Hungary and Italy. No man of humanitarian and liberal sympathies could be expected to stay mute in face of the brutalities used against the rebels after the risings had been crushed. Palmerston's handling of the Haynau episode, when the Austrian general was manhandled in London, may not have been in accordance with diplomatic etiquette but it echoed what the ordinary man felt.

Just before Palmerston's dismissal from the Foreign Office, there occurred the Don Pacifico incident, which has been criticised as an over-dramatic use of British power against a small country. The small country concerned, Greece, had been persistently obstructionist and wrong over the repayment of debts to British subjects. Palmerston's knack of going straight to the point was precisely the method required to bring the Greeks to their senses. His action proved sufficient to secure redress from the Greek Government. While, as a matter of diplomatic form, he should first have consulted Russia and France, the co-guarantors of Greek independence, this would have been an over-elaborate and slow procedure merely to settle a matter of debt-collecting.

Palmerston made clear his determination to take strong action against Russia as the Crimean War drew nearer. It is true that the causes of the war seem trivial and that it might have been avoided; but this ignored the fact of the persistent scheming of the Russians to take advantage of Turkish weakness. It may be that Russian motives were primarily defen-

sive, and that they wished to use a docile or a conquered
Turkey in the first place as a barrier against attack by the
Western powers. But once they were established in Turkey
these defensive motives might well become secondary. The
prospect of a hostile Russian fleet in the Mediterranean was
one which Palmerston would rather not face — and understandably. On the other hand the developments which led to
the Crimean War gave the British an opportunity to cripple
Russian sea-power in the Black Sea, and to remove for some
years at least the annoyance of the Russian policy of pin-
pricks against Turkey. No one believed that this would settle
the Eastern Question, but it gave a breathing-space from intrigues against Turkey — much needed after the schemings of
the last twenty-five years. The military conduct of the
campaign was badly handled in many respects, as is well
known, but eventually Sevastopol was captured; indeed, as
A. J. P. Taylor has pointed out, the Crimean War has been
the only successful invasion of Russia in modern times.[1]
The Treaty of Paris, concluding the war, admirably fulfilled
Palmerston's purpose of securing a respite from further
Russian activity in the Near East.

Palmerston's last period of power, as Prime Minister from
1859 to 1865, is the one in which he is most vulnerable to
criticism. The weight of work and responsibility was a heavy
one for a man in his late seventies; even so the consistent protection of British interests and the sympathy for liberal
causes which characterise the earlier periods of Palmerston's
career are markedly present in this last phase also. There was
one exception, however, namely Palmerston's handling of
relations with China. As in the Opium War of 1840-2, Palmerston allowed his determination to protect British nationals to
blind him to all other considerations after the *Arrow* incident
of 1856. The result was a minor war and some hard bargaining
from which neither side emerged with much credit; the upshot was that by the Treaty of Pekin the English and French
extorted further trading and diplomatic privileges from the
Chinese. There are legalistic and commercial arguments
which could be put in Palmerston's favour, but they do little
to counteract the overall impression that in this instance

[1] A. J. P. Taylor, *The Struggle for Mastery in Europe 1848-1918*
(Oxford: Clarendon Press, 1954), p. 82.

D

Palmerston's judgment was faulty, though we should not underestimate the difficulty of assessing and directing events taking place at the other side of the world in days when communications were still in their infancy.

Nevertheless, even if the harshest judgment is made of Palmerston's handling of this episode, it is only one of a series of other decisions from which Palmerston emerges with much greater credit. From the outset of this ministry Italian affairs had been the focus of interest. The movement for Italian independence had Palmerston's sympathy, but at the same time he was anxious not to alienate Austria. Help was therefore confined to the negative role of non-interference when Garibaldi crossed from Sicily into Italy. This proved sufficient to ensure the success of the project without any direct British confrontation of Austrian influence in Italy. It was an exactly judged and successful policy. There was no open break with Austria. Indeed the Austrians, if they laid aside their prejudices, might well have seen the wisdom of Palmerston's view that the Austrian Empire was too unwieldy to be manageable; the political surgery involved in the loss of the Italian provinces would do the Empire no disservice. Italy, for her part, would have cause to be grateful to Britain, and this, it was hoped, would lead to a stronger trading connection since one of the expected consequences of the unification would be a lowering of tariffs in Italy. It should not be forgotten either that this policy, beneficial to Britain, had to be put into effect by Palmerston and Russell, the Foreign Secretary, in the face of tetchy and hostile interference from the Queen, who shared the pro-German sympathies of Prince Albert.

The final acts of foreign policy during this ministry seem very vulnerable to criticism, yet on close examination there is very little substance in the charges. British opinion at the beginning of the American Civil War was fairly evenly divided between the two sides. The southern states had forged a strong trading link with Britain in supplying her with raw cotton, and, at first, Lincoln did not make an issue of the widespread existence of slavery in the southern states. Accordingly there were those in Britain who believed that the southern states were merely exercising the right to secede from a Union which no longer represented their viewpoint adequately. These states, therefore, deserved to some extent the sympathy which Britain had extended throughout the century to those countries where constitutional movements were struggling for independence. The parallel is not exact, but it was close enough to lead to some speculation as to how far Britain would follow a policy of strict neutrality. Palmerston and Russell showed a wise determination, however, to give no hope to the supporters of either side that Britain would accept any major involvement in American affairs. The first comment, therefore, on the *Alabama* and *Trent* episodes is that these were minor matters compared with the complications which might have followed if Palmerston and Russell had paid any attention to the hotheads on either side. It would have been practicable for instance for the British Navy to have played an active role in the war in lifting the blockade of the southern ports, but politically such an action would have been the height of folly.

It is true that the escape of the *Alabama* indicated an error of judgment, though primarily by Russell rather than by Palmerston, and it is true that at the end of the war the matter of compensation for the destruction of northern shipping by the *Alabama* was evaded. But relations between Britain and the northern states were then bad, the faults were not confined to one side as the *Trent* episode showed, and it was accordingly much easier for Gladstone some six years later to arrange the matter of compensation when passions had subsided. It should be remembered, too, that after the escape of the *Alabama* there was no repetition of the affair. British merchant ships occasionally slipped through the blockade of the southern ports but this was merely for the profit of the owner and at his own risk. Neither in public nor in private did the British Government condone these activities. Nor were Palmerston and Russell tempted out of their neutrality by the considerable provocation of the interception of the British ship *Trent* by an American warship. The American captain removed two envoys from the southern states on their way to Britain. There was no shadow of legal justification for this high-handed act. It was entirely reasonable to demand the return of the envoys and an apology. A firm dispatch was sent to the Americans, though Prince Albert was able to secure that its terms should be softened; but, whatever the firmness of the original draft, sending a dispatch is a very different matter from sending a fleet. Had Palmerston taken more violent action the northern states at this stage of the war in 1861 would have been in serious difficulties. Palmerston knew this but his sound judgment enabled him to keep the incident in proportion, though the American, Adams, writing from London, made clear his belief that '999 out of every thousand would declare for immediate war'. Palmerston has acquired such a reputation for gun-boat diplomacy that it is easy to overlook his caution in dealing with the great powers. The only occasion on which he gave whole-hearted support to armed British intervention against a great power was in the Crimean War; his motives in that episode have already been explained.

It was impracticable for the British to intervene in defence of the Poles rebelling against Russia in 1863. It has therefore been suggested that Britain was unwise to join with Austria and France in a protest against the suppression of the Polish rebels, since the protest was meaningless and calculated to raise false hopes among the Polish patriots. This is a mistaken view. Armed intervention was never promised nor could the Poles have expected it. The prospect of a war with Russia in defence of Poland was, as Russell said, 'a very cloudy one'; it would have been folly for the British to engage in such a project even with French support. Nevertheless, the joint protest was worth making. It at least made it clear to the Russians that the three major powers who made it were not indifferent to the fate of the Poles, and that they were sharply critical of the Russian policy of repression. Silent acceptance of the repression would have reflected no credit on Britain.

It was unfortunate for Palmerston that the final episode in foreign policy in his career, the Schleswig-Holstein question, was the one where his judgment served him less well than it had in the past. But he was old and he leaned more heavily on the erratic judgment of Russell than he would have done in his prime; even so Palmerston, though he mishandled the episode in one particular, namely his promise to give help to Denmark if her independence were violated, still retained enough grasp of the realities of military power not to engage in quixotic and futile adventures in support of Den-

mark when his bluff was called by Bismarck's shrewd diplomacy and prompt military action. The old order was changing
and Palmerston had been a little slow to understand this.
Up till the last moment he underestimated Bismarck and the
power of the Prussian army. For this he cannot be greatly
blamed. The Schleswig-Holstein episode was the first real
opportunity Europe had of realising the power of Bismarck's
Prussia. Palmerston had not been the only statesman to
underestimate Prussia; Napoleon III would continue to do so
until 1870: yet Palmerston, when confronted with the un-
palatable fact, had the sense to recognise it, and saw immediately the impossibility of naval or military action. It was
possible for his critics to strike aggrieved moral attitudes over
the abandonment of Denmark: none of them could suggest a
realistic alternative.

One other matter, differing in nature from the alarms and
crises which make up the staple material of foreign policy,
deserves attention in assessing Palmerston's policies. This was
his humanitarian concern to secure the abolition of the slave
trade. Legislative enactments were not enough. To prevent
the continued passage of slaves from Africa it was necessary
to maintain patrolling squadrons off the coast of West Africa,
with the right of search. Palmerston's determination to stamp
out the slave trade was backed by his customary practical
sense. Negotiations with other countries over the right of
search involved delicate diplomacy, but Palmerston handled
the matter so ably that all the great powers except the
United States accepted the arrangements which he devised.

The most lasting impression left by an examination of
Palmerston's foreign policies is of his abundant common
sense. 'He was not a common man', wrote Bagehot in 1865,
'but a common man might have been cut out of him. He had
in him all that a common man has, and something more.'
Palmerston's skill lay in his ability to import into international affairs the plain good sense of the intelligent citizen.
This is an infinitely harder task than it sounds. National
pride, personal feelings, and political expediency can make it
almost impossible in practice to apply the direct simple solutions which seem so obviously right to outside observers.
Palmerston was more successful than most in this respect.
His long direction of foreign affairs coincided with a singularly

unstable period in European affairs Yet, when Britain's
fortunes during these years are contrasted with those of the
other great powers, the scale of Palmerston's achievement is
more readily seen. France suffered from the unpredictable
foreign policies pursued under Louis-Philippe and Napoleon
III; Austria was bundled out of Italy and humiliated at
Sadowa; Russian intrigues against the Turkish Empire were
sharply checked by the Crimean campaign; Prussia, it is true,
advanced in strength during the period but only by means
which in the end proved self-destructive. Meanwhile Britain,
under Palmerston's direction, and at the cost of one successful
war, steadily pursued a policy of prosperity and strength.
Problems were dealt with as they arose, unhampered by
abstract propositions about the balance of power, or the rule
of law, or other slogans of theorists. Relations with the great
powers were handled with firm confidence, yet, it should be
noted, with the minimum loss of British lives. Italian unification and political development owed much to Britain, as did
the cause of liberalism in Europe generally. There was under
Palmerston a solidity in Britain's influence in the world which
has been patently lacking since. The changes have been too
complex to be explained merely in terms of personal leadership, but at least it can fairly be stated that no other Victorian
statesman recognised more clearly than Palmerston where
Britain's 'eternal interests' lay, and none pursued them with
greater vigour and common sense.

5. GLADSTONE
STATESMAN OR BIGOT?

Prelude

For Gladstone a political career was a means by which he could influence the mass of the community with his own powerful sense of moral purpose. In his long parliamentary career, stretching from his entry into the House of Commons in 1832 at the age of twenty-three until his retirement sixty-two years later in 1894, there were occasional episodes when his actions seem to have been decided by reference to his own or his country's advantage rather than by reference to principle. His sharp suppression of the nationalist movement in Egypt in 1881–2 contrasts oddly, for instance, with his sympathy for nationalist movements in Ireland, Italy, South Africa, the Balkans, and Afghanistan. There are a few other occasions, too, where it is difficult to reconcile his actions with his own stern judgment of what constituted a proper standard of conduct in political life. The use of the Royal Warrant method, for instance, to secure the abolition of commission purchase in 1871, though constitutional, was regarded as being somewhat sharp practice since it was used to by-pass the opposition of the House of Lords who were acting in full accordance with their constitutional rights in opposing the Bill. Yet, even if the qualification has to be made that Gladstone was apt at times to justify actions of his own which he would have roundly condemned in others, the fact remains that he was conscious of the moral responsibilities of political power to an extent which cannot be matched among his political contemporaries.

Like Peel, whose career has its parallels with that of Gladstone, he was strongly influenced by his home background both in his youth and as an adult. His father, John Gladstone, came from Scotland originally, but later established himself in Liverpool. John Gladstone had a sharp eye for business. The Napoleonic War and the Continental blockade gave the opportunity to British merchants to enrich themselves and Gladstone's father took fuller advantage of the situation than most, by means of trading with America, India, and the West Indies. He was himself the owner of slave plantations in the West Indies, but this caused no troubling of Gladstonian consciences since both father and son believed that slavery was not wrong in principle provided that the slave-owners exercised their powers responsibly. William Gladstone was to retain throughout his life the view, allied closely to this, that power was a trust to be exercised over the masses for their own benefit by those better gifted by nature and training. Gladstone also imbibed from his father, for whom he had genuine respect and affection in spite of later quarrels, a strong but narrowly based religious sense. In his early years his preoccupation with religion made him priggish and self-centred. His contempt for the religious indifference he found at Oxford, where he became a member of the college of Christ Church after schooling at Eton, sprang in part from an over-awareness of his own superiority, a characteristic which never quite left him. Later in life, particularly when he became Prime Minister, he showed a tolerance towards Dissenters and non-Christians which was in advance of the opinion of his contemporaries, but this was far from being so in the early years of his political career. This later tolerance was in no way whatsoever associated with laxity. His appetite for sermons never deserted him. Even in his last years he regretted that his ill-health prevented him from attending morning services, though he was as regular as ever in attendance at evening services.

Religion meant far more to him, however, than regular attendance at church. It was the weft and warp of his life without which he would have been nothing. He was an emotional excitable man who, without a religious sense to give purpose and meaning to his life, would have been more vulnerable than most men to impulsive, irrational decisions. For him politics and religion were not separate spheres. He would have vehemently repudiated the belief that 'politics is the art of the possible' as a cowardly cynical approach, appropriate for Disraeli, but entirely out of keeping with his own lofty principles. On all the great political issues of his time his first instinct was to consider the moral implications involved, and to shape his actions in such a way that his formidable support was given to the course of action which was in his estimation most righteous; whether his proposals were practicable, expedient, or popular was for the most part a matter of supreme indifference to him. There were exceptions at times, as perhaps there were bound to be in so long a period of heavy political responsibility. The electoral programme which he put forward at Newcastle in 1891 shows, for example, an uncharacteristic tendency to win votes by promising everything to everybody. Yet even here, and this was an exceptional instance, Gladstone was obsessed with the belief that the nation needed the light of his guidance on the Irish question. Vote-catching was reprehensible, but on this occasion he believed it to be pardonable on the grounds that his leadership was indispensable to the nation; besides, he was eighty-one, 'an old man in a hurry', and if he was to act as an instrument of the Almighty — and he firmly believed that this was his function in political life — his time was running short.

There were, therefore, special circumstances at work in Gladstone's mind in this episode which modified his political behaviour and make it superficially but not fundamentally different from his reaction to political issues in earlier years. But if one takes a mountain-top vision of Gladstone's career, looking back over that long span of sixty-two years in Parliament, the striking point is that on every decision with which he was associated, whether on great matters or small, his first and sometimes only point of reference is a moral one. Sometimes he could see a moral issue where no one else was aware of one. The adoption of Free Trade, the preservation of the lowest possible rate of income tax, and the reduction of the salaries of government officials, these are not at first sight moral issues; but they were for Gladstone. Only Gladstone could make a budget sound like the announcement of a crusade. If these drab financial issues could rouse Gladstone to such fervour it is easy to anticipate the strength of feeling which social reforms, the Irish problem, prison conditions in Naples, and the massacre of Balkan Christians by the Turks would produce.

On these and all other matters Gladstone's approach was too universal to be boxed in the little confines of party politics. He has been described as 'a tremendous old Tory' but no label fits. He began as a Tory and finished as a Liberal; neither

*

party commanded his full allegiance. If political issues are essentially moral ones, as Gladstone believed, God is relevant but parties are not. Like Luther, whom he resembled in temperament, he believed in the sovereign power of a man's conscience. Like Cromwell, and like the great preachers, he believed he had a God-given mission to perform. His writings and speeches give ample evidence of this. 'The Almighty seems to sustain and spare me for some purpose of his own, deeply unworthy as I know myself to be.' So wrote Gladstone in his diary in 1868 just after the beginning of his first ministry. The statement shows a curious blending of arrogance and humility, characteristic of the man. When after much heart-searching he joined Palmerston's Government in 1859 as Chancellor of the Exchequer he justified himself ultimately by asserting that he was obeying the call of duty and the will of God. In everything he saw the will of God, with himself very often as its interpreter. 'The expenses of war', he said, when defending the increase in income tax made necessary by the Crimean War, 'are a moral check which it has pleased the Almighty to impose upon the ambition and lust of conquest that are inherent in so many nations.' He attacked Disraeli's foreign policy because it had endangered 'all the most fundamental interests of Christian society'. For Palmerston and Disraeli the Eastern Question was a military, political, and economic issue; for Gladstone it was a moral one. They hoped to solve it with maps, treaties, ships, and soldiers; Gladstone believed that the central issue was to preserve the Balkan Christians from Turkish persecution.

It is plain then that Gladstone's strong religious sense was a permanent accompaniment to his thinking in all aspects of policy. This had advantages for him since it gave him intensity of feeling and power over men: whether it gave him political wisdom is another matter and it is this which is now to be considered.

Attack

In 1843 Gladstone became President of the Board of Trade during Peel's second ministry. He had served in the same Government as Vice-President of the Board of Trade from

STATESMAN OR BIGOT? 99

1841, though with no great enthusiasm at first, since his interest in the controversy over Free Trade was slow to develop. Like his leader, Peel, he eventually found the arguments of the Anti-Corn Law League convincing. 'Every day that I served at the Board of Trade beat like a battering-ram on the unsure fabric of my official protectionism': these were Gladstone's feelings in 1842. He had the highest respect for Peel's judgment in financial matters and was content to follow his lead. Peel did not have the opportunity to complete the work of freeing trade, but he had of course moved a long way in that direction in the budgets of 1842 and 1845 and in the repeal of the Corn Laws in 1846. During the next twenty years his disciple, Gladstone, followed in the direction which Peel had indicated. Gladstone became Chancellor of the Exchequer in the Whig–Peelite Coalition Government headed by the Earl of Aberdeen in 1852, and in the following year devised a budget which carried Free Trade a stage further by reducing duties on food-stuffs. This affected fruits and dairy produce in particular. The Anti-Corn Law League had pressed for years that the people should have the benefit of the 'free breakfast table', by which they meant that breakfast food-stuffs should be freed of duties, and Gladstone was now fulfilling their policy. In 1860 he took the further step of abolishing altogether duties on fruits, dairy produce, and all manufactures. The timber duty, whose retention Gladstone regarded as 'the very essence and quintessence of political folly', was removed in 1866. The Cobden–Chevalier trade treaty with France in 1860, leading to a mutual reduction of duties between that country and Britain, was also a result of Gladstone's persistent advocacy of Free Trade.

To much of this activity there can be no objection. Free Trade was probably a stimulus to the British economy in the middle of the century, though economists both at the time and later have thought that improvements in communications by rail and by ship, and the extension of industrialisation in other countries, may have been no less significant. Mid-century prosperity was not confined to Britain; it was to be found in Protectionist countries too. However, the arguments on this issue are necessarily speculative, though not unimportant on that account. It may well be that Gladstone overrated the importance of Free Trade. Influenced overmuch perhaps by Peel's views on the issue in the 1840s Gladstone, who lacked Peel's flexibility of mind, clung on unimaginatively to Free Trade when its period of usefulness was at an end. In his ministry of 1868–74 Free Trade seemed to have justified itself. By the time of his second ministry of 1880–5 and his last ministry of 1892–4 the merits of Free Trade seemed less convincing. Agriculture was hard-hit in the 1870s and 1880s by foreign competition, and manufacturers were alarmed at falling prices and at the resurgence of Protectionism in Europe. Protection was adopted by Germany in 1879, and increased tariffs were imposed by France, Austria, Italy, and Russia in the 1880s. The United States steadily maintained a high tariff rate. In these circumstances the policy which had seemed so inspired in the 1840s looked much less convincing.

If Gladstone had been capable of being influenced by economic considerations in fiscal policy there might have been some hope of a reassessment of the implications of Free Trade during his later ministries. He still regarded financial affairs as his own special preserve, and took an almost parental interest in the policies of the various Chancellors of the Exchequer who served under him. But on the principle of Free Trade he had long ago made up his mind, partly because of the economic arguments which the Anti-Corn Law League advanced and which Peel accepted, but more fundamentally because Free Trade made an overwhelming moral appeal to Gladstone. Protectionism was wrong because it was contrary to the will of God. The freeing of trade, quite apart from any economic benefits it might bring, would encourage sturdy self-respect and hard work. Free Trade was the right policy because it was morally right. This was an attitude which left no room whatsoever for manœuvre. If Free Trade was morally right it could be neither abandoned nor modified. Once Gladstone had completed the removal of the major duties on manufactures and food-stuffs the matter in his estimation was at an end, and there could be no going back. If a man is to merit the title of 'statesman' he needs a degree of responsiveness to the people and circumstances of his own time; he needs sensitivity to new developments and the foresight which takes into account changes in outlook. In this Gladstone was totally lacking. He preferred the comfort of obsessions to the challenge of new thought.

This obtrusively moral approach likewise coloured his attitude to income tax. His intention when he became Chancellor of the Exchequer in 1852 was to remove this tax altogether. Men must be encouraged to work hard and to save so that wealth might 'fructify in the pockets of the people'. Public expenditure had to be reduced to the minimum. Administrators were in a sense parasites. They did not contribute directly to the nation's wealth, and therefore their numbers and salaries should both be as low as possible. Defence expenditure could be minimised if the nation accepted Gladstone's view that nationalist policies were an obstacle to the development of a European Concert of Powers basing its actions on Christian principles. Schemes for social expenditure were wasteful and misguided since they robbed men of their moral fibre; it was part of the natural order that men should learn to master circumstances by their individual strivings, and that they were entitled to their earnings in the fullest possible measure. Gladstone's hope of a swift abolition of income tax was frustrated by the onset of the Crimean War. Income tax had to be raised from 7d to 1s 2d in the £ but in 1868 Gladstone was able to reduce it to 3d in the £, and in the 1874 election he promised its total abolition. He remained adamant in his opposition to direct taxation throughout his life. He was infuriated by Sir William Harcourt's proposals for a death duty tax in 1894, and his anger over this precipitated the divisions of opinion in the Cabinet which were the major reason for his resignation in 1894. When one considers the growing rivalry from Germany, particularly over naval construction, and the sluggishness and inadequacy of social reform in the late nineteenth century in Britain, Gladstone's inability to adapt himself to changing situations becomes cruelly clear. Public expenditure is not an evil in itself. Wasteful spending is reprehensible, but so is parsimony. Gladstone's inflexibility of outlook blinded him to this plain fact. His attitude played a part in developing a belief that State help for those not able to help themselves is objectionable. It is of some significance that Britain lagged some twenty years behind Germany in the provision of State schemes for the relief of old age and sickness. Nor was it helpful to Britain in the Boer War and in the naval competition with Germany that Service expenditure had been so firmly controlled in the preceding years.

Even if it is conceded that those aspects of social reform which depended on an increase in public expenditure were unlikely to make much headway under Gladstone, it might be argued that in Gladstone's ministries there were many other reforms which were measures of social justice and which show a statesmanlike vision on his part. Certainly a tremendous amount of energy was devoted to domestic reforms, particularly in his first ministry when the Irish situation was not quite so much an obsession for Gladstone as it was to become in later years. The chief reforming measures make an impressive list on their own, quite apart from the numerous measures to pacify the Irish. The 1870 Education Act was an important preliminary to the establishment of a national system of primary education; reforms of the Civil Service entrance system meant that, except for the Foreign Office, administrative posts were now open to competitive examination; a thoroughgoing reform of army organisation and of the terms of service added significantly to the nation's military efficiency without imposing heavy charges on the revenue; the tendency of employers and judges to treat trade unions as conspiracies was frustrated by the 1871 Trade Union Act which recognised the unions as legal corporations; the University Tests Act of 1871 prevented men from being barred from holding lay posts in the Oxford and Cambridge colleges because of their religious beliefs; the Local Government Act of the same year showed some awareness of the need to administer public health more efficiently; the Ballot Act in 1872 helped to reduce intimidation and improper influence at elections: finally the Licensing Act of 1872 was a well-meant attempt to reduce the social evil of drunkenness by limiting the hours of sale of alcoholic drinks.

It was this extensive legislative activity which moved Disraeli in 1872 to compare the occupants of the government front bench to 'a range of exhausted volcanoes'. His comparison was more flattering than it need have been. The mountains had heaved, but when the movement died down were found to have produced very small mice. Moreover, they would have produced even fewer had it not been that Gladstone's Cabinet contained men with a more positive interest in social advance than he had himself. The two most important reforms of the first ministry, the Education Act and the army reforms, owed much more to Forster, the Vice-President of the Privy Council, who was responsible for education, and to Cardwell, the Secretary of State for War, than they did to Gladstone. The arguments that a national system of education would assist citizens in the future to work more efficiently, to use their votes with fuller understanding, and to develop their intellects a little more fully, made little impact on Gladstone. For him, as ever, the issue was a moral one. The main virtue of a national system of education to his mind was that it would extend a wider knowledge of the Christian religion among the nation's children. Had it not been for this fact it is unlikely that Gladstone would have had much sympathy with the Education Act. He had a paternal interest in the welfare of the people but it was a paternalism based on the expectation of obedience and uniformity; these same qualities incidentally, but revealingly, were at work in his treatment of his own family.[1] He was far removed from the belief that governments had a duty to provide educational step-ladders across the barriers of social divisions. He had no vision of the part education would one day play in loosening the grip of the established order on society, and he would certainly have found the idea repugnant. The 1867 Reform Act had made the Education Act necessary. 'We must educate our masters,' said Lowe, one of the opponents of the Reform Act, when that measure was finally passed. It was in this reluctant spirit that the Education Act was introduced. Forster piloted it through the religious squabbles which followed as the Nonconformists and the Church of England tried to assert their special interests in education. Gladstone was uneasy at the clauses in the Act which provided that religious teaching in Board Schools should be undenominational, but he was ultimately content to leave this matter and the others arising from the Act to Forster.

His interest in the army reforms was likewise limited rather than whole-hearted. The Services are traditionally more vulnerable to governmental financial economies than the civil departments of State. Gladstone, when Chancellor of the Exchequer, had employed a policy of financial stringency to-

[1] Philip Magnus, *Gladstone* (London: John Murray, 1954) is informative on this aspect of Gladstone's life, and also provides a very full assessment of his political career.

wards the Services which had resulted among other things in
a totally inadequate standard of barrack accommodation.
He was not likely therefore to sanction as Prime Minister any
reforms which added to Service expenditure. Cardwell naturally had to accept this from the outset. The result was a series
of useful but minor reforms which made the Army more
efficient for dealing with minor colonial wars in Afghanistan
and Egypt but which in no way fitted Britain for Continental
wars, nor even for dealing effectively with the Boers, as the
military set-backs of 1899 were to demonstrate. Since Gladstone had such a high regard for economy and for negotiation
as a means of avoiding war it is hardly surprising that the
Services had to accustom themselves to 'shoe-string' expenditure. Whether this policy was beneficial to Britain either in
diplomacy or in the wars she was eventually obliged to fight,
both in Europe and elsewhere, is very much open to question.

Few of the other domestic reforms of his first ministry can
be regarded with unqualified satisfaction. It is notorious that,
having granted legal status to the trade union movement
with one hand in the 1871 Trade Union Act, Gladstone then
proceeded with the other hand to make the movement ineffectual by making picketing illegal in the Criminal Law
Amendment Act of the same year. The two actions, so contrary to each other, seem at first sight to be a mixture of
obtuseness and ignorance of working-class conditions, but
this would be an over-simplification. Gladstone has indeed
been charged with knowing nothing of working-class conditions and this has been advanced as a reason for his opposition to 'collectivist' improvement of social conditions, but his
work of rescuing women in London from prostitution must
have made him thoroughly aware of the squalid conditions
there. The more important point is that he believed that man's
struggle for mastery over circumstances was part of the God-
given order. He was prepared to take legislative action to
remove gross inequalities of opportunity. This was why he
secured the reform of the methods of entrance into the Civil
Service, and the abolition of commission purchase, for instance. It was his distaste for the corrupting effects of privilege
which was at the root of his Liberalism. But he found equally
repellent the notion that the State had a duty to safeguard the
citizen against every occupational hazard; by doing so it

might remove a stimulus to honest endeavour. He was prepared to hold the ring to ensure that the contest in society
between the privileged and unprivileged did not become too
one-sided, but he had no sympathy for State welfare legislation of the kind introduced by the Liberal ministries in the
pre-1914 period. His Liberalism had more in keeping with
modern Conservatism than it has with the Radical movement
in English history. There are times when such an approach
is healthy and useful in society, but the industrial unrest and
occasional rioting of the last quarter of the nineteenth century
suggest strongly that Gladstone's moral prejudices blinded
him to the needs of the working classes.

The other outstanding feature of Gladstone's domestic
legislation in his first ministry is its incompleteness, not only
in respect of legislation which he failed to introduce but in the
comparative ineffectiveness of the legislation which he did
introduce. His treatment of the trade unions is one instance,
the long delay before the Ballot Act of 1872 was given the
effective force it needed by means of the Corrupt Practices
Act of 1883 is another. A third instance is the way in which
the opportunities for more effective control of public health
problems were not imaginatively used. The legislation of
1871–2 created a Local Government Board and sanitary
districts in England and Wales but, in keeping with Gladstone's public parsimony, public health continued to be administered in the spirit of the harsh 1834 Poor Law. This
grudging aid fell far short of the real needs of the situation.

The outstanding example of the misconceived nature of
Gladstone's legislation is his handling of the Irish problem.
The history of the Irish question between 1868 and 1894
mirrors Gladstone's unsoundness of judgment. His bigotry, his
sense of mission, his delusion that he understood the masses
and that they understood him, and his muddle-headedness in
legislative activity and in acts of policy, all of these characteristics are to be seen. The disestablishment of the Irish Church
in 1869 was a reasonable step in itself, but quite irrelevant to
the central problems of Ireland which in the nineteenth
century were primarily political and economic. Yet when
Gladstone tackled the land question the first result was the
botched First Irish Land Act of 1870. This was the kind of indecisive reform at which Gladstone excelled. He had too much

respect for the sanctity of property rights to make the radical
reforms which were plainly needed in the land-holding system
in Ireland. The Act provided that compensation should be
paid to tenants who were arbitrarily evicted and that they
should also receive compensation for any improvements they
had made to the land during the tenancy. In addition, a
scheme was introduced by which the State would advance
loans to tenants enabling them to buy land themselves and
thus be freed of the uncertainties of tenant holding.

These measures were quite inadequate. Very few Irish
tenants were in a position to take up a loan even at the low
rate of interest asked. Moreover, the eviction clauses of the
Act were extraordinarily badly devised. There was nothing to
prevent landlords from raising rents and then evicting tenants
who could not pay the new rent. This was not the same as
arbitrary eviction and consequently imposed no obligation
upon the landlord for the payment of compensation. As the
agricultural depression in Ireland worsened in the late seventies the temptation to raise rents became increasingly attractive, and the Irish tenant farmer suffered. It was not surprising that the violent tactics of the Irish Land League won
new adherents, and for this the ineffectiveness of Gladstone's
Land Act is at least partly to blame.

By the time of his second ministry (1880–5) Gladstone had
learned to avoid some of the errors he had made earlier in his
Irish policy, but not to avoid new ones. The Second Land
Act of 1881 not only gave the Irish tenants security of tenure
and freedom to sell their holdings when they wished, but it
also arranged for the establishment of tribunals to determine
fair rents. Had this measure been passed in 1870 it might have
reduced the bitterness of the Irish towards the English. By
1881 it was too late. Under Parnell's guidance the Irish boy-
cotted the Land Courts set up to establish fair rents. They
wanted no more half-measures: now their aim was Home Rule
to be achieved not by co-operation with Britain but by
political propaganda and violence. This was a state of mind
which Gladstone could not comprehend and it led him to
oscillate uncertainly between appeasement and harshness.
When, as a result of the obstructionist influence of Parnell,
the Act failed to make the impact for which Gladstone had
hoped, his response was to imprison Parnell in Kilmainham

Gaol under the terms of the 1881 Coercion Act. It was an action of naïve clumsiness which indicated Gladstone's total failure to grasp the realities of Irish politics. The deep-seated hatred of English rule, and the difficulty posed by the religious division in Ireland were matters which he overlooked. He thought that the Irish people would share his own belief that his leadership, being founded on the highest altruistic motives, would make more appeal to them than Parnell's policy of violent non-co-operation. Then there would be a dignified and orderly advance to Home Rule.

This was a grave error of judgment and in the end he was forced to recognise it himself. Yet even when at last he directed his attention away from land reform towards Home Rule his political tactics were incomprehensible by any rational standard. His overweening confidence in the wisdom of his own policies led to his ridiculous secretiveness in 1886, when he hoped that Parnell might ally with the Conservatives to secure the passage of a Home Rule Bill through the Commons and the Lords. The whole scheme was speculative in the extreme. Even if it had not broken down through Herbert Gladstone's indiscreet disclosures of his father's hopes, the Conservatives were unlikely to give the Irish independence on the terms they wanted. The Conservative reaction to the Third Home Rule Bill of 1912 is sufficient indication of that. The price Gladstone paid for this misjudgment was firstly the loss from his party of a hundred Liberals who eventually drifted across to the Conservative side; included in their number was the formidable Joseph Chamberlain whose talents were thus lost to the Liberals. Secondly, Gladstone's aptitude for consulting his conscience rather than his common sense led him to make the useless atonement of introducing two Home Rule Bills in 1886 and 1893 as a gesture of goodwill towards the Irish, although he knew quite well that the Bills would never become law. Ireland had become the cuckoo in the nest, crowding out the measures with which Parliament should have been occupying itself at a time when restive social discontent was strongly marked. Gladstone's obsessive belief that he had a God-given mission to solve the Irish problem made his later ministries extraordinarily unproductive in the social legislation which Britain so patently needed.

So far as there was any social advance in the Liberal
ministry of 1880–5 it owed its impetus to the driving force of
Joseph Chamberlain. Chamberlain had none of his leader's
deferential respect for authority. He was a formidable critic
of the established order. At different times the monarchy, the
House of Lords, and the Church of England became the
victims of his tongue, and the weight of his attacks was reinforced by the growing sympathy for Socialist doctrines far
removed from Gladstone's conservative Liberalism. The
Lords, for instance, were opposed to the extension of the
franchise envisaged in the 1884 Bill, the impulse for which
came from Chamberlain, not Gladstone. It was Chamberlain
who then took the lead when the Lords threatened the Bill,
and exposed the selfish hollowness of their dull mechanical
opposition to change. Yet Gladstone had no more reason than
Chamberlain to love the Lords. It was only too plain that their
solid opposition to Gladstone's schemes for Irish Home Rule
seemed destined to frustrate indefinitely any hope of advance
in that direction. But Gladstone was too preoccupied with his
conscience over Irish and Egyptian affairs, and too inhibited
by respect for the old order to give Chamberlain the support
he deserved. Nevertheless the Bill became law when the
Lords' resistance was bought off by a promise to introduce a
Redistribution Bill, reorganising the constituencies. Admittedly Gladstone's parliamentary skill was valuable in
devising and presenting the details of the Reform Bill. This
was not surprising; his capacity for burying his head in the
sand of detail was a well-marked characteristic. Perhaps it
helped him to forget his earlier view on the 1832 Reform Act
which he had once succinctly described as 'anti-Christ'.

The central weakness in Gladstone's handling of affairs was
his lack of realism. He had an interest in minute administrative detail, appropriate for a lesser Treasury official but not
for a Prime Minister. Yet with this he combined a fondness for
high-sounding but irrelevant principles appropriate for an
academic visionary but not for the man responsible for the
nation's interests. His unrealistic approach has been demonstrated in his handling of affairs at home; it is plainer still in
his handling of affairs abroad. If grandiose conceptions were
the measure of statesmanship Gladstone's claim to the description would be impregnable; in practice much more is

needed than visions, and Gladstone's hope for recreating a
Concert of Europe in an age of militant nationalism was an
almost ludicrous misreading of the European situation. Far
from winning friendship from other countries by his moderation, Gladstone gained contempt and distrust. That his
policies were applied with characteristically bad timing made
them appear inept as well as misconceived.

Evidence of his misjudgment quickly accumulated during
his first ministry. Gladstone secured a promise from each side
to respect Belgian neutrality when the Franco-Prussian
War broke out in 1870. This was orthodox, sensible and, in its
military effects, favourable to Prussia. It is not a matter on
which Gladstone can reasonably be criticised. Nevertheless
the misguided sentimentalism which was never far from the
surface in his political thinking led him to propose collective
action by the neutral powers to prevent Germany annexing
Alsace-Lorraine at the end of the war. This was a totally unrealistic suggestion. There was no hope that Russia and
Austria would support such a move, no hope that negotiations would serve any purpose, and no hope that Bismarck's
policies would be influenced in the least degree by the tiny
British expeditionary force in the unlikely event of Gladstone turning from words to action. Fortunately Gladstone's
Cabinet showed more sense than their leader and his suggestion was firmly rejected.

Gladstone's preference for abstract principles rather than
political realities is clearly marked in another episode arising
from the Franco-Prussian War. This occurred when Russia,
with Bismarck's encouragement, denounced the clauses of the
Treaty of Paris neutralising the Black Sea. It was impossible
for Britain to prevent this. Instead of a blunt recognition of
the realities of the situation a solemn farce was played in
London in 1871 in which a conference of the powers condemned unilateral denunciation of treaties but agreed in the
next breath to the action which Russia had taken; it was
scarcely a moment of high statesmanship. It was not surprising that a nation accustomed in recent years to Palmerston's rumbustious diplomacy should chafe under Gladstone's
obscure idealism. It was his misfortune rather than his fault
that shortly after this Britain agreed to pay the United
States compensation for the havoc created by the *Alabama*, a

sea-raider which had been allowed to escape from Liverpool during the American Civil War and which had fought for the the southern states. This was an issue where a high-minded policy was also the most sensible, but in conjunction with the earlier episodes in foreign policy it stimulated further criticism of Gladstone.

That Gladstone had learned nothing by the experiences of his first ministry in foreign affairs is plain from the events of his second ministry. In Afghanistan and the Transvaal he reversed Disraeli's forward policy. This was reasonable, except that the Transvaal withdrawal followed the British defeat at Majuba Hill and gave the Boers an inflated notion of the strength of their own military power. Gladstone's policies in Egypt and the Sudan are even more vulnerable to criticism. From the start of the crisis in Egypt, resulting from Arabi Pasha's nationalist rising, to the dramatic and un-necessary death of Gordon at Khartoum, Gladstone behaved with a bewildered clumsiness which was the negation of statesmanship. When Disraeli had been Prime Minister Glad-stone sharply criticised his Egyptian policy on the grounds that it would lead inevitably to political control of Egypt by Britain with all the attendant risks of strained relations with France and Turkey, and the prospect of increased public expenditure to defend British interests there; more funda-mentally than this Gladstone, as his later policy towards Ireland and the Transvaal showed, was opposed to the domi-nance of the lesser powers by the greater ones. A statesman with a more practical turn of mind might have had doubts about the wisdom of a policy conducted by reference to abstract principles, but when Gladstone was in opposition his attitude at least had the merit of consistency. In office this quality deserted him, as did his judgment. When Gambetta, the French Prime Minister, pressed for joint Anglo-French action against Arabi Pasha, Gladstone would have none of it. In January 1882 the Gambetta Government was defeated. The new Prime Minister M. de Freycinet — like Gladstone, so one might reasonably think, in his distaste for overseas com-mitments for his country — tried to placate Arabi by negotia-tion.

Gladstone in his unpredictable way had now decided that the prospect of a tyranny headed by Arabi Pasha in Egypt was more of an affront to morality than the use of physical force to establish British political control over Egypt. The trouble with principles was that there were so many from which to choose. Gladstone, however, was now firmly of the opinion that his most recent beliefs were the right ones, and authority was given to Admiral Seymour to bombard the coastal batteries at Alexandria. This action the French refused to support, but Gladstone was quite content to act alone as guardian of international morality. Accordingly the bombardment took place and Arabi Pasha's troops were defeated a few months later at Tel-el-Kebir by British troops led by Sir Garnet Wolseley. In effect this led to British control of Egyptian affairs for another seventy years. The normally peaceful Gladstone showed all the pleasure of an old soldier at the news of the British troops' success. Had he been able to foresee the consequences in the twentieth century his pleasure would have been diluted. To sympathise with nationalism in Ireland and the Transvaal, but to regard it as pernicious in Egypt, was inconsistent. Moreover, there was little doubt at this stage that the British Navy, with the probability of French support, was amply capable of securing that Britain's major interest in the area, the Suez Canal, would be strongly protected. Coupled with a holding force in the Canal Zone itself this would have been entirely adequate to meet the needs of the situation. Tel-el-Kebir was as superfluous as the death of Gordon.

The latter episode does illustrate, however, the harm which was caused by Gladstone's spasms of indecisiveness and his tendency to lose his grasp of the full range of policy issues. The delays in sending the relief force to Khartoum cruelly expose Gladstone's immunity to common sense. At one level his mind was absorbed with the details of the Third Reform Bill; at another his will to action was sapped by a sentimental regard for the Dervish rising as another symptom of struggling nationalism. Meanwhile the delays lengthened from days, to weeks, to months, and Gordon waited in alternate hope and despair for the relief which came two days after his death. That Gordon was the wrong man for the task of evacuating the garrisons from the Sudan in no way weakens the case against Gladstone: it was Gladstone who had sanctioned his appointment.

It was fortunate for Britain that Gladstone was seldom in a position to exercise much influence on events at the time when international relations were most complex. The blunders which he made when in power have already been indicated; those which might have been made had Gladstone been given the opportunity can be deduced in part from his criticisms of the policies of Palmerston and Disraeli in particular. Whatever their faults they at least had a firmer grasp of the realities of politics than Gladstone possessed. There was one notable instance of this during the Crimean War. Gladstone in the spring of 1855 pressed strongly for a negotiated peace with Russia, as an alternative to Palmerston's policy which aimed at the capture of Sevastopol and the neutralisation of the Black Sea. Palmerston knew that his policy was not a long-term answer to the Eastern Question but at least it was a short-term one; Gladstone's policy was neither. Palmerston was too shrewd to be misled and nothing came of Gladstone's proposal. Gladstone's opinions, though frequently expressed, were of equally little consequence when the Eastern Question flared up again during the Balkan crisis of 1875–8. His support for the Balkan nations and his detestation for Turkish brutality are well known. These were admirable sentiments, as Gladstone was at pains to point out: 'Gladstone', said Disraeli, 'is worse than any Bulgarian atrocity.' Nevertheless there were other considerations, no less relevant, to be weighed in the settlement made at the Congress of Berlin. The settlement was imperfect, but this is to be expected. No one has yet found the answer to the Eastern Question. On the other hand the prospect of Gladstone fishing for principles in those troubled waters is not one calculated to rouse the feeling that he would have done any better. Much the same considerations apply to the possibility of Gladstone and Bismarck being thrown into closer contact than they proved to be in practice. Gladstone had none of the wariness of Disraeli or Salisbury and his headstrong impulsiveness would have been the worst possible counter to Bismarck's devious intrigues. Even Gladstone himself recognised how readily he was apt to lurch into blunders as a result of his emotional approach to the great issues of the day. At Newcastle in October 1862 he shocked opinion in Britain and elsewhere in a speech whose wording suggested that he, the

Chancellor of the Exchequer, and therefore a leading member
of the Government, felt the strongest sympathy for the
southern states in the American Civil War. 'Jefferson Davis
and other leaders of the South have made an Army. They are
making, it appears, a Navy. And they have made — what is
more than either — they have made a Nation.' As a means of
exciting applause this was excellent; as a public utterance on a
complex and undecided issue it was lamentable.

Ultimately then the same theme underlies every criticism
of Gladstone. He lacked the saving grace of common sense. He
could theorise, sermonise, and trace great principles in small
actions; at the other extreme he could absorb and neatly
organise intricate masses of detail. Yet when it was a matter of
seeing what was necessary and possible his complex mind
recoiled from the obvious, and he blundered on from one mis-
calculation to the next. When he was twenty-one he had expressed a wish to enter the Church. His father gently dis-
suaded him from an immediate decision, and perhaps was mistaken. Had his father judged the situation differently — and
it is an intriguing vision — we might have had Gladstone as
Archbishop of Canterbury and Joseph Chamberlain as Liberal
Prime Minister: the talents of both of them would have been
better used.

Defence

Criticism of Gladstone's policies presents no great difficulty.
His political career lasted for sixty-two years and it would be
miraculous if he had made no error of judgment. Statesmanship consists of much more than a capacity for avoiding mistakes. It has a positive quality discernible to contemporaries
and even to the jaundiced eyes of later historians. Gladstone
was 'the Grand Old Man', 'the People's William', nicknames
showing that compound of respect and affection which the
British reserve for those whose greatness they sense; his rival
they called 'Dizzy'. Gladstone so clearly had the attributes of
greatness — a physical presence more compelling than that of
Napoleon, a vision of society as he would like it to be, a
strength of will to spurn distractions and opposition, and yet,

with all this, a concern for the welfare of each individual in the community which communicated itself clearly to the masses, even when, in his characteristic way, he was addressing them on matters which they had little hope of understanding. There cannot have been many Prime Ministers who would have been capable, as Gladstone was at Greenwich in 1871, of addressing a mass audience of twenty-five thousand, in an explanation of his policies lasting for two hours; and there cannot have been many occasions in our history when the audience would have stayed. Nor can Gladstone be dismissed as a mere demagogue. There is ample evidence of his intellectual power from the early days of his double first at Oxford to the comment made by Edward Grey, a first-rate judge in these matters, that 'Gladstone was the greatest man in whose presence I have ever been'.

Ultimately it was precisely Gladstone's concentration on the moral issues of politics, which has been criticised as his chief weakness, which was in fact his greatest strength. 'Too fond of right to pursue the expedient' he saw the futility and danger of opportunist policies and short-term solutions. This gave to his political thinking a breadth and individualism which inevitably earned him critics, especially among those who lacked these qualities themselves. Yet even when his policies were unpopular the masses retained their respect for him. They may lack political discernment but have an eye for character and can tell a St Bernard from a Pekinese.

Gladstone's first opportunity to exercise an important influence on public affairs came in the 1840s. He became Vice-President of the Board of Trade in 1841 and President in 1843. That Free Trade would be adopted was already a foregone conclusion. Adam Smith had provided the text and the trade returns of the early nineteenth century provided the sermon. Gladstone's views had changed from unreflecting Protectionism to energetic support for Free Trade as soon as his work at the Board of Trade brought him into contact with economic reality. His role at first was naturally subsidiary to that of Peel in the measures of the 1840s — the budgets of 1842 and 1845, and the repeal of the Corn Laws in 1846 — which mark the abandonment of Protectionism as a principle. Gladstone differed from his leader at times over methods but he was a whole-hearted supporter of the main tendencies of

Peel's policy, and it was Gladstone who completed Peel's
work in the budgets of 1853 and 1860. Other factors may have
contributed to Britain's prosperity as a trading nation in the
mid-Victorian period, but it would be a mistake to belittle the
influence of the decision to adopt Free Trade. Britain experienced the Industrial Revolution many years in advance of
her potential rivals in Europe and the United States; in
addition, in many of these countries progress was hampered
by political and social disorders which gave Britain an additional advantage. In the key industries of iron and steel, coal,
and textiles, Britain had a huge lead over her rivals even as
late as 1870. Protectionism was an anachronism. Britain, 'the
workshop of the world', with production rapidly expanding,
had no cause whatsoever to shrink from the adoption of Free
Trade. Its economic benefits were plain, and Gladstone, influenced perhaps by Cobden, was statesmanlike enough to see
the political benefits of a policy which was based on the
concept of co-operation among the nations rather than on
the cut-throat tactics of mercantilism. The 1860 Cobden–
Chevalier treaty with France was an important step in this
direction; had it not been for the nationalist hysteria created
in Europe by Bismarck's narrow-minded power politics this
1860 treaty was potentially a healing agent for the social and
political maladies of Europe. Gladstone had secured that it
would contain a 'most favoured nation' clause, which meant
that the mutual benefits obtained in the treaty by Britain and
France would be extended to other nations subsequently
entering into trade treaties with either of these two powers.
It might therefore have become a nucleus of the utmost value
in creating peaceful conditions in Europe. It might even have
helped to avert the First World War. This concept was characteristic of the pacific liberalism of Gladstone which is perhaps his strongest claim to statesmanship.

It can be claimed, however, against Gladstone that while
Free Trade was probably advantageous up to 1870 its merits
were less plain afterwards, and that Gladstone clung on to the
policy in a way which says more for his determination than
for his common sense. This view is fallacious. It is true that in
the twenty years after 1870 Germany and the United States,
our chief competitors, came near to doubling the value of
their foreign trade; in the same period Britain increased the

value of her foreign trade by less than half. But expression of development in this way conceals the fact that Germany and the United States, both of whom were well equipped with natural resources and an expanding population, were going through the exhilarating spurt in production which was the natural accompaniment of the Industrial Revolution wherever it was experienced. Britain had passed through the same phase herself some forty years beforehand and obviously could not expect to repeat indefinitely sensational advances in her share in foreign trade. If, however, the foreign trade figures for 1870–89 are examined in terms of absolute advance the results are not nearly so flattering to Britain's rivals. In millions Britain's foreign trade rose from £547m. in 1870 to £740m. in 1889, an increase of £193m. Germany's foreign trade rose from £212m. in 1870 to £367m. in 1889, an increase of £155m. The United States 'foreign trade rose from £165m. in 1870 to £320m. in 1889, an increase of £155m. also.[1] Even at this stage, therefore, when other countries were becoming industrialised and many of them were adopting Protection, the absolute increase in Britain's foreign trade was greater than that of either of her two main rivals. Her total share of foreign trade was greater than the two of them put together. Expansion of this kind does not suggest any short-sightedness on Gladstone's part in maintaining Free Trade.

Nevertheless it is true that the prosperity of the mid-century was less easy to maintain in the changed circumstances of later years. Agriculture undoubtedly suffered from foreign competition, emigration figures rose sharply between 1880 and 1893, prices fell, the word 'unemployed', Ensor points out, is first recorded in use as a noun by the Oxford English Dictionary in 1882,[2] and the phrase 'the Great Depression' has been bandied about as a description of the period from 1873–96. Undoubtedly there were pockets of social discontent and unemployment but 'depression' is a gross misnomer, except for agriculture; and if Protection had been adopted for agriculture this would have been followed by a reversion to the pre-1846 situation in which British industry, still thriving as the production and export figures

---

[1] These are Mulhall's figures quoted in R. C. K. Ensor, *England 1870–1914* (Oxford: Clarendon Press, 1936), p. 104.

[2] Ensor, *England 1870–1914*, p. 112.

show, would have been penalised for the deficiencies of British agriculture. Protectionism is not divisible. Protection for British agriculture would have greatly increased the risk of retaliatory duties being imposed by other countries on British manufactured goods. In 1846 Free Trade had been a stimulus to more scientific farming; now it was a stimulus to adaptation to other types of farming than the production of grain. The period of transition would present difficulties and, for some, distress, but this was preferable in the wider view to a revised tariff policy. In modern times the strains of such a transition would have been eased by State help for agriculture and for the agricultural labourer, but is it realistic to criticise Gladstone for not being Lord Beveridge? Besides, some of the arguments supporting the idea of a depression during this period rest on a slender basis. The price fall may have made manufacturers depressed, but the real wages of industrial workers benefited by the fall, and the continued expansion of trade and production ensured that unemployment was not widespread.

Gladstone's stringent views on the need for public economy are well known. In the words of Sir Philip Magnus 'he loathed waste because he regarded all money as a trust committed by God to man'.[1] This is now an unfashionable view on more counts than one. In 1853 income tax stood at 7d in the £. In 1967 it stood at 8s 3d in the £. Two world wars, shifts in the balance of political and economic forces in the world, and the growth of the Welfare State explain much of the difference, but not all. Students of modern parliamentary procedure know well how strongly the present methods of controlling expenditure have been criticised both inside and outside Parliament. It would be interesting, and perhaps instructive, to know how a resurrected Gladstone would react to the vote on account involving large sums of public money being passed 'on the nod', or what he would think of the history of missile development expenditure since the Second World War, or of social welfare schemes which assist the rich as well as the poor. Gladstone's philosophy on these matters was totally different. He believed that the nation's wealth would 'fructify in the pockets of the people'. Circumstances have changed and it would no longer be appropriate to apply

[1] Magnus, *Gladstone*, p. 112.

in their entirety the simplicity of Gladstone's financial principles to the more complex problems of the modern State.
Nevertheless in his own time his vigilance over public expenditure had its merits both in saving money and in encouraging individual thrift and hard work. When one contrasts on the one hand the enormous expenditure of the
modern State, and on the other Gladstone's saving of £300 a
year by reducing the salary of a Parliamentary Secretary by
that amount, the modern tax-payer may feel that a touch of
Gladstonian cheese-paring would not be out of place. There
is no doubt that Gladstone's financial policies proved their
worth in his own times. It is a platitude, but an important
one, that Britain's wealth is a matter of its productivity and
export levels. Gladstone's acknowledged dominance in
financial affairs set the pattern in taxation even when he was
not Prime Minister or Chancellor of the Exchequer himself.
The result was a great growth in capital accumulation which
provided ample funds not only for industrial expansion at
home but also for investment on a massive scale abroad,
bringing with it all the advantages of returns of interest and a
host of trading contacts to stimulate the export market.

The characteristic which most clearly distinguished Gladstone from most politicians of his times was the breadth of
mind and vision which enabled him to keep clearly in focus the
interests of the nation to the exclusion of the narrower claims
of party and class interest. With this he combined another
attribute of a stateman in his remarkable sensitivity to the
changing circumstances of his time; this resulted in a spate of
legislation which cleared the way for the considerable advances
made by the Balfour Government of 1902–5 and the Liberal
Governments between 1906 and 1914. He had given ample
indication of his fearless and liberal-minded approach long
before he became Prime Minister. As President of the Board of
Trade he had been responsible for the Parliamentary Train
Act of 1844. This showed a characteristic concern for the well-
being of the masses and made it clear to the railway companies that they existed for public service as well as private
gain. They owed their existence to Acts of Parliament; this
privilege carried with it responsibility too. Every company
therefore had to provide at least one train a day which would
stop at every station. The maximum charge was to be one

penny a mile and covered seating had to be provided for the passengers. It was symptomatic of Gladstone's long-sighted handling of affairs that he made a strong attempt to have clauses inserted in the Bill which would have enabled the State to have had the option of taking over the railways after a period of twenty-one years. Had this been successful it would have obviated the cut-throat competition in which the railway companies were forced to indulge later in the century.

His respect for principle and his indifference to unpopularity led him in the years before he became Prime Minister to press several measures which he believed to be right; whether his colleagues, still less his opponents, thought so or not left him unmoved. In 1853 as Chancellor of the Exchequer, in the face of the initial opposition of the whole Cabinet and the fury of the landed interests, he forced through the House of Commons a measure to extend the legacy duty to all successions to property. In 1866, when Lord Russell was Prime Minister, Gladstone introduced the Representation of the People Bill, the Bill which was subsequently borrowed and adapted by Disraeli in 1867 to become the Second Reform Act extending the franchise to a million new voters. Disraeli thus brought the Bill to fruition because of his skilful political handling of his party. The impetus to the reform came from Gladstone. In 1832 he had been convinced that the Reform Bill was premature. By the early 1860s changing circumstances and his own experience of public affairs had led him to form a different view. He was impressed by the moderation and constitutional approach of the working classes in their desire to be given the vote. He knew, at first hand, the sufferings of the cotton operatives in Lancashire as a result of the interruption of raw cotton supplies during the American Civil War, and he had also seen how, in spite of this, they had recognised the merit of a war which had as part of its aim the suppression of slavery. This self-discipline and his own strong faith in the innate wisdom of the masses weighed more strongly with him than choosing phrases on the subject which would not irritate Lord Palmerston or the Queen. Both of them were indignant over Gladstone's outburst in 1864 when he stated: 'I venture to say that every man, who is not presumably incapacitated by some consideration of personal unfitness or of political danger, is morally entitled to come within the pale of the Constitution.' These sentiments would become commonplace in the twentieth century; for a minister of the Crown to utter them in mid-Victorian Britain was like whistling in church. Gladstone's speech may not have been tactful, but he regarded tact as one of the lesser virtues. His words cut through the knot of prejudice. He was voicing what many had felt, and gave a huge impetus to the movement to franchise reform. The Second Reform Bill, which was fundamentally the consequence of Gladstone's belief in the masses, was by far the most important landmark in the history of the extension of the franchise. The 1832 Bill had been conceived in a grudging and restrictive spirit. Gladstone's attitude on franchise reform was completely different. It sprang from a respect for democracy. Subsequent Acts in 1884, 1918, and 1928 extended the vote more widely, but neither these Acts nor that of 1832 have the significance of the Act of 1867. As in so many matters Gladstone laid the foundations and others built.

The record of Gladstone's legislative achievement after he became Prime Minister is impressive by any standard. It is even more impressive in the context of his time. Palmerston's liberalism was for export only; in domestic affairs he showed a resistance to change which exceeded that of the Tory party. The Statute Book was full enough in his estimation; 'We cannot go on legislating for ever.' The Conservative Prime Ministers contemporary with Gladstone were Disraeli and Lord Salisbury. The former belonged to the progressive wing of Conservatism which was finding its inspiration at this stage in borrowing the more popular reforms of its opponents. Lord Salisbury was Prime Minister from 1886 to 1902, except for a short Liberal interlude between 1892 and 1895. His policy was largely one of benevolent passivity.

Gladstone's legislative record therefore presents a startling contrast with that of his contemporaries. Moreover, many of the changes made were not in trivial or transient issues but in aspects of policy having far-reaching consequences extending into modern times. The 1870 Education Act, the adoption of open competitive examination for the Civil Service, the Ballot and Corrupt Practices Acts, and the University Tests Act, all show the distaste for privileged cliques and a fundamental concern for the welfare of all the people which is the mark of

PLATES

THE MODERN JOB! or JOHN BULL and his COMFORTS! 1816

The Red Book refers to the campaign against the appointment of Government supporters to sinecure positions.

From left: Lord Liverpool, with his hand on McMahon's shoulder, the Prince Regent, John Bull, Canning, Viscount Sidmouth, Lord Ellenborough.

Robert, 2nd Earl of Liverpool, K.G. (1770–1828). Painting by Sir Thomas Lawrence, 1804.

The features are those of a man disciplined by the exercise of power. Self-control and decisiveness are suggested in the firm lines of the face; at the same time the eyes have an uncertainty of expression oddly at variance with the rest of the face. The loose lines of the mouth owe more to Lawrence's characteristic style as a portrait-painter than to any trait of Liverpool himself. Liverpool's long neck and nose gave ample scope to the political cartoonists.

THE UNITED CABINET, 1832

From right: Earl Grey, Lord Durham, Lord Brougham, C. Grant (*in background*), Marquis of Lansdowne, Viscount Althorp (*in background*), Viscount Palmerston, Lord Holland (*in background*), unidentified minister, Lord John Russell.

Charles, 2nd Earl Grey (1764–1845). Artist unknown, c. 1830.

Grey is remembered for his legislation rather than his personality, and his personal inconspicuousness is suggested by this portrait. There is no strongly individualistic feature of dress or appearance. A slim man, with dark, lively eyes, he might well be taken for a lawyer; the precise pose adds to the impression of dapper neatness.

THE FALLEN MINISTER, 1846

From left: Disraeli, Peel, Lord Bentinck, O'Connell, and Lord John Russell (*standing together*).

Sir Robert Peel (1788–1850). Painting by John Linnell, 1838.

Peel retained a youthful appearance longer than most, though in his later years he became heavily built and, according to Greville, his complexion became pallid and even yellow, a marked contrast with the radiance which Disraeli had noted in an earlier description. He was light in colouring with sandy hair and large blue eyes. The painter has brilliantly conveyed here in the expression of the eyes the combination of vivacious intelligence and sensitive wariness which colleagues found so puzzling. The restless nervous energy of the man is evident in the unrelaxed pose.

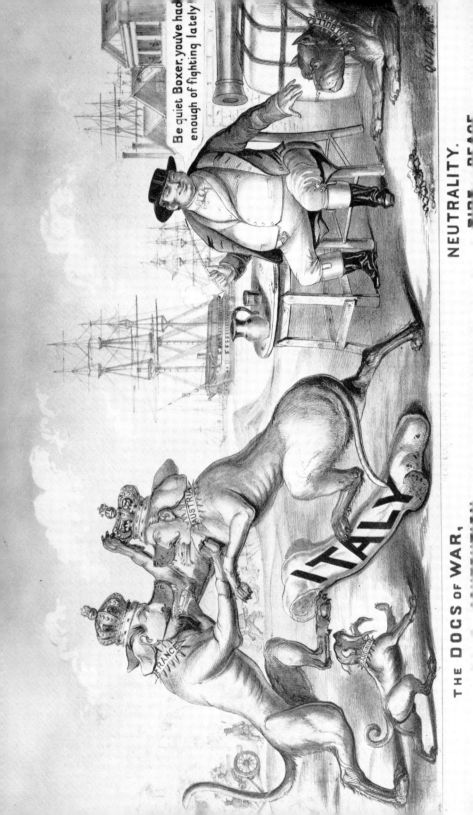

THE DOCS OF WAR, NEUTRALITY.

THE DOGS OF WAR, 1859

The power and self-confidence of Palmerston's Britain are strongly evident in this contemporary cartoon.

Henry, 3rd Viscount Palmerston (1784–1865). Painting by F. Cruikshank.

The better-known and more flattering portrait of Palmerston is that by John Partridge painted in 1845 and now in the National Portrait Gallery. There he is shown in an artificially languid pose, dressed as a dandy, his features sensitive to the point of femininity. The portrait shown here is more revealing. The strength and irascibility of the man are clearly marked in this leonine head with its thick mane of hair and strongly lined face. There was a toughness or coarseness of character about Palmerston which can be glimpsed here in the eyes and the obstinate lines of the mouth. Strength of will rather than sensibility or intellectual power is the prevailing impression left by the portrait.

Tom Merry

William Gladstone (1809–98). Painting by Sir John Millais, 1879.

The strength of Gladstone's character is perfectly expressed in this famous painting. The large features, deeply-set dark eyes, the intent expression, and the strong line of the mouth powerfully suggest the almost hypnotic force of will which Gladstone generated at times of crisis; so, too, does the firm stance — erect, composed, but permeated with a sense of energy. The air of severity and moral authority is striking but is tinged perhaps with the self-righteousness which Disraeli resented.

THE FIRST HOME RULE BILL, 1886

From left: Lord Hartington (*in top hat*), G. J. Goschen, John Bright, Joseph Chamberlain, Lord Randolph Churchill, Lord Salisbury, Sir Stafford Northcote (*probably*).
Above: Gladstone.

THE CHAMPIONS, 1872

Disraeli's apparently simple patriotism appealed more to the Victorians at times than Gladstone's moralistic approach.

Earl of Beaconsfield (1804–81). Painting by Sir John Millais, 1881

The beard and long hair give a curiously Elizabethan air to Disraeli. His obtrusively courtly manner and romantic, but practical, nature would have made him very much at home in that age. The hooded eyes and firm sardonic mouth and chin give some indication of the resilient elusive strength which enabled him to match the fiery power of Gladstone in debate. His dark eyes contrasted strikingly with the pallor of his face and gave him a dramatic appearance which he accentuated by his manner and dress.

Joseph Chamberlain (1836–1914).
Painting by J. S. Sargent, 1896.

The political cartoonists needed to look little further than the famous eye-glass and flowered buttonhole, but there are other features of Chamberlain's dress and appearance which are equally interesting. The neatness of dress, a shade too immaculate, and the stiff posture suggest the basic social unease of the respectable Radical. His intelligence, disciplined by concentration, is well conveyed here; so, too, is the cold defensiveness, the natural recourse of a sensitive man subjected, as Chamberlain was, to virulent criticism.

POLITICAL TRINITY AT LOGGERHEADS, 1885

From left: Joseph Chamberlain, Lord Hartington, Gladstone. Chamberlain, the Radical, Hartington, the Whig, and Gladstone, the vague idealist, here typify the conflicts which weakened the Liberal party.

Queen Victoria and the Prince Consort. From the painting by Sir Edwin Landseer, 1845

The domesticity and mutual devotion shown in this painting strongly influenced middle-class attitudes. Prince Albert's death prematurely ended this happy phase of the Queen's life.

liberalism as its best. The significance of these Acts in relation to later developments is self-evident. Their advantages can be hedged around with little qualifications. No doubt by twentieth-century standards the Education Act, for instance, was a modest measure. It may well be true that Gladstone hoped for no more from these schools than a greater diffusion of knowledge of Christian principles and a knowledge of how to read and write. If so it was not a small hope where four out of five in the adult population had been estimated to be illiterate, and training in moral conduct is still not superfluous.

Several of the measures passed in Gladstone's ministries owed much to leading ministers. Forster piloted the Education Bill through the religious squabbles which developed out of its terms; Cardwell planned the detail of the army reforms; Joseph Chamberlain pressed for the introduction of the Third Reform Bill; Fowler initiated the Local Government Act of 1894. The last-named Act was passed in the year of Gladstone's retirement and his personal contribution to its passage was negligible. He was now in his mid-eighties, his energies had been absorbed in the introduction of the Second Home Rule Bill in 1893, and the Local Government Act, though a useful administrative advance, was merely the logical continuation of the Local Government Act of 1888. On the other issues mentioned Gladstone was far from providing mere figure-head leadership, in spite of the heavy claims made on his time by a varied legislative programme, the disorders in Ireland, and the vexed issues arising in political developments overseas. The Education Act was the sequel and obvious corollary to the 1867 Act; it had Gladstone's complete approval in principle, and it was natural enough to leave to the minister in charge the task of reaching a balance between the competing sectarian claims. Similarly Gladstone was content to leave the details of the army reforms to Cardwell, but the economies involved in these reforms bear the unmistakable impress of Gladstone's thinking; it is indicative too of his influence that when Cardwell encountered the stumbling-block of the opposition of the House of Lords to the abolition of commission purchase, it was Gladstone who cleared the way by the use of the Royal Warrant procedure. On the other matter, the Third Reform Bill, it is true that the pressure applied by Joseph Chamberlain and the Radicals stimulated

E

the onset of this Bill. There needs to be set against this the heavy burden of responsibility which Gladstone shouldered during this ministry for the handling of imperial and Irish affairs, which precluded him from giving to domestic affairs as much attention as he would have liked. Moreover, the new Bill, though important, did not represent such a breakthrough as the 1867 Act whose debt to Gladstone has already been described; nor should it be overlooked that once the decision had been taken to push through the Reform Bill Gladstone made the passage of this complex measure very much easier by his oratory, his mastery of detail, and his massive concentration.

It would be patently false to claim that Gladstone's legislative enactments were without fault. His most conspicuous misjudgment in home affairs was his mishandling of the legislation affecting trade unions. It is familiar enough that Gladstone, having recognised the right to existence of the trade unions, partly nullified this advance by depriving them of the power of picketing in the Criminal Law Amendment Act of 1871. This was a misjudgment though well-intentioned. It sprang from Gladstone's strong liberal belief that decisions should be freely arrived at both by employers and by employees. Coercion of a man's opinions, even in the common interest of the group to which he belonged, was repugnant to Gladstone. The restriction on picketing was removed by Disraeli in 1875 and trade unionism, still a fragile growth at this stage, was correspondingly strengthened. Nevertheless Gladstone's views on picketing, though an obstacle to the group movement, showed a creditable respect for the individual. It could be pointed out too in Gladstone's defence that had it not been for his willingness to accept the minority report of the commission of inquiry into trade unionism that movement would have lacked the advantages which it acquired by the Act of 1871. Official opinion, interfused with and supported by vested interests, was still strongly hostile to trade unionism. Legally the trade unions had been able to make no advance since 1824 until Gladstone characteristically hauled out into the open a national issue which had been neglected for too long.

Gladstone had no sympathy with the common Victorian belief that difficulties could best be solved by not thinking

about them. His policies therefore carried greater risks, but
they had the hallmark of honesty. Irish affairs between 1868
and 1894 are an outstanding example of this directness.
Superficially his efforts can be written off as a failure. The
First Land Act had too many loopholes, and the Second Land
Act came too late. The arrest of Parnell alienated the Irish
without stopping violence; the secrecy of Gladstone's conversion to Home Rule, and the events of 1885, are a little
melodramatic and absurd. The Home Rule Bills of 1886 and
of 1893 were doomed to failure and it might have been more
profitable for Gladstone to have washed his hands of Ireland
and to have concentrated on social problems at home. None
of these criticisms touches the central point, of greater merit
than any of them, that, alone among Prime Ministers of the
second half of the nineteenth century, Gladstone recognised
that Ireland deserved something better than the diluted
Cromwellianism which was all that his opponents could offer.
His mission, as he recognised in 1868, was to pacify Ireland,
not to punish her. Whatever the immediate provocation from
Fenians and later from the Land League, Ireland deserved
something better than a further dose of the repression and
neglect of which she had had more than her share for over two
hundred years. These facts Gladstone not only discerned but
made the basis for action. Tactically Gladstone made blunders
but few would now quarrel with his strategy.

That Anglo-Irish relations have remained bad in the
twentieth century is not the responsibility of Gladstone. He
disestablished the Church in Ireland, unmoved by Disraeli's
flamboyant attack. He worked out a solution to the problems
of tenant-holding in Ireland which was frustrated a little by
the imperfections of his own legislation, but much more so by
Disraeli's neglect of Irish affairs between 1874 and 1880, and
Parnell's ruthless selfishness in the 1880s. Finally when he
saw that the Irish would only be satisfied with Home Rule, he
believed Britain's responsibility towards them to be so great
that he braved violent opposition in the Lords and the
Commons, and remained resolute in the face of desertion by
many of his own party as he vainly attempted to give the
Irish what they wanted. His policy failed, in one sense, but
no man could have made a more herculean effort; by forcing
Home Rule upon public attention he won converts among

liberally-minded people and prepared the way, as no one else had done, for the subsequent independence of the Irish.

Honesty in politics is not likely to be a popular virtue, least of all perhaps in overseas affairs when nationalist prejudices and self-advantage predispose politicians to following the safe course of jingoism. When Gladstone recognised the justice of the United States' claim for the damage inflicted by the *Alabama*, the sea-raider which the British Government had allowed to escape to join the southern forces during the American Civil War, he knew that the British public, accustomed to the heady nationalism of Palmerston and *Punch* cartoons, would not be pleased. This did not deter him in the slightest. He had the confidence which stems from depth of thought and sound moral principles. He replaced the simple formula of ' Rule Britannia ' with the impartial doctrine of the rule of law in international relations. His influence was on the side of peace and mutual respect among nations. He regretted Russia's violation of the Treaty of Paris since it was a breach of the rule of law. At the same time he had the practical sense to recognise that the spirit is more important than the letter of the law, and that it would be as nonsensical to deny Russia access to the Black Sea as to deny Britain access to the English Channel. He showed precisely the same kind of long-sighted moderation in his handling of the circumstances arising out of the Franco-Prussian War. He not only secured the neutrality of Belgium but also made an energetic effort to mediate between Prussia and France over the peace terms. Had he secured the backing which he deserved it is possible that he might have been able to avoid the cession of Alsace and Lorraine to Prussia, with all the bitter consequences which that entailed.

Respect for the rule of law in international affairs was a valuable antidote to the insular selfishness of his times but it naturally led Gladstone into conflicts of opinion with his contemporaries, particularly when in opposition he was obliged to watch his wider approach to international problems being set aside by men of more limited vision. He recommended, for instance, that peace should be made with Russia in 1855 before Sevastopol fell, on the grounds that the cause of public law had been served by the action taken so far. Russia had been shown that her policy of aggression had not paid; to persist with the campaign in order to humiliate her would be to lay up trouble for the future, as indeed happened, and would give more encouragement to Turkey than that country deserved in view of the ill-management of her empire. Gladstone exhibited precisely the same breadth and humanity of outlook in the later crisis in the Near East which culminated in the Congress of Berlin in 1878. It says much for Gladstone's steadiness of purpose that he resolutely opposed the anti-Russian hysteria of a large section of the population at this time. The Queen pressed for war against Russia, Disraeli showed his customary aptitude for floating with the tide of public opinion, Gladstone was snubbed by the upper classes, deserted by some of his fellow Liberals, and jeered at in the streets. In the face of all this he continued to criticise the abuses of Turkish government in the Balkans; he attacked Disraeli's decision to send a fleet to Constantinople on the grounds that as the Russians were already negotiating for peace it was an unnecessarily provocative action; finally he deplored the conduct of affairs by Disraeli at Berlin. He believed, with justice, that the settlement had been made on the grounds of military expediency and he despised the paltry intrigues which gave Cyprus to Britain. His own view was that the best defence against aggression in the Balkans was 'the breasts of free men'. Cynics may doubt this, but the history of the Balkans between 1878 and 1914 does not give any assurance that they are right.

It was logical and reasonable that Gladstone should apply exactly the same principles in imperial affairs as in foreign affairs. In his withdrawal of British forces from Afghanistan, and in recognising the independence of the Transvaal in 1881, he was able to do so with very little trouble. It is too far-fetched to lay at Gladstone's door the troubles which developed later in Britain's relations with the Boers. He would have had no sympathy at all with the expansionist policies in South Africa of Rhodes and the Conservative Government, which were at the root of the Second Boer War. In his handling of affairs in Egypt and the Sudan Gladstone is more vulnerable. On the other hand the evasion of financial obligations by the Egyptians, the prospect of a tyrannical government led by Arabi Pasha, and the importance of the Suez Canal in promoting peaceful trading relations, all weighed heavily with Gladstone. Even so his military intervention in Egypt in 1881 was reluctant, but forced upon him by circumstances for which he could not be blamed. 'I affirm, and will show, that the situation in Egypt is not one which we made, but one that we found. I shall show that we never had any option. . . .' As one studies the development of the Egyptian crisis and Gladstone's slow conversion to the need for military action, so characteristic of him, and so far removed from the jingoism of the Opposition, it is difficult to doubt the truth of these words uttered to the House of Commons in 1884. In the tragic but politically less important episode of Gordon's death at Khartoum, Gladstone was undoubtedly at fault. Gordon had contributed to his own death by his impulsiveness. 'I own to having been very insubordinate to Her Majesty's Government,' he wrote in his diary, but this does not pardon Gladstone's indecision over the relief expedition.

From time to time Gladstone thus made errors of judgment, but in any long view of his career the outstanding impression is of a man who is firmly buttressed by a strong moral sense and by a vision of the nation as it might become if it developed its greater qualities instead of its lesser ones. Men of this kind are uncomfortable companions for those who prefer the cosy self-interest of the *status quo*. At the same time the people in general are generous in their recognition of statesmanship; they know it is in short supply. Nor is there any substance whatsoever in the charge that Gladstone was a bigot. His moral approach, as has been amply demonstrated, was part of his statesmanship. One has only to compare him with bigots such as Mary Tudor or James I to see that the charge is not worthy of serious consideration. They had an essential smallness of mind which was the antithesis of Gladstone's broad humanity. Mary and James the nation distrusted or despised; for Gladstone it had the greatest respect. If people broke his windows they did so because they felt that he was worth it; they would not have wasted their energies on a lesser man.

6. DISRAELI
STATESMAN OR CHARLATAN?

Prelude

That Disraeli should have become Prime Minister at all is one of the more surprising contradictions of the Victorian Age. Prejudice against Jews was still strong enough to prevent until 1858 the admission to Parliament of those who followed the Jewish faith, and though this did not affect Disraeli himself, since he had been given Christian baptism at the age of thirteen, he still had to contend with a certain amount of anti-Semitic feeling, especially during the early years of his political career. Nor had his education followed the stereotyped pattern of his great contemporaries. He went neither to a public school nor to a university. Until the age of fifteen he attended a private school where he showed an independence of mind and a flair for acting, both of which qualities earned him the resentment of his headmaster. The more valuable part of his early education then followed at home where he made full use of the extensive library of his bookish father.

Even Disraeli's physical appearance told against him. Gladstone had the bearing and outlook of an Old Testament prophet, Peel the representative primness of the middle class, Palmerston a confident John Bull solidity. Disraeli had none of these qualities. His stooped shoulders, sallow complexion, and eyes shrouded from expression, suggested at first sight a man with very little zest for the part he was required to play in politics. He might be a man of the world but not of the people. Gladstone was nicknamed 'the People's William' largely because at his greatest moments they discerned in him qualities which at their best they would have liked to possess themselves — strength of will, fine principles, and the gift to express them. No such identification was possible with Disraeli. Could he ever have been 'the People's Benjamin'? The idea is absurd. Far from seeking this identification with the people Disraeli went out of his way to avoid it. For many years he increased the distance between himself and normality by a foppish taste in dress and appearance. In early middle age he was wearing clothes which would have been startling even for an adolescent — green trousers, yellow waistcoat, a shirt with ruffles, and lest these should make him too inconspicuous he wore large rings, and his hair was arranged in carefully pressed ringlets. His style of speech in the House of Commons was at first as pretentious as his dress. What was even worse was that the good sense which he wished to convey was so overloaded with flowery and pompous language that his maiden speech made him a laughing stock in the House, except to a more discerning minority.

Disraeli was far too able a man to ignore the lesson of this experience. He adopted a flat, almost prosaic style in his speeches in the House but his unemphatic voice, his perfect sense of timing, and sharp awareness of the vulnerable points in the arguments and temperaments of his opponents, made him outstanding even among the great orators of his time. The brilliance and flexibility of his mind made its mark on the House of Commons, particularly in the verbal duels with Gladstone where the House, a little grudgingly, was driven to realise that Disraeli could at least hold his own against his opponent's thunderous denunciations. Nevertheless the feeling long remained in the Commons, and even in the Conservative party, that Disraeli though in them was not of them. There was an alien quality about him which would lead, one might reasonably expect, to a feeling that any ideas coming from this strange, and possibly tainted, source would be unacceptable.

His career, when seen in gaunt outline, gives some substance for this belief. Peel, Gladstone, and Palmerston had all had resounding influence on the course of national affairs before achieving Prime Ministerial office. Disraeli's brief experiences of ministerial office had been almost universally unfortunate. He became Chancellor of the Exchequer in 1852 and produced a budget which Gladstone felled as if it were some offending tree on his Hawarden estate. By the end of the year the Government itself had fallen and Disraeli was out of office. He returned as Chancellor of the Exchequer, a post for which he had little aptitude or liking, in the Derby Government in 1858. His most conspicuous activity was characteristically not financial but political. He introduced a Bill for parliamentary reform, saw it defeated, and shortly after, in the summer of 1859, the Derby Government, never a match for the Whigs in spite of the divisions in the latter party, was ousted from power. In 1866 Derby once more became Prime Minister, with the faithful Disraeli in support as Chancellor of the Exchequer, 'the Jew and the Jockey' as they were not too affectionately called. The extension of the parliamentary franchise was a more pressing issue than it had been in 1859. The Liberal failure to secure the passage of a new Reform Bill had whetted the country's appetite for reform without satisfying it. Disraeli, sensitive as ever to trends in political opinion, was quicker than most of his colleagues to see the need for the Conservatives to wean themselves from unthinking opposition to change. Accordingly he introduced the Second Reform Bill which was duly passed in 1867. No doubt Conservatives had second thoughts about the wisdom of this change when the Liberals won the 1868 election with a majority of 112 seats.

There had been little in Disraeli's ministerial career so far to suggest that his influence would be of any great significance in the country's history. The one major measure with which he had been associated, the Second Reform Act, had had a boomerang effect on his party's electoral fortunes, and his opponents could claim with some appearance of justice that his introduction of the Bill had been a piece of political opportunism which had deceived nobody. 'In the Reform Act,' wrote Bagehot, 'as a strategist he unquestionably outflanked himself.' Shortly afterwards, in February 1868, Disraeli became Prime Minister upon the resignation of Lord Derby through ill-health. His hold on power was weak and brief. Gladstone and the Liberals secured the defeat of the Government in April 1868 on a Liberal proposal to disestablish the Anglican Church in Ireland. Time was needed to revise the electoral registers to take into account the changes made by the Second Reform Act. By the autumn this work was completed, the elections were held, and the Liberals, brimming with reforms, were back in power.

Disraeli led the Opposition skilfully during the next six years. He bided his time as the Liberal reforms cascaded out until, as Disraeli picturesquely remarked, the ministers on the

*

Treasury bench resembled a South American landscape. 'You behold a range of exhausted volcanoes. Not a flame flickers on a single pallid crest.' The Government was defeated in 1873 on the Irish University Bill, designed to give equality of status in a new university at Dublin to Roman Catholics and to Protestants. Disraeli wisely refused to take office in the existing state of the parties in the Commons. For the time being Gladstone was left to flounder in uneasy leadership while the Conservatives under Disraeli's guidance prepared themselves thoroughly at national and local levels for the coming elections. When the results were declared early in 1874 the Conservatives had gone much of the way to reversing the set-back of 1868. They had an advantage over the Liberals of more than a hundred seats, and an overall majority of fifty.

The result was a tribute to Disraeli's political astuteness, but this was to be his last chance to make a distinctive contribution to the development of his country and of his party, and it had come very late. He lacked the physical vigour which Gladstone retained even when he was in his eighties. Disraeli was now in his seventieth year, asthmatic and gouty. His wife, Mary Anne, whose devotion had buoyed him up against the violence of his enemies, had died in 1872. For a man so dependent on feminine company and admiration this was a shattering loss. Even the large majority which he now enjoyed was more impressive in numbers than in fact. His connection with the Conservative party had so often been ill-starred in the past. He had been more instrumental than anyone else in securing the overthrow of Peel in 1846 in the debate on the repeal of the Corn Laws. Three times since then he had flitted in and out of office as Chancellor of the Exchequer; on each occasion the ministries in which he served had been of short duration, and a critic might well consider that it was Disraeli's activities primarily which produced their downfall. His principles seemed uncertain. Having lashed Peel over the latter's abandonment of Protection he had quietly followed the same course himself within a few years' time. He had secured the passage of the Second Reform Act but his motives for doing so were uncertain, and the reform had a speculative quality not usually associated with Conservatism. Disraeli seemed to have moved a disconcertingly

long way from the romantic semi-feudal version of Conservatism which he and the Young England group had propounded
in the 1840s.

When Parliament reassembled in 1874 it seemed, in the first
excitement of power after the frustrations of the last thirty
years, that the Conservative party had perhaps set aside its
doubts about their leader. He was greeted with great acclaim.
But prejudices acquired over a long period of years are not so
easily put aside. Disraeli had no illusions on this score. He
knew that as yet his contribution to Conservatism had been
slight. If he was to achieve the greatness on which he had set
his mind since his youth everything would now depend on the
success of this ministry — almost certain, in view of his age
and strength, to be his last. In any assessment of Disraeli's
political stature it is this ministry of 1874–80 which must be
pre-eminently considered: by its achievements or its failures
he stands or falls.

Attack

Disraeli's reputation rests largely on his contribution to Conservatism. Until his time the appeal of that party had been
narrowly based and its objectives narrowly conceived. Peel
had rebelled against this restrictive outlook, and Gladstone,
irked by the strait-jacket of reactionary Toryism, had left the
party to join the Whigs. Between 1846 and 1874 the Tory
Party was equally ineffective whether in power or in opposition. The one major Act with which it was associated —
against the wishes of many of its members — was the Second
Reform Act; and this measure they owed to the Whigs and to
the political opportunism of Disraeli. When therefore at long
last the Conservative ministry under Disraeli not only survived for a few years but actually appeared to have achieved
something, Conservative satisfaction became disproportionately great. Dr Johnson's comment on the preaching of a
sermon by a woman is apposite: 'It is not done well but you
are surprised to find it done at all.'

As a consequence Disraeli's activities in the different
aspects of policy acquired a mystique which was to dominate

Conservative thinking for many years to come. Through half-closed eyes he might seem great, a quality in short supply in the party at that stage of its existence. He had an air of confidence, much needed in the party after the tribulations of the past thirty years. Moses would lead them out of the wilderness and in return they would overlook his past. But, beyond this, Disraeli had an imaginative flair, and at times came close to achieving the politician's dream of belonging to a party and speaking for the nation. In practice the dream faded, but there were a few exhilarating moments during his ministry when it seemed as if Conservatism and the nation were at one. His grandiloquent statement on the principles of Conservatism, 'to maintain the institutions of the country, to uphold the Empire of England, and to elevate the condition of the people', became accepted as unquestioningly by the party as if it were a chemical formula in a successful experiment. Undoubtedly he gave to Conservatives a coherence of thought from which they profited; it was fortunate too that he bore in mind the condition of the people, even if it came last in his list of priorities. Nevertheless, when one probes behind the slogans of Conservatism and examines Disraeli's achievements, it soon becomes apparent that there were flaws in the principles of which he was chief advocate, and that there were times too when Disraeli's conduct was dictated purely by the opportunism which was his characteristic weakness. This was to be expected. He had spent a lifetime appeasing hostility, in schooling his character, and in making himself agreeable. Lord John Manners, his colleague in the Young England movement some thirty years before Disraeli became Prime Minister, had summed it all up: 'If I could be sure that Disraeli believes all that he says I should be happier.' Disraeli had climbed the greasy pole. What he would do at the top of it remained to be seen; only an invincible optimist would expect the actions of such a man to be likely to bring any lasting benefits to his nation or to his party.

Imperialism was not invented by Disraeli. The British had been an effective imperial power from the middle of the eighteenth century, and the extension of the Empire and its interests had continued steadily in India, Afghanistan, China, Malaya, Africa, New Zealand, the Pacific Islands, and elsewhere during the nineteenth century. Frequently these

activities had been accompanied by all the unpleasant characteristics of early colonialism. Might was right, a reassuring
doctrine for the strong — as it was in the Stone Age. Native
rulers were superseded, or subdued. Pockets were filled and
consciences salved by the export of textiles, hardware, and
Bibles. By the time Disraeli became Prime Minister, however,
this first phase of simple-minded greed was giving way to a
more sophisticated and creditable approach. The Durham
Report, 'the Bible of the new imperialism', had been published as long ago as 1839. The Report had been concerned
with Canadian affairs but its recommendation for the grant
of self-government in internal affairs was applied over the
next forty years not only to Canada itself, but to most of the
Australian states, to New Zealand, and to Cape Colony. One of
the strongest criticisms of Disraeli is that instead of attuning
himself to this new and promising development in colonial
affairs his policy was a reversion to the aggressiveness of the
old colonialism already partly discredited even by this stage.

In South Africa it seemed at first that the financial difficulties of the Boers and their fear of the Zulu warriors might lead
to a federation combining the two Boer states of the Transvaal
and the Orange Free State with the two British colonies of
Cape Colony and Natal. Lord Carnarvon, the Colonial Secretary, had been primarily responsible for the British North
America Act of 1867, by which Canada had been federated,
and it was natural for him to think in similar terms over the
problem of Anglo-Boer relations. The federation was eventually successfully achieved in 1909 by the Union of South
Africa Act. That it took so long to achieve, and that before
it had been achieved the Boers and the British twice went to
war against each other, cannot be wholly blamed on Disraeli.
Others played their part in the blunders of the 1870s. There
was no telegraphic communication with South Africa in those
days and the immediate decisions had to be taken by the
men on the spot. Shepstone, the Minister for Native Affairs
in Natal, was commissioned to arrange the federation of the
two British colonies with the Transvaal, the Boer state most
immediately vulnerable to Zulu attack. He handled the matter
clumsily and the upshot was the annexation of the Transvaal
instead of the wiser remedy of federation. Frere, the High
Commissioner for South Africa, added another blunder by

involving Britain, on his own initiative, in what was intended
to be a punitive war against the Zulus. The British forces were
not fully equipped for war against the large Zulu force, num-
bering some 40,000 warriors, and this, coupled with the care-
lessness of their commander, Lord Chelmsford, led to the
disaster of Isandhlwana where over eight hundred British
troops were killed. In 1879, however, the Zulu army was defeated at Ulundi and their leader Keshwayo was deported.
Up to this stage it can reasonably be claimed on Disraeli's
behalf that while mistakes had been made the errors in
judgment had not been his; but in the decisions which now
followed Disraeli committed blunders which make those of his
underlings seem insignificant. In the first place Zululand was
divided among eight chieftains, whose ambitions were unlikely to be satisfied by a partition of this kind. Secondly, and
more unwisely still, Disraeli continued to treat the Transvaal
as if it were a defeated enemy state rather than a possible
partner in a South African federation. This naturally stimulated Boer nationalism — the nationalist Afrikaaner Bund,
for instance, was founded in 1879 — and contributed to the
outbreak of the First Boer War in 1881. What was equally
serious, however, was that Disraeli's handling of the episode
associated the Conservative Party with a cavalier disregard
for the rights of weaker states, and it was to be a long time
before the more obtuse members of the party became capable
of grasping any other approach on this subject. Indeed, the
two other major episodes in imperial policy — in Egypt and
in Afghanistan — merely served to reinforce their impression
that the British had a divine dispensation to rule, a view not
widely shared outside the ranks of the Conservative Party.

Disraeli's intrusion into Afghan affairs was even more
flagrant than his policy over the Transvaal. In the latter country there was a real threat to British interests, if a remote one,
in the existence of a large Zulu army; in Afghanistan the
threat to British interests was a figment of the imagination.
The supposed enemy here was Russia. Ever since Russia became a major power in the eighteenth century the British
have experienced periodical bouts of Russophobia. Public
opinion was particularly hysterical on this issue in the late
1870s following the Congress of Berlin and the events which
had preceded it. When the Amir of Afghanistan accepted a

Russian mission at Kabul but rejected a British one this was made an excuse for war. Disraeli's handling of the affair was inept and ill-judged in the extreme. He failed to overrule Lord Lytton, the belligerent Viceroy of India, who pressed for military action which was manifestly pointless, and he allowed himself to be borne along on the unthinking tide of anti-Russian public opinion. The result was a war to impose a British minister by force in Kabul, the subsequent assassination of the minister and his staff by Afghan soldiers, and a further war to chastise the Afghans for this action. The absurdity of Disraeli's policy was plainly demonstrated when Gladstone in the next ministry withdrew the British troops from Afghanistan. If Disraeli had judged the situation accurately one would have expected this withdrawal to be followed by an onrush of Russian troops into Afghanistan and the development of a menacing situation on the north-west frontier of India. Nothing of the kind happened, nor has it happened since. There was abundant evidence available, even in Disraeli's own time, to indicate the improbability of a Russian threat to India. The Russian territories adjacent to Afghanistan had not been effectively occupied by the Russians until the 1860s. They were trackless wastes for the most part, two thousand miles from Moscow. The impossibility of the Russians mounting an attack upon India through the narrow and difficult passes of the Afghan–Indian frontier was plain; the absurdity of the idea could be demonstrated with a map and ruler. But Disraeli, fresh from the pseudo-triumph of the Congress of Berlin, could not resist the opportunity to pose as the hammer of the Russians. Pandering to his self-esteem in this way led to wholly useless bloodshed and, once again, to an overbearing disregard for the rights of an independent people too weak to defend themselves against physical force. The human consequences of the irresponsible approach which envisages the world as a diplomatic chess-board were clearly exposed in Gladstone's Midlothian campaign: 'Remember that the sanctity of life in the hill villages of Afghanistan, among the winter snows, is as inviolable in the eye of Almighty God as can be your own.' It was an obvious sentiment, but one which Disraeli and his followers had forgotten.

In Egypt the consequences of Disraeli's loose direction of imperial policies were not quite so immediately apparent as in Afghanistan, though they were to become so in the next few years. The purchase of Khedive Ismail's shares in the Suez Canal Company had been an act of quick-witted opportunism for which Disraeli can fairly be praised. He can equally fairly be criticised for the weakness he showed in allowing himself to be persuaded by the French to participate directly in the management of Egyptian affairs. Egyptian finances were chaotic, and the object of this Anglo-French control was to ensure that interest payments would be made to European bond-holders of the Egyptian debt. It was an understandable policy but a mistake. It was the prelude to a long period of misunderstanding and bad relations between the British and Egyptians, culminating in the unfortunate Suez Canal campaign of 1956. If Gladstone had been in power in the 1870s the entanglement in Egypt might have been avoided. With Disraeli in power, dazzled by imperialism, there was never much doubt that Britain would be increasingly enmeshed in the web of Middle East politics.

Imperial policy was characterised by a narrow-minded, self-seeking approach; predictably, the foreign policy of Disraeli shared the same weakness. During his ministry the Eastern Question, always smouldering, flared into brief life. Most of the Balkan peninsula was under Turkish rule, as it had been since the fifteenth century. The Turks ruled their subjects there with a particularly obnoxious mixture of harshness, inefficiency, and corruption. The Greeks had won their independence after the war against the Turks which ended in 1829, and only the isolation and backwardness of the Balkan peoples had prevented mass risings of a similar nature. Even so, their inaccessibility and the inefficient administration of the sprawling Turkish Empire had enabled some of the Balkan nations, notably Romania, Serbia, and Montenegro, to obtain virtual independence before the 1875 crisis had developed at all. This crisis, which began with risings in Bosnia and Herzegovina against the Turkish tax-gatherers, looked therefore as if it might be the prelude to the ejection of the Turks from the Balkans. Changes in the *status quo* in the Balkans were a matter of close concern to Russia, Austria, France, and Britain, because of their interests, present or prospective, in the Eastern Mediterranean. Bismarck, in spite of his assertion that all the affairs of the Balkans were not worth the bones of

a single Pomeranian grenadier, could not in fact be indifferent
to the possibility of an Austro-Russian conflict which might
follow from the rivalry of these two countries over the
Balkans.

The first imperative need, therefore, was to localise the
fighting and to end it as soon as possible. If the great powers
were to act unitedly to secure this result the Turks were too
weak to oppose any decision they might reach. Accordingly,
when Austria, Russia, and Germany sent a joint note to the
Sultan demanding reforms in the Turkish system of government, and when Disraeli added his support too, it looked as if
an international settlement of the situation might be
achieved; this collaboration of the great powers was greatly
to be preferred to the nationalist free-for-all to obtain parcels
of Turkish territory which was virtually inevitable if the co-
operation of the powers failed at any point. In practice this co-
operation broke down and the man who was primarily responsible for its failure was Disraeli. In Afghanistan he had
allowed Lord Lytton to take decisions which pertained to the
Prime Minister; in the Transvaal he had leaned too heavily
on the advice of Frere; in Egypt on the matter of Anglo-
French control he had been swayed by Baring. Now on the
Turkish question he lamely followed the advice of the pro-
Turkish British ambassador at Constantinople, Sir H. Elliott.
Advice of the men on the spot is not a substitute for leadership by the Prime Minister. In this instance acceptance of
Elliott's advice was particularly disastrous. Austria, Germany, and Russia had just sent a further note to the Sultan,
the Berlin Memorandum, pressing for an armistice with the
rebels and implementation of the reforms in Turkish government previously proposed. Elliott advised Disraeli not to
support the note. Disraeli accepted this advice and the consequences of this foolish decision were to trouble the peace
of Europe for years to come.

The effect upon the Turks and the Balkan nations of this
open split among the great powers needs little amplification.
The Turks were confident now that they need not take the
suggestions for reforms seriously. The Balkan nations saw that
if they were to improve their situation they could only do so
by force. The separate ambitions of Austria and Russia which
could have been held in check by joint international action

were now unleashed. When Disraeli returned in 1878 from the Congress of Berlin in a state of ill-justified complacency, it presumably never occurred to him that this Congress would have been a much better one for Europe if it had taken place two years previously, before the fighting rather than after it. It is a clear instance of one decision changing the course of history, and in this instance very much for the worse.

The rebellion therefore duly spread. Bulgaria joined in; so did Serbia. The Bulgarian atrocities perpetrated by the Turks took place in 1876, though it took three months to convince Disraeli that they had happened at all. A further and belated attempt was now made, in which Britain collaborated, to secure reforms of Turkish government. The Turks, however, had ample cause to suspect British determination on this issue and confidently looked for British support in the event of a war against Russia. Russia, after further delays in negotiations with Turkey, declared war against her in April 1877. When one considers that the rebellions had begun about two years previously it gives the lie effectively to the belief that Russia was poised to leap on Turkey at the first opportunity, yet this was the fundamental assumption on which Disraeli's policy had been based.

Words had now given way to actions and Disraeli could happily revert to the spectacular opportunism which served him as a substitute for policy. By January 1878 the Russian troops had seized Adrianople. Superficially it might seem that Constantinople itself was in danger of occupation by the Russians, a view which appealed to the over-dramatic imagination of the Queen and to the more exuberant music-hall performers of the time. Disraeli did not share these illusions but he pandered to them by ordering the Mediterranean fleet to Constantinople. When the Russians and the Turks made peace in the Treaty of San Stefano a few months later, Disraeli again indulged the nation in its hysteria by ordering the call-up of reserves and by summoning Indian troops to Malta. These were meaningless gestures. The Russians had already exhausted their impetus in the campaign against Turkey. The diplomatic pressures which Britain, Austria-Hungary, and Germany could bring to bear at this stage were entirely adequate to ensure Russia's presence at the conference table, so that the terms of the San Stefano treaty could be revised. The military movements which Disraeli ordered were a mere charade. He had never heard of 'government by gimmick' but it is doubtful whether any other Prime Minister has had a better grasp of its meaning.

The essential narrowness of his political vision was made sharply apparent in the peace negotiations which followed Russia's inevitable acceptance of a European Conference to amend the San Stefano treaty. Secret negotiations with the other powers preceded the Berlin Congress. Russia agreed to a reduction in size of the large Bulgaria which had been created by the San Stefano treaty, and to abandon her claims to Armenia. Both changes were ill-judged. The anti-Russian nature of Bulgarian nationalism showed itself a mere seven years later when the northern section of Bulgaria expelled its Russian puppet ruler, Alexander, and united itself with Eastern Roumelia. The latter state was the southern section of Bulgaria, separated in the most arbitrary way from the northern half by the peacemakers at Berlin.[1] Disraeli persisted in the belief that the Balkan nations were willing accomplices in furthering Russian ambitions in the Middle East; in reality their behaviour now and later showed that they were fiercely independent and had no more love for the Russians than for the Turks. The Armenian situation involved different considerations. Armenia could scarcely be established as a separate State, but to hand over two million Christian Armenians to Turkish rule without making any effective provision for their freedom from persecution was an irresponsible act, whose consequences became only too plain when over six thousand Armenians were massacred in 1894.

Other agreements gave Austria a protectorate over Bosnia and Herzegovina and the right to garrison Novibazar; Britain acquired Cyprus in return for guaranteeing to defend Turkey-in-Asia. The former agreement was consistent with Disraeli's mistaken belief that the Balkan states needed to be put under forcible restraint to prevent them from becoming willing agents of Russian imperialism; one of its historical by-products was the assassination of the Archduke Franz Ferdinand of Austria at Sarajevo in 1914. The acquisition of Cyprus perhaps gave Disraeli more pleasure than any other feature of the settlement. Britain had thus gained an island, rich in

[1] See pp. 140–1.

historical associations, without having to fire a shot; no street-trader driving a hard bargain with a customer could have been more pleased. 'An act of duplicity not surpassed and rarely equalled in the history of nations,' was Gladstone's description of this gain. Satisfaction at the completion of a sharp-thinking deal outweighed in Disraeli's mind the fact that the island was of negligible military importance, for even by 1878 it was becoming obvious that Egypt, a better base anyway, could be available as a centre for British operations in the Middle East, if required.

When the Congress met the main lines of the settlement had therefore already been agreed. Moreover, some features of the San Stefano treaty were acceptable and required little further discussion. The independence of Serbia, Montenegro, and Rumania was confirmed. They had been independent in practice for some years before this crisis had developed and it was a matter of common sense to accept this position. The terms of San Stefano by which Romania had been obliged to cede Bessarabia to her ally Russia, receiving in exchange the inadequate compensation of being allowed to take the Dobruja from Bulgaria, were allowed to stand; in Disraeli's mind the basis for this decision was that when thieves fall out interference is unnecessary: the consequences of this decision were not serious and his policy on this issue can be justified. By other clauses of the treaty Russia was allowed to retain Batum and Kars since for political and military reasons it was hardly feasible to adopt any alternative course.

The major dilemma facing the powers at the Congress itself arose from the decision to reduce drastically the size of the large Bulgaria created by the San Stefano treaty. The Russians had accepted this reduction in principle but there was a good deal of manœuvring for advantage in working out the details. In the end Disraeli won his way by ordering a special train to take the British delegation back home unless the Russians accepted his proposals — a device which impressed Bismarck and which might have impressed historians too had it been used in a better cause. Disraeli's scheme for the trisection of Bulgaria was not worthy of these histrionics. The Russians were to remain in control of northern Bulgaria. Southern Bulgaria, known as Eastern Roumelia, was separated from its northern neighbour and remained under the

Turks though it was given a Christian governor. The reason for the separation was a military one. Between these two sections of Bulgaria lay the Balkan mountains. Disraeli's suspicion that the Bulgarians were hand-in-glove with the Russians led him to attach more importance to the military value of having a mountain range as a barrier between the Russians and Turks than to the legitimate desire of the Bulgarians for independence. The Bulgarians were only too well aware that Greece, Rumania, Serbia, and even the small state of Montenegro had all attained independence. Disraeli underestimated the strength and usefulness of Balkan nationalism which during the next twenty-five years became a much more dynamic force in this quarter of Europe than either Russian ambition or Turkey's failing strength. One other undesirable off-shoot of the trisection of Bulgaria was that Macedonia was returned to the Turks. The population consisted of Greeks, Bulgars, and Serbs; none of them could expect much consideration from their Turkish masters after the events of the last few years. Greece itself, its frontiers much more contracted than they are now, had hoped that the peace-makers would grant her territorial concessions at the expense of Turkey, but Disraeli's pro-Turkish policy made this impossible. When one considers the dismal history of the Balkans between 1878 and 1914 it is reasonable to think that Gladstone's advocacy of support for Balkan nationalism was not only morally justified but also politically wise. Disraeli's support for Turkey alienated Russia and frustrated the Balkan states; eventually it did not even secure the friendship of Turkey itself since pro-German feeling developed during the next twenty years and Turkey joined the First World War on Germany's side in 1914.

Between 1874 and 1876 social legislation had received a degree of attention which was markedly lacking between 1877 and 1880. The argument usually advanced in explanation of these two contrasting phases is that in the latter period imperial and foreign affairs distracted Disraeli from domestic legislation. This is too glib to be acceptable. In home affairs particularly the burden of work falls far more heavily on the ministers concerned than on the Prime Minister himself; work at the Home Office does not come to a standstill because the Prime Minister is attending a conference at Berlin: the whole notion is absurd. It is plain, for instance, that the considerable legislation undertaken in the early years of Disraeli's ministry was dominated by Richard Cross, the Home Secretary, and that Disraeli confined himself to the traditional role of the Prime Minister in these matters of sanctioning legislative change but leaving the detail to his ministers. Gladstone too had foreign and imperial problems to exercise his mind during his first and second ministries, but this made no difference to the pace of social legislation; in fact the most prolific period of legislative change during Gladstone's first ministry coincided with the Franco-Prussian War and the London Conference on the Black Sea question.

The essential point is that Disraeli had very little interest in domestic affairs, and was much more happily occupied pursuing the will-o'-the-wisp of international and imperial prestige than in giving his attention to paving stones, bricks, and drains. He was politically shrewd enough, of course, to see that there might be electoral advantage in improving living conditions, but the persistent drive towards social change which is so marked a characteristic of Gladstone was simply not present in Disraeli. His reputation as a social reformer is based in part on his book *Sybil* with its concept, scarcely novel, that England was divided into two nations, the rich and the poor. The book is full of the froth and sentiment of secondhand knowledge; its stilted style is the natural consequence of its insincerity. Once in power Disraeli's primary concern was to stay there. At first it seemed politic to win the favour of the recently enfranchised masses by social legislation; once it became plain that Tory support in Parliament for these changes was beginning to falter, Disraeli's transient interest in these affairs lapsed too. By chance this decline in interest coincided almost exactly with the period when a depression was beginning to develop in agriculture, as the large scale production of grain in North America and Eastern Europe began to reveal some of the cracks in the outwardly imposing façade of Britain's Free Trade policy. Industry, too, had lost some of the momentum of its earlier advance. Social distress began to be felt in Britain and in Ireland, leading in the latter to the violence of the Land League and in the former to restiveness and to growing sympathy for the then revolutionary doctrines of Socialism.

Governments need to be judged by their omissions as well as by their deeds, and on this basis Disraeli's ministry is extremely vulnerable.

There are considerable reservations, therefore, to be made about Disraeli's domestic policy as a whole even though the individual Acts, considered in isolation, had some value for the community. The most influential of the Acts passed were those affecting the trade union movement and those affecting public health. The abandonment of a *laissez-faire* attitude to public health can be traced at least as far back as 1848. An outbreak of cholera in 1866 and of smallpox in 1871 had emphasised the need for continued attention to the combating of disease. Gladstone in 1872 had created sanitary districts responsible among other matters for the safeguarding of the water supply and the disposal of sewage. The Public Health Act of 1875 consolidated this work of organisation by extending the powers of local authorities over health matters. Linked with this Act were the Artisans' Dwellings Act and the Sale of Food and Drugs Act, both of which were also passed in 1875. The former, though only permissive in form, encouraged local authorities to get rid of slums, and the latter was part of the concerted attack made by both parties at this period to improve public health standards.

The legislation on trade unions was also of a follow-up kind. Gladstone's moral qualms about picketing have already been described.[1] Disraeli was not the man to be deterred by considerations of this kind, but he could see the political advantage which might accrue to Conservatism if the trade unions gained their objectives on strike action as a result of Disraeli's help. The risks were negligible anyway. In 1875 the trade union movement numbered less than half a million; it was not particularly militant and if it were to become so it lacked the funds as yet for prolonged strike action. It was therefore safe and politic to pass the Conspiracy and Protection of Property Act legalising picketing; at the same time it was asserted that no action performed by a trade combination would be illegal if it were not illegal when performed by an individual citizen. In 1875 the Employers and Workmen Act made employers and workmen equally liable in law for breach of contract. Previously workmen had been at a disadvantage

[1] See p. 122.

in this respect in that breach of contract made them liable to
prosecution by criminal law; now, both for employers and
employees, action could only be taken under civil law. The
working classes were expected to be grateful for this rectifying
of Liberal legislation; how little they were impressed with
Disraeli's wooing is evident in the result of the 1880 election
where the Liberals gained the large majority of 135 seats over
the Conservatives.

That Disraeli did not possess much personal urge 'to elevate the condition of the people' is clear from his policy
which, as has been seen, involved no new principle and owed
its origin chiefly to the ideas of his opponents. The way in
which Plimsoll had to struggle so hard in order to obtain the
passage of the Merchant Shipping Act of 1876, securing greater
safety for seamen by insisting on owners painting a loadline
on their ships, is equally significant in revealing the Government's lack of independent enterprise on social issues. In the
last analysis Disraeli's policies are in every respect consistent
with those of a man of small vision who, a little luckily,
found himself in power. 'He knew how to climb to power,'
wrote Bagehot, 'but not how to use it when there.' He had
spent a lifetime accommodating himself to the wishes of
others; he was clever, adaptable, a seeker after popularity,
an opportunist; he made an impression upon the Conservative Party from which perhaps it has not fully recovered yet:
but he is not part of that older Conservative tradition which
stems back to Edmund Burke. Disraeli's Conservatism did
not rest on principle. He was a master of expediency, crowing
over his little gains.

Defence

Disraeli is so closely associated with the development of
modern Conservatism that objective assessment of his
achievements is peculiarly difficult. Gladstonian Liberalism
is dead and rouses no partisan feelings; the Conservatism of
Disraeli still retains much of its vigour as a political ideal and
attracts exaggerated support or criticism according to the
political views of the writer. That this is so is in itself a tribute

to Disraeli. Like Peel he saw the need for a more flexible
version of Conservatism; unlike Peel he succeeded in achieving this without splitting his party. Nor is it fair to equate
this greater flexibility with vote-catching. Presumably his
critics only approve of those reforms which are likely to irritate the majority of the electorate. In practice Disraeli was
little influenced in his political behaviour either by popularity
or unpopularity. His long political experience before he became Prime Minister had trained him to evaluate public
opinion at its true worth; in this important respect his age was
far more of an asset than a liability during his last ministry.
His cool resistance to the anti-Turkish hysteria which Gladstone fomented in 1876 is a conspicuous instance both of
Disraeli's refusal to be stampeded by public opinion and of his
ability, essential in a Prime Minister, to disentangle emotional
reactions from political fact. There were compelling reasons
for shoring up the Turkish Empire, as will be seen later, and
his policy was far more realistic than that of Gladstone. Disraeli wrote to his Foreign Secretary, Lord Derby: 'What the
public meetings want is nonsense not politics.' It was a sensible appraisal of an inflammatory situation in which a lesser
man would have been tempted to play to the gallery of public
opinion.

A Prime Minister who is thus capable of detaching himself
from the hurly-burly of immediate events and seeing the
implications of policy decisions in a wider context runs the
risk of being regarded as a cold-blooded creature incapable of
idealism or humanity, 'a dessicated calculating machine', to
borrow a phrase. To believe this of Disraeli is a fundamental
source of error. His idealism was not so obtrusive as Gladstone's; it was of a different nature, but it was equally for him
a mainspring of action evident in both domestic and overseas
affairs. To see the domestic legislation of 1874–80 merely as
a vote-catching gambit, inspired by the extension of the
franchise in 1867, overlooks completely the fact that Disraeli's
concern for the welfare of the people was not something of
recent growth. The evidence for this concern rests on a more
substantial basis than the writing of *Sybil*, though his sympathetic descriptions in that book of the living conditions of
the poor in the 1840s served as a useful reminder that government should be for the people as well as of the people. His

opportunities to put this belief into practice were necessarily limited before his last ministry by the short duration of Conservative Governments; yet the brevity of these governments throws into still sharper focus Disraeli's determination during the brief months of Conservative power to introduce measures beneficial to the mass of the people.

It is not always realised, for instance, that the virtual adoption of Free Trade in the 1840s was not followed by instantaneous prosperity. For agriculture, employing about half the working population of the country, 1846 to 1852 were lean years. Disraeli had more respect for facts than slogans, and it was he who took the lead in pressing for the reduction of rates and taxes for the farming community. His attempt failed as did his budget of 1852, also favouring the countryman; but the more significant point was his obvious willingness to relieve immediate difficulties with immediate action. Nor can he fairly be accused of favouring one class or interest in the community rather than another. A reduction in rates and taxes, by easing the pressure on the landowner and tenant farmer, would be of general benefit also to the agricultural labourer. That his interest in the welfare of the mass of the people was removed from the myopic selfishness of some of his colleagues is clear in other directions too. Following the working-class unrest of the 1840s one of the few constructive attempts from any party to deal with their grievances was the Act of 1852, which Disraeli persuaded his colleagues to support, legalising the formation of Industrial and Provident Societies; this gave the co-operative societies legal status, and channelled working-class energies into activities useful to themselves and to the community. The episode is characteristic of Disraeli's activity in home affairs and of the best kind of Conservatism. The Liberals provided the furore and the philosophy, followed all too often by botched legislation. Disraeli's objectives were less ambitious but they were measured against the criterion of practicality. Limited but certain advance was more useful than grandiloquent failure.

He showed precisely the same attitude on the subject of the extension of the franchise. He had the formidable task as leader of the House of Commons in 1866–8 of steering a middle course between the reactionary opposition to any change of some of his colleagues and the indiscriminate enthusiasm of many of his opponents for a widespread extension of the vote. Lowe's famous comment after the passage of the Bill that 'we must educate our masters' sharply exposed the weakness of the Bill which was eventually devised. The Bill almost doubled the electorate which was not yet ready for so extensive a change. Disraeli knew this but the Conservatives had taken office in 1866 without a majority; each of the safeguards which he carefully devised — double votes for the more financially substantial householders, votes for those with certain educational qualifications, or with £50 or more in the savings bank — was swept away through the inadequate support given to Disraeli by his colleagues and through the rashness of his opponents. For Disraeli the choice lay between accepting a mutilated Bill or no Bill at all; the first option was bad but the second one was worse, and Disraeli, always a realist, piloted the Bill through its final stages. The right to vote has become so much the sacred cow of democracy that any attempt to limit it is regarded as heinous. Yet in the circumstances of his time Disraeli was right. An extension of the franchise was justified, but not so wide an extension as the one thrust upon the community against his advice. Furthermore, to claim that Disraeli was merely borrowing this legislation from the 1866 Bill of the Whigs is more plausible than accurate. Electoral reform had been well aired as an issue for some years and was not the monopoly of any one party; in fact there had been a positive attempt, frustrated by the Whigs, to extend the franchise in 1859, and the author of that Bill was Disraeli.

It would clearly be unjust, therefore, to treat Disraeli's legislation of 1874–80 in isolation, as if his concern for the welfare of the people were a hypocritical attitude hastily adopted to suit the occasion. There is abundant evidence that Disraeli had a long-standing belief in orderly progress, and the 1874–80 ministry — the first one in which he could count on adequate parliamentary support incidentally — was the logical culmination of this process. It is true that much of the legislation of these years involved modification and improvement of statutes already in existence. This does not make it less valuable; on the contrary it was an asset to the community that Disraeli had the clarity of mind to convert Gladstone's muddled benevolence into statutes of some practical effectiveness. The trade union movement, for instance, had been hamstrung in its vital right to engage in strike action by the absurdity of Gladstone's ban on picketing. This anomaly was removed by the Conspiracy and Protection of Property Act of 1875. In the same year the Employers and Workmen Act virtually removed altogether the penalty of imprisonment for breach of contract; henceforth the contract between employer and employee was governed purely by civil law, and legally they were thus given equal status. This Act replaced the iniquitous Master and Servant Act, which had been weighted so heavily in the employer's interest. As recently as 1872, for instance, the Master and Servant Act had led to the imposition of sentences of between six weeks' and twelve months' imprisonment on London gas-stokers who had fallen foul of their employers as a result of strike action. The need for an amendment of the law had been clear for some time but it was Disraeli, not the Liberals, who took the necessary action. In doing so, incidentally, he made concessions to trade unionism considerably greater than those advocated by the Royal Commission on Trade Unionism in the report issued during Gladstone's first ministry.

The same shrewd judgment is reflected in the Acts to improve living conditions. This legislation is concentrated into one year, 1875. Sometimes Disraeli is criticised on the grounds that, dazzled by his adventures in imperial and foreign policy, he lost interest in domestic affairs. This is nonsense. The folly of an overcrowded legislative programme had recently been demonstrated in Gladstone's first ministry, where an abundance of good intentions had not compensated for the lack of common sense. The effectiveness of a ministry cannot be judged by the number of pages it adds to the statute-book. The Artisans' Dwellings Act and the Public Health Act of 1875 were far-reaching changes. It would take some years before their full effect was felt but it is a highly defensible proposition that the destruction of slum property, the building of small but well-constructed houses, the provision of an adequate sewage system, and the paving of streets, were more likely to add to the sum of human happiness than Gladstone's high sentiments and woolly actions. It is worth remembering that it was during this ministry that the ten-hour day which had been the subject of agitation for some forty years was

finally attained in practice by the Factory Act of 1874. This
established the 56-hour week, which meant five working days
of ten hours each and six hours on Saturday. A consolidating
Act of 1878 codified and rationalised the miscellaneous collection of factory regulations which had followed the Act of
1833. The essential point about all the social legislation of this
period is its strong sense of practicality. Dr Johnson once
pointed out that a poor man would rather be given a shilling
than hear a lecture on morality, a comment with which Disraeli would have wholeheartedly agreed; whether Gladstone
would have done so is much more open to doubt.

Disraeli's critics could almost forgive him for his domestic
policy; its aims were the same as their own though the
greater efficiency of his methods was galling to them. On
foreign and imperial policy the divergence between Disraeli's
views and those of his opponents was greater, and criticism
correspondingly more bitter, though not necessarily more
justifiable. The fashionable modern guilt complex about imperialism adds to the difficulty of objective interpretation of
Disraeli's policies.

On some of the issues involved Disraeli's actions have little
need of defence at all. His promptitude in purchasing the
Khedive Ismail's shares in the Suez Canal Company was of
immense benefit to Britain both commercially and strategically. Britain was henceforth assured of a shorter sea route
to Aden, to the coast of East Africa, and to India; at the same
time her influence in the Eastern Mediterranean and the
Middle East was greatly increased, reducing the risk of the
troubles which had disturbed those areas between 1821 and
1841. Her hold on Egypt was also to be a factor which the
Russians had to take into account in deciding to bring the
Russo-Turkish War to an end in 1878 when the Russian troops
were temptingly close to the city of Constantinople itself.
The dual control of Egyptian finances established by the
British and French in 1878 was essential, unless one believes
that there is a sacred duty to promote chaos by neglect in a
country whose only hope of orderly development lay in the
support given by European money and skills. That British
handling of Egyptian affairs since then has so often been
characterised by vacillation punctuated by violence is hardly
the fault of Disraeli.

In the Transvaal and in Afghanistan the course of events and the criticisms made of Disraeli follow broadly the same pattern. An external threat — in the Transvaal from the Zulus and in Afghanistan from the Russians — was countered by the actions of the men on the spot. The charge levelled against Disraeli is that in each instance a minor threat to British influence was exploited in order to advance British imperialism. It is claimed, too, that at this stage imperialism acquired symbolic value and that it became a quasi-sacrosanct duty of the British to extend the imperial frontiers, and to impose British habits of thought on unwilling native peoples. Enough has been said of Disraeli's pragmatic approach to make this explanation of his actions inherently improbable. He was, of all Britain's nineteenth-century Prime Ministers, one of the least likely to guide his conduct by missionary zeal and abstract conceptions. His policies in Afghanistan and in the Transvaal are entirely explicable within the framework of practicality. In the former country it was a fact that the Russians had steadily been extending their influence eastwards in the nineteenth century. An intensification of their activities in this quarter of the world was only to be expected after the set-back administered to their ambitions nearer home by the Congress of Berlin. Kabul was two thousand miles from Moscow but it was even further from London. The danger to India was a real one, not a figment of Disraeli's imagination.

Ever since the Americans had opened up Japan to the Western world it had become likely that there would be a scramble for influence in the Far East just as there was to be 'a scramble for Africa'. When the Russians were successful in establishing a mission in Kabul the threat to British India, comparatively lightly held by British troops, was increased, particularly when the Afghans refused to accept a British mission. In view of the great interests of Britain in India and the risk of the infiltration of Russian influence into India itself, still somewhat restive after the recent Mutiny of 1857, the British request to the Amir was reasonable. Gladstone thundered on about the independent rights of the Afghans; it made a fine sermon but bad politics. In the end force had to be used to establish British influence in Afghanistan. To Lord Lytton, the Viceroy in India, and to Disraeli the use of force seemed justified. Prompt action now would be a rebuff to Russian ambitions in this area sufficient to deter them for some years to come. It is at least arguable that this demonstration of force served precisely the purpose which Lytton and Disraeli had intended, and averted the much more disastrous conflict which might have occurred in India itself. When Gladstone withdrew British troops from Afghanistan in 1881 the Russians offered no threat to India: this might be interpreted as evidence that they never intended one; it could also be interpreted as evidence that Disraeli's firm reaction in 1879 had served its purpose. The Penjdeh incident in 1885, when Gladstone had to issue a strong warning to the Russians against infringement of Afghan independence, shows that the Russian threat was not a product of Disraeli's imagination.

In the Transvaal the problems posed by the Zulu warriors were of less strategic consequence; nevertheless their warlike presence on the borders of the Transvaal clearly involved dangers to British lives and property in Natal and Cape Colony. Frere and Shepstone, the men on the spot, made misjudgments, as did the military commander Lord Chelmsford. The strongest criticism of Disraeli personally is his unwillingness to remove the British troops from the Transvaal once the Zulus had been defeated, and Keshwayo deported. This argument glosses over the practical difficulties facing Disraeli. The Zulus had been defeated but not destroyed. His subdivision of their lands into eight chieftainships was a sensible arrangement to reduce the risk of another mass Zulu rising, but this risk could not be wholly ignored. The Transvaal had shown itself to be wholly incapable of self-defence in 1877, and it was perfectly reasonable to leave troops in the Transvaal until it had been established beyond doubt that the Boers there were capable of dealing with any recurrence of the Zulu problem. The gold discoveries at Johannesburg had not yet been made; to all appearances the Transvaal was poverty-stricken and still militarily vulnerable along its extensive eastern frontier. The country, in short, at this time was a liability not an asset to any power having the invidious task of managing it. Had Disraeli immediately evacuated the Transvaal after the defeat of the Zulus at Ulundi his critics would attack him for an irresponsible withdrawal exposing the Boer and British states in South Africa to further attack. Any objective assessment of the risks would show that Disraeli's caution was richly justified.

Disraeli's determination to safeguard British interests is as characteristic of his handling of the Eastern Question as it is of his imperial policy. One of the essential points to grasp at the outset is the extraordinary complexity, and the attendant risks, of the rival ambitions of the European powers most closely concerned, and of the Balkan nations themselves. The latter were as likely to fight against each other as against the Turks, a fact which was clearly demonstrated in the Balkan Wars of 1912–13. Russia's strategic and commercial interest in the area had been demonstrated time and again since the end of the seventeenth century. Austria was equally sensitive to changes in the *status quo* in the Balkans and had engaged in intermittent warfare against the Turks for centuries. The statesmen with whom Disraeli had to deal, Andrássy of Austria, Gortchakov of Russia, Bismarck of Germany, and Abdul Hamid, Sultan of Turkey, were clever, untrustworthy, and ambitious. Moreover, Austria, Russia, and Germany were banded together by the League of Three Emperors, and there was an obvious risk that the secret conversations and intrigues between the powers which preceded the Berlin Conference might lead to a settlement beneficial to Austria and Russia, in particular, at the expense of Turkish control in the Balkans. The Turkish Empire, propped up by British sea-power, was an invaluable barrier for British interests in the key area of the Middle East. Its governmental system was badly organised and occasionally tyrannical but not beyond the hope of reform. In the immediate crisis of 1875–8 the objective which Disraeli pursued correctly, coolly, and persistently, was to deprive Russia of the profits of war, thus minimising the risk to Constantinople itself. His skill in doing so was remarkable.

When the crisis began with the risings in Bosnia, Herzegovina, and Bulgaria, Disraeli soon found himself confronted with the awkward dilemma posed by the Berlin Memorandum. This note, supported by Austria, Russia, and Prussia, advocated reforms in the Turkish system of government. Only a political simpleton could imagine that this note was sent merely as an act of benevolence. Had Disraeli added his support Britain's position in the event of a Turkish rejection of the note would have been extremely invidious. Such a rejection would have paved the way to military intervention against Turkey by the powers concerned in order to secure the reforms by force. Reforms were desirable in Turkish methods of government, but not at the expense of exposing the Turkish Empire to wholesale interference by Russia in particular; one might as well cure a headache by surgery. There had already been one instance of collusion between the Eastern European powers in 1870 when Russian ships entered the Black Sea, thus infringing the 1856 Treaty of Paris. Disraeli's suspicions about the Berlin Memorandum were eminently justified.

Disraeli next had to endure the furore created by Gladstone's pamphlet *The Bulgarian Horrors and the Question of the East*. He had too steady a vision of Britain's primary interests in the crisis to be swamped by this emotionalism. Nevertheless a conference on reform took place at Constantinople, but the dubious motives of the other European powers present there and the evasiveness of the Turks made a settlement impossible. Since this device had failed the Russians resorted to force. Any illusions that the Russians engaged in this war from an altruistic interest in the welfare of the Balkan peoples can be swiftly dispelled by studying the terms of the Treaty of San Stefano, hastily made when Disraeli checked Russian ambitions by sending the British Mediterranean fleet to Constantinople. Further military pressure, involving the calling up of reserves and the sending of Indian troops to Malta, was designed to persuade the Russians to accept a European conference to amend the San Stefano treaty. Austria, belatedly alarmed at the extent of Russian ambitions, likewise pressed for a conference. To force the Russians to accept this conference after a hard-fought war and extensive gains was a considerable achievement itself; to pretend that this could have been accomplished without the military movements which Disraeli organised is absurd.

The terms of the Treaty of Berlin were entirely consistent with the attitude which Disraeli had steadily maintained throughout. The problem in the first place was a military one. The straits had to be safeguarded, and the greater the distance which separated the Russians from Constantinople the

F

better. The Balkan mountains separating Bulgaria from Eastern Roumelia made a good barrier against any future Russian advance. It is argued that this took no account of Bulgarian nationalism, and Gladstone asserted that the best barrier against Russian attack would be 'the breasts of free men'. Whether these 'free men' would fight among themselves to the advantage of the Russians was a matter which he did not consider. Disraeli, not having the gift of prophecy on this issue, rightly placed more value on the tangible military protection of a range of mountains defended by Turkish troops who had shown their fighting qualities in the recent war. The arrangement broke down seven years later, it is true, when Eastern Roumelia was reunited with Bulgaria forming an anti-Russian nationalist state. No one in 1878 could have predicted the unusual circumstances which led to this situation, which is in itself a further indication of the incalculable nature of Balkan nationalism. To have put one's trust in Balkan nationalism, as Gladstone advocated, would have been to build on sand indeed.

During the negotiations which preceded the Congress Disraeli secured Cyprus from Turkey in return for a promise to defend the Turkish Empire in Asia Minor. Cyprus would provide a nearer base for any action needed to defend Turkey than either Malta or Egypt; moreover, in the latter country at this stage Britain was merely sharing control with the French who had long-standing interests there, and use of Egyptian bases would be a matter of consultation not of right. The promise to defend Asia Minor gave the opportunity for the British to establish military consuls there, and the presence of these British representatives in Armenia, for instance, would do much to minimise the risk of persecution of Armenian subjects by the Turks. The removal of these consuls by Gladstone in 1880 was a blunder, and is much more directly a cause of the Armenian persecutions than any action taken by Disraeli.

The other arrangements made by the Congress were largely beyond Disraeli's powers of control. Nothing could prevent Austria securing the protectorate of Bosnia and Herzegovina; nor was it feasible to insist that Russia should restore Bessarabia to Romania though Disraeli toyed with the idea for a time. The restoration of Macedonia to Turkish control was similarly unavoidable. If the Turks were to be the front line of defence against any further Russian advance — and they had already shown their worth in that respect — they would be justifiably aggrieved if in return Disraeli were to insist on robbing them of territory for the benefit of the Balkan nations, who at this stage at least were far more likely to be anti-Turkish than anti-Russian.

It is not difficult to see why Disraeli attracted so much feeling both in his own time and since. His approach represents something permanent and valuable in politics. His conservatism was not of the die-hard kind which had already outlived whatever usefulness it had. He showed his party, as Peel had tried to do though less successfully, that social reform need not be the monopoly of the radical party, and that in some respects the Conservative Party with its pragmatic cautious approach can secure orderly, well-founded progress more effectively than its opponents. He showed precisely the same sense of practicality in imperial and foreign affairs. He was not concerned with striking attitudes, with visions and sermons. He was content to be merely Prime Minister of Britain. His duty, as he saw it, was to protect British interests and the interests of those nations which had become dependent on her. His aims, whether in Afghanistan, Egypt, the Transvaal, or in the Middle East, were to secure order and peace — and Britain would not be the sole beneficiary. 'Statesmanship' is sometimes used as if it were merely a synonym for flamboyant oratory; by definition it means 'skilful management of public affairs'. Can anyone doubt that Disraeli was a statesman?

7. JOSEPH CHAMBERLAIN
EGOTIST OR VISIONARY?

Prelude

The inequalities of Victorian society made it virtually certain that political power would be monopolised by a privileged group. At the beginning of the century the background and careers of the leading politicians varied very little. Wealth, derived from the possession of land or inherited as a result of business enterprise, a public school and a university education, followed almost immediately by entry into the House of Commons, these were the badges and the basis of success. By the end of the century the pattern had changed hardly at all. There were a few exceptions. Measured by conventional standards Disraeli was never quite a gentleman, though he was constantly harping on the importance of being one. At ministerial level W. H. Smith and Bright were even odder fish to swim in so select a pool. But these deviations merely confirmed the norm. The widening of the franchise in 1832 and 1867 had made no appreciable difference to the composition of Cabinets and very little to the membership of the House of Commons itself. The self-made man who occasionally established himself in politics was much more likely to be engulfed, like a stone thrown into the sea, than to produce any waves on his own. The interest of Joseph Chamberlain's career lies in the fact that it marks a rebellion against absorption. He was too important to be engulfed, too self-important his critics would say. Compromise was not one of his talents, and he had an aptitude for creating political furore which delighted newspaper editors and cartoonists, but not his colleagues. No one could ignore him. He had no intention of allowing them to do so. As mayor of Birmingham between 1873 and 1876 his gas, water, and improvement schemes made his name nationally prominent. Subsequently, as an M.P. and as a minister, one might say that he envisaged Britain and the Commonwealth as a greatly enlarged Birmingham in which he could deploy his extensive talents as a business man and as a social reformer.

His highly charged individualism could be deduced, at least in part, from his career before his entry into the House of Commons in 1876. He came of a prosperous middle-class family. An ancestor on the father's side had settled in London in the eighteenth century and had made a fortune there in the leather industry. Sons and grandsons, including Joseph Chamberlain's father, successfully carried on the business. Joseph was brought up to appreciate the virtues of shrewdness, hard work, and individual enterprise, and having acquired these qualities put them to good use in making a personal fortune for himself in the screw-making trade, in company with his cousin Joseph Nettlefold. The Nettlefold family was already established in Birmingham and it was in this way that Chamberlain's personal connection with the city began. His move to Birmingham took place in 1854, when he was aged eighteen. The next twenty years were spent in forging his outstanding talents as a business man. The business had become a very large one by the 1860s, providing screws for the English market and for the Continent too; its success owed much to Chamberlain's shrewd insight into what we should now call 'sales psychology' and to his ability to think broadly enough not to confine the marketing activities of the firm to Britain itself. Some of the qualities he was to show later in his political career clearly matured during this formative stage of his life.

The other element in his individualistic approach sprang from earlier influences. The Chamberlains were a Unitarian family. The Unitarians were, as they are today, a small minority group still subject at the time of Chamberlain's birth to civil disabilities, depriving them, for instance, of the right to marry in their own chapels, and of the right to enter Oxford or Cambridge. Education therefore presented special problems for Dissenting families, but the Chamberlain family's wealth, coupled with the existence of Unitarian academies where the quality of work was very high, eased the difficulty. After attendance at two private schools Chamberlain attended University College School, London, between 1850 and 1852, before entering his father's business at the age of sixteen, and then moved, as has been seen, to Birmingham in 1854.

The contrast between a career of this kind, limited by narrow-minded religious restrictions which no longer served any useful purpose, and the careers of men like Gladstone and Lord Salisbury, later to be his colleagues, could hardly escape Chamberlain's attention; this was to be a powerful force in moving him later in his career to press for the removal of the religious and educational disabilities of Nonconformists. Similarly, first-hand knowledge of the conditions of working-class life in Birmingham obviously motivated Chamberlain's interest in social reform, at first locally and then nationally. At the time of his mayoralty of Birmingham there was no doubt of his horror of the foul living conditions to be found in the courts and alleys of the city's back streets. Reform of these conditions became for him a crusade. He showed the greatest determination in the wearisome business of convincing rate-payers that other people's health was no less important than their money, and in pushing the improvement schemes through committees and the council.

At the same time his mind was considering wider issues. In the early 1870s he flirted a little with the idea of Republicanism, but his admiration for that form of government was merely academic, though his speeches on the subject show how much more individualistic he was than those who were shortly to be his colleagues in Parliament. Of greater immediate relevance was the programme which he suggested for the Liberal Party in an article he wrote for the *Fortnightly* in 1873. He advocated as an aim four freedoms — freedom for labour, by which he meant the removal of restrictions on trade union activity, freedom for the transfer of land, leading he hoped to the creation of a very large number of small properties, a free church to end jealousies of rival sects, and free education which ought to be a right in any justly organised state. These then were his long-term aims for the Liberal Party. How far they were achieved when Chamberlain was in a position to influence the course of political events more directly remains to be seen.

Chamberlain stood as a Liberal for the Sheffield constituency in 1874. He was narrowly defeated, but in 1876 victory in a by-election in Birmingham enabled him to take his seat in the House of Commons. He soon showed himself to be an effective speaker, quiet, persuasive, skilful in argument,

though at times bitingly sarcastic. Members who expected
from his reputation as a radical that he would be something
of a wild man in appearance and ideas were astonished to be
confronted by the elegant Chamberlain complete with the
famous eye-glass. For the time being, however, only his dress
was conservative. Gladstone was clearly impressed with the
newcomer's strength of character and administrative energy,
and the latter found no cause yet to disagree with his leader's
political opinions. Furthermore, Chamberlain was able to add
immeasurably to his stature in the party by the creation of
the National Liberal Federation in 1877, linking together the
local associations. The Federation was founded at Birmingham itself and Gladstone visited the city to mark the importance of the occasion. The value of the Federation in help-
ing the Liberals to win the 1880 election was soon made plain.
Chamberlain's apprenticeship was over. He became President of the Board of Trade in the new Government, and was
at last in a position to put into effect some at least of the
policies which he had advocated for so long. For the best part
of twenty-five years he was to become the stormy petrel of
English politics. Clearly his actions at times were damaging
to the parties he joined; whether his actions were beneficial
in the wider context of national needs is the crucial issue
which is discussed next.

Attack

If it is true that the British have a sentimental regard for
failure, and it is easy to find historical support for this, then
Chamberlain deserves a special niche in history alongside
Charles Stuart, General Gordon, and other popular failures.
An outline of his ministerial career begins with the useful
reforms devised by him in Gladstone's second ministry, con-
tinues with the widening breach with his leader, reaching its
climax in Chamberlain's opposition to the First Home Rule
Bill, and his abandonment of his party, proceeds with the
failure to secure the German alliance, with the blundering
entry into the South African War, with Chamberlain's bitter
opposition to the 1902 Act, 'a social revolution of the first

magnitude' as Halévy has described it,[1] and ends with his inability in the Tariff Reform campaign to achieve anything
except a huge majority for his opponents, the Liberals. As
a catalogue of failure it is impressive. Failure so extensive has
an almost wilful quality in it as if Chamberlain, like some
political lemming, were consciously seeking his own destruction.

This would matter less for Chamberlain's historical reputation if it were the only element in the situation. If he were
merely another Don Quixote tilting at windmills of partisan
obstructionism it would be easy to sympathise with him,
however many times he was unhorsed. No one who has
studied his career would cast him for that role. After his desertion from the Liberal party his ex-colleagues looked upon
him as a Judas, until it occurred to one of them, Labouchère,
that this was an over-estimate. Speaking at Bury in 1891 he
said:

> Still there was something to be said for Judas. After be-
> traying his Master he did not attend public meetings; he
> did not revile his associates; he did not sponge upon the
> priests, the Pharisees, and the Sadducees in order to be
> received into their society; he did not go swaggering
> about Judaea saying he had now joined the gentlemen of
> Jerusalem. No. Judas was contrite; he was ashamed; he
> went out and hanged himself. In some things Judas appears
> advantageously with Mr Chamberlain.[2]

Failure is one matter but the destructive influence of Chamberlain upon both the major parties is quite another. He was
an ambitious, strongly individualistic man, who had entered
politics late in life. He was also extremely able, with a keen
eye for publicity. In many ways he was admirably equipped
for a successful political career. His weakness was an overweening egotism which clouded his judgment and made
loyalty a secondary consideration. His background differen-
tiated him sharply from his colleagues in the Government, but
his constant clashes with them came about not because they

[1] E. Halévy, *History of the English People in the Nineteenth Century*
(London: Benn, 1961), vol. 5, p. 205.

[2] J. L. Garvin, *The Life of Joseph Chamberlain* (London: Macmillan,
1933), vol. ii, p. 480.

would not accept him, but because he would not accept them. He was ingenious but wayward and inconsistent in devising policies, and fundamentally was more concerned with imposing his own will than with the merits of the issues about which he temporarily generated so much destructive heat.

In his first years at the Board of Trade Chamberlain introduced a number of useful but unspectacular measures which merely whetted his appetite for a larger role in government. He secured the passage in 1880 of a Seamen's Wages Act and a Grain Cargoes Act, and to do so had to out manœuvre in the House of Commons the spokesmen for the vested interests of the shipowners. A Bankruptcy Bill in 1883 made it harder for bankrupts to evade their obligations, and a Patents Bill in the same year encouraged inventiveness by reducing the payment for patent rights. The first inkling of the future pattern of Chamberlain's career came with his failure to win enough support for his Merchant Shipping Bill. Disraeli's Act of 1876 to prevent overloading and over-insurance of merchant ships had been ineffective. Chamberlain hoped to remedy its weakness. Opposition to the Bill was so strong that Gladstone, much harried by troubles in Ireland and by criticism of his policy in the Transvaal, persuaded Chamberlain to withdraw the Bill. Reluctantly the latter did so. It was his first serious difference of opinion with his leader, but it brought closer to the surface an antagonism always latent between the Radical Chamberlain and Gladstone, 'that tremendous old Tory', as he was once ironically described. Chamberlain briefly toyed with the idea of resignation, but sensing that the occasion was not sufficiently dramatic changed his mind.

Instead he brought increasing pressure to bear on his leader to concentrate greater attention on domestic reform. The major consequence was the Third Reform Act of 1884. This added two million new voters to the electorate. Chamberlain was well-satisfied with his achievement. It was a Radical measure; it had been secured in the teeth of strong opposition within the Cabinet itself; it had given Chamberlain the opportunity to launch a devastating attack on the constitutional rights of the House of Lords, who did their best to block the Bill until bought off with a bargain over the redistribution of seats; it added to Chamberlain's hope that his policy of Free

*

Land, Free Schools, and a Free Church would gain wider
acceptance since it was well calculated to appeal to the new
voters; above all the decisive part played by Chamberlain in
the reform tilted the balance of influence within the Liberal
Party a little more in his direction and a little more away
from Gladstone. For the time being it was power by proxy,
but it was no less sweet on that account. It is not given to
many Presidents of the Board of Trade to be so influential.

Whether the time was opportune for this franchise reform
is controversial. If the Bill is isolated from its political context there is no doubt that the country labourer in 1884 deserved the vote as much as the town artisan in 1867, and if the
implication is that neither deserved it particularly there is
something to be said for that. A wholesale extension of the
vote at a time when education was still rudimentary and when
the sources of information on political issues were infinitely
more limited than they are today was not necessarily a virtue.
Secondly, Chamberlain's insistence on the abolition of the
plural member system strengthened the Irish nationalist
movement to a dangerous extent. Previously in two-member
constituencies it had generally proved possible to return a
Liberal along with an Irish nationalist, thus diluting the
strength of the latter movement. Now this was no longer so.
Chamberlain justified the change as a matter of abstract
justice, but this was not the only consideration. The Irish had
steadily followed a policy of obstructionism at Westminster
and violence in Ireland. To strengthen their representation
would earn no gratitude — Parnell was not that kind of a
man — and would add to the difficulties of securing more
settled conditions. Chamberlain's poor sense of political timing was often in evidence during his career, and this episode
is one more instance of that deficiency.

Chamberlain was becoming increasingly restive about Gladstone's lack of urgency over social reforms, though in public
he still supported his leader. 'We radicals,' he said on one occasion, 'do not think it necessary to upset the coach every
time the pace does not come up to our expectations.' 'He that
speaketh of himself speaketh false' is a shrewd piece of ancient
psychology, and it is sufficiently evident that if any coaches
were to be upset Chamberlain would play a major part
in the mishap if his will were overruled. When the clash

with Gladstone did come, however, it was not over social reform but over Gladstone's conversion to the idea of Home
Rule. Chamberlain's views on the Irish Question were clear
and strongly held, like most of his views while they lasted.
He believed in a slow preparation of the Irish in the art of
self-government, though he discounted altogether any idea
of separating Ireland completely from the rest of Britain. He
believed that Irish participation in local government to the
fullest possible extent was reasonable, but Home Rule was not.
There had been rumours for some months before the First
Home Rule Bill was introduced that Gladstone was no longer
content with a moderate step-by-step movement to self-
government for Ireland. Chamberlain knew of these rumours
and in a speech at Birmingham in 1885 pointedly reminded
Gladstone of the need to maintain the integrity of the Empire,
a strange sentiment for a Radical but apparently deeply felt.

It would take little to create a split between the two men
now. Chamberlain, dissatisfied with the official Liberal programme, had already put forward his own unauthorised programme for the election to be held at the end of 1885. This
programme advocated free schools, encouragement of the
ownership of small holdings, and a system of graduated
taxation. Gladstone could not be expected to be delighted
with its terms nor with its success since it was clearly much
more influential than the official programme in securing the
victory of the Liberals in the 1885 election. Chamberlain on
the other hand felt that his strength was growing; a contemporary cartoon represents Chamberlain as the young bantam
and Gladstone as the old rooster. When Gladstone tried to conceal from his colleagues his conversion to Home Rule,
although the concealment was with the best intentions, the
affront to Chamberlain's vanity was greater than he could
bear. He had believed himself to be at the centre of power;
now he found himself relegated to the circumference and his
often expressed views on Ireland ignored. After a brief uneasy
tenure of the post of President of the Local Government Board
he resigned. That he acted according to his principles in this
episode is not denied, though Chamberlain's political principles
were of a conveniently adaptable nature; a few years later
when guiding the Australian Commonwealth Bill through the
House of Commons he was emphasising the importance of the

colonies' 'free will and absolute consent' in their relations with
Britain. Presumably what was sauce for the Australian goose
should have been sauce for the Irish gander, but this does not
seem to have appealed to Chamberlain with equal force on each
occasion. The merits of Gladstone's policy also deserved
closer consideration than Chamberlain was prepared to give
them.[1] In short, there are overtones of personal pique, of
muddled thinking, and of rigid prejudice in Chamberlain's
attitude on the Irish question which reflect gravely on his
political judgment.

   These criticisms are serious enough, but they are dwarfed
by Chamberlain's abandonment of his party. On 23 December
1886 Chamberlain suggested a 'round table conference' in an
attempt to settle differences between leading Liberals. 'We
Liberals,' he said, 'are agreed upon ninety-nine points of our
programme.' When the conference took place, however, in
January 1887 it was plain enough that Chamberlain wanted
surrender not negotiation. He remained immovable on the
Irish Question and since the Liberals were now irrevocably
committed to Home Rule the conference became pointless.
Had Chamberlain remained within the party and co-operated
with Gladstone in putting into effect some at least of the
'ninety-nine points', as he termed them, on which they were
in agreement, his intransigence on the Irish Question would
merit respect. His radical Liberalism would have been of the
greatest service to the party. Socialism instead of becoming
a destructive rival of Liberalism might well have been absorbed within it, to the advantage of both. Chamberlain was
not unaware of his influence in this respect. Nor was he unaware of the strong personal following he had among the
Liberal Party. He could therefore have had no illusions of the
effect on Liberalism as a party and as a principle if he were
to secede to the Conservatives. With the latter he had nothing
in common except antagonism to Gladstone. Even on the
Irish Question it seemed unlikely for the time being that the
Conservatives would offer the Irish anything but coercion;
Chamberlain's own scheme for local self-government and land
reform was therefore not likely to be hatched for many years
yet by a Conservative Government. Imperialism, except in
the negative sense of preventing the separation of Ireland

[1] See pp. 123–4 for a defence of Gladstone's policy on this issue.

from the United Kingdom, was as yet no bond between
Chamberlain and the Conservatives. During Gladstone's
second ministry, for instance, Chamberlain had faithfully followed the same line as his leader on the problems arising in the
Transvaal, Egypt, and the Sudan. All these facts Chamberlain
wantonly ignored. To gratify his ambition he ranged himself
and his fellow Liberal Unionists alongside the Conservatives.
In 1895 Lord Salisbury rewarded him with the office of
Colonial Secretary. No Greek playwright could have devised
the history of the ten years which followed with a keener
sense of dramatic irony than the events themselves display.

Chamberlain had first made his name in politics as a social
reformer. It was curious that he should now accept the office
of Colonial Secretary; his rejection of the office of Chancellor
of the Exchequer, offered to him by Lord Salisbury, is odder
still. Fair taxation had been one of the pillars of the unauthorised programme, but it was not until Lloyd George's
budget of 1909 that any extensive progress was made with the
principle of a graduated income tax. Had Chamberlain accepted the Chancellorship in 1895 he would obviously have
been well placed to press his ideas on this subject. His refusal
throws an interesting sidelight on his character. As a genera-
tor of ideas he had few equals, but he was fundamentally
lacking in the persistence and patient political management
needed to convert visions into reality. Imperialism had
acquired a new vogue with the acquisition by Britain of territories in East Africa, and with the activities of Rhodes in
South Africa. Chamberlain gladly sacrificed the dull but valuable work of a Chancellor of the Exchequer for the excitements of Empire-making.

The qualities of the new Colonial Secretary were soon
revealed in his dealings with the two Boer states in South
Africa. There were complexities in the relationship between
Britain and the Boers which might easily precipitate violence
unless negotiations were handled deftly and with a willingness to accept compromise solutions. There is nothing in
Chamberlain's career to suggest that he had much respect for
anyone's opinion except his own; one might as well expect
compromise from an incensed rhinoceros. Part of the difficulty sprang from the presence of the Uitlanders in the
Transvaal, and President Kruger's refusal to grant them full

civic rights. Chamberlain and Lord Salisbury, the Prime Minister, made much of this issue. There is no doubt that the Uitlanders, many of them British, were subject to irksome restrictions. When the gold discoveries had been made at Witwatersrand Reef in 1886 a minor tidal wave of fortune hunters from Europe had descended upon the Transvaal. The Boers, accustomed to isolation, poverty, and social backwardness, found themselves engulfed in a gold rush. They needed the mining expertise of the new arrivals if they were to benefit fully from the gold discoveries; at the same time there were fundamental differences of outlook between the Boers and the Europeans. Kruger was determined that the newcomers should not acquire so much wealth and influence that the Boers themselves would be relegated to a secondary position in the State. The Boer Government therefore taxed mine profits heavily, imposed heavy duties on equipment imported for mining, and refused to grant the Uitlanders full citizen status including the right to vote. Tension between Britain and the Transvaal increased. The Boers feared British intentions as Rhodes and the British South Africa Company penetrated into the heart of Bechuanaland on the western border of the Transvaal; the British feared that their own ambitious plans for the extension of their influence in Africa might be frustrated by collaboration between the Boers and the Germans who were already established in German South West Africa. At first these mutual fears found open expression primarily in arguments about the degree of independence which the Transvaal might rightly enjoy. The Pretoria Convention of 1881 had granted the Transvaal independence, subject to British suzerainty, and forbade the Boers to make treaties with any other country, except the Orange Free State. The Boers were dissatisfied with this arrangement and a second agreement was made, the London Convention of 1884. This was more ambiguous in its wording on the suzerainty issue and, as resentment against Britain grew, so did Boer objections to the idea of British suzerainty over any of their affairs. Chamberlain flatly refused to accept any diminution of British rights whatsoever.

Against such a background of suspicion and resentment the Jameson Raid now took place. Jameson and 470 cavalry, mainly from the British South Africa Company, crossed the border into the Transvaal on 29 December 1895 with the object of linking up with the discontented Uitlanders in Johannesburg. By 2 January the raiders were outmanœuvred and rounded up by the Boers at Doornkop. Chamberlain's complicity in the raid has been the subject of much discussion since.[1] A Select Committee of the House of Commons investigated the allegation in 1897 and agreed that Chamberlain had no fore-knowledge of the raid. Doubt remains whether the committee was provided with all the relevant evidence, but the more important issue to consider is not the extent of Chamberlain's knowledge of the raid but whether in a wider context his whole attitude and policy, both before and after the raid, were creating precisely the conditions in which such acts of folly were likely. In the long run his major interest was not the defence of the rights of the Uitlanders, still less an honourable settlement of differences with the Boers, but the assertion of unchallenged British supremacy in South Africa. 'Never again', said Chamberlain exultantly at the height of the Boer War, 'shall they be able to endanger the paramountcy of Great Britain.' He could hardly have made his intentions more plain.

Once the raid had taken place the prospects of a full-scale war obviously increased and Milner, the High Commissioner in South Africa, whom Chamberlain had set in charge of negotiations with the Boers, showed little disposition to avoid it. A conference at Bloemfontein in 1899 between Kruger and Milner broke down; the political antagonism of the two men, one an unyielding nationalist and one a convinced imperialist, made agreement out of the question. Chamberlain made proposals for fresh negotiations, more moderate in tone than had been the habit so far, but still giving not the slightest hope to Kruger that the Transvaal would ever be recognised as a sovereign independent state. Kruger would be satisfied with nothing less; he regarded the treatment of the Uitlanders as a matter to be decided by the government of the State in which they had chosen to live. Ever since the 1884 London Convention Kruger had been determined to remove Britain's claim to suzerainty over the Transvaal's affairs. Negotiations had proved useless. The Jameson Raid had been ominous,

[1] See for instance Halévy, *History of the English People*, vol. 5, p. 30, and Ensor, *England 1870–1914*, pp. 233–6.

more especially when Chamberlain in a House of Commons debate had fulsomely praised Rhodes in spite of the fact that the latter had recently been censured by a Select Committee for his complicity in the raid. It can hardly be a matter of surprise to anyone that Kruger's exasperation and his resentment of British imperialism should cause him to resort to war. He knew that the risks were enormous, and this in itself is a measure of the unease which British policies under Chamberlain's direction had created among the Boers.

By this stage, however, Chamberlain's impatient mind had darted away to concern itself with more spectacular possibilities in another direction. Lord Salisbury, the Prime Minister, had so far combined that office with that of Foreign Secretary. Ill health and Salisbury's aristocratic indifference to the full exercise of his powers gave Chamberlain increasing opportunities to advance his own opinions on foreign policy. Whatever office Chamberlain happened to hold, whether under Gladstone, Salisbury, or Balfour, merely became a stalking horse behind which Chamberlain developed his own spectacular ambitions. Gladstone had already experienced this; now it was Salisbury's turn. The essence of Chamberlain's policy was the creation of a new Triple Alliance between Britain, the United States, and Germany. Salisbury in his more cautious way favoured the same idea. The Russian acquisition of Port Arthur in the Far East, the existence since 1893 of the Franco-Russian alliance, and the violent tone of the French newspapers towards Britain, particularly when the interests of the two countries clashed over the occupation of Fashoda on the upper waters of the Nile, strengthened the doubts, never far from the surface, over the splendours of isolationism.

The opportunity of being in the forefront of a spectacular change of policy was irresistible for Chamberlain. Salisbury with his long diplomatic experience knew only too well that the conclusion of an alliance with a great power could not be handled as if it were a contract for making screws. During much of 1898 and 1899, however, Salisbury's ill health and his reliance on Liberal Unionist support enabled Chamberlain to secure a dominance in the negotiations with Germany. The effects were unfortunate. Whether the alliance itself would have been beneficial can only be a matter of speculation; the point which does emerge without any qualification is Chamberlain's blunt clumsiness in his handling of the negotiations. Lord Salisbury's departure to the South of France in March 1898 to convalesce after an illness increased Chamberlain's authority. By the end of the month the latter had proposed to the German ambassador that Britain should join the Triple Alliance which existed between Germany, Austria, and Italy. Relations with Germany over the colonies, naval competition, and industrial rivalry, were far too complex to be handled in this impulsive way. Predictably the German Emperor rejected the offer. Following a visit to Windsor in 1899 the Kaiser and his foreign minister, Count Bülow, induced Chamberlain to make a public speech advocating an alliance between Britain, Germany, and the United States. Although the Kaiser had rejected Chamberlain's offer of an alliance in 1898 he had some sympathy with the scheme, and was quite content to exploit Chamberlain's fondness for dramatics to test Anglo-German reactions to the idea in 1899. Chamberlain duly made the required speech at Leicester on 30 November 1899, and for good measure added some provocative remarks on the attitude of the French press to Britain and to Queen Victoria. On the central issue of the panteutonic alliance the response in Germany, the United States, and in Britain made it abundantly plain that the plan was unacceptable. Bülow on his return to Germany snubbed Chamberlain by making no reference to the scheme for an Anglo-German alliance; furthermore he pressed the Reichstag to give its full support to increasing the size of the German Navy, obviously in rivalry to Britain. Chamberlain's grandiose hopes were thus frustrated. Throughout the negotiations there is a strong impression that, in his eagerness to unite 'the greatest naval nation in the world and the greatest military nation', he became so obsessed with his own importance in bringing about the alliance that he grossly underestimated the need to manage the negotiations with the skill and caution so plainly required. Having failed, it was characteristic of Chamberlain that by 1902 he was gratuitously making acid remarks about atrocities committed by the Germans during the Franco-Prussian war.

If perpetual activity were the mark of a statesman few could rival Chamberlain. An imminent war in South Africa and the possibility of a new alliance with Germany and the United States would be enough, one would think, to absorb the energies of most ministers. Chamberlain thought otherwise. His over-heated imagination was simultaneously busy with another project, the development of imperial federation, from which the split in the Conservative party over the Protectionist issue was to spring. In 1897, the year of the Queen's Diamond Jubilee, a Colonial Conference was held in London. Chamberlain put forward to the colonial leaders suggestions for the closer integration of the Empire. Ideas for a closer political, economic, and military relationship between Britain and the colonies had been bandied about for some time among politicians and intellectuals. The success of the Prussian Zollverein, which had been strongly established by 1833, had been duly noted in Britain and continued to influence opinion at the end of the century. Disraeli had toyed with the idea of an imperial federation and closer military co-operation with the colonies. Chamberlain's ideas were clearly not original. To some extent then the ground had already been prepared; moreover, international affairs were in a state of flux to an unusual degree at this stage, and circumstances were favourable to the emergence of new alignments and groupings. There was, in short, a real hope that more effective imperial unity might be achieved. On the other hand there was always an element of uncertainty in dealing with Chamberlain. He had abandoned his party, and had an aptitude for being concerned with spectacular developments in policy in a way which raised doubts whether he was concerned with anything else except the advancement of his own career. The exact nature of his imperialist feeling was thus a matter of some doubt, doubt which was already being reinforced by his high-handed treatment of the problems in South Africa. When Chamberlain sketched out at the conference his proposals for an imperial federation the response, predictably, was not enthusiastic. The older colonies in particular were looking forward to an increasing degree of independence. Their leaders were suspicious that behind the smoke-screen of Chamberlain's words there lay the reality of a federation in which Britain would be permanently dominant. Chamberlain never abandoned lightly schemes with which he was personally associated, but in this instance he saw that there was no hope yet of creating a unified political structure within the Empire.

There was, however, one offshoot of the negotiations where progress might be possible, namely the idea of imperial preference. While Britain retained a Free Trade system the value of preferential tariffs for the colonies could only be hypothetical. Nevertheless the attractions of the idea began to make increasing impact on Chamberlain's mind. In the first place if Britain were to revert to Protection, and imperial preference were to be linked with this move, it would be an important step towards the unity which Chamberlain was currently advocating. But this was not all; there were wider implications. The increased revenue from duties would facilitate the introduction of social legislation, such as old age pensions, favoured by Chamberlain, and would cut the ground from under the feet of Socialism. The first stirrings of Labour political activity were already evident and Chamberlain was in no hurry to abandon his role of leader of the progressive movement in British politics. Above all, so fundamental a change in Britain's economic policy would cause a tremendous stir and bustle comparable to the excitements of 1846; at the centre of the furore would be Chamberlain himself, wiser than his leaders, galvanising them into energy with his directing genius. It was his favourite political role, combining the maximum of publicity with the minimum of responsibility.

This judgment would plainly be too harsh if it could be shown that Protection was in the national interest. Then, whatever Chamberlain's motivation may have been, at least Britain would have derived benefits from his proposals. But in fact Protection had become superfluous precisely at the time that Chamberlain's advocacy of it reached its climax. Undoubtedly Britain had been experiencing economic difficulties during the last quarter of the nineteenth century. The Fair Trade League as early as 1880 had blamed the retention of Free Trade for these set-backs. Chamberlain had studied the writings of the Fair Traders and paid them the compliment of borrowing their ideas. The adoption of tariffs by the leading powers in Europe, and the adoption of the stringent McKinley tariff in the United States in 1891, undoubtedly created anxiety about a situation in which Britain would remain an open door for foreign producers yet find herself restricted as a seller in foreign markets by the existence of tariffs. But this is altogether too naïve a view of the situation. Free Trade had been retained because it was still commercially valuable. Its adoption had never meant at any stage that governments had washed their hands of their economic responsibilities. Statistics on trade and production were now a familiar part of the apparatus of government. If the evidence which they furnished justified tariff reform no one imagined that Free Trade was so sacrosanct a principle that it could never be abandoned. The Fair Trade League had brought the issue of Protection to the fore during the difficulties of the 1880s, but had been given no encouragement, not because of doctrinaire support for Free Trade but because the view was taken that the trading difficulties of this period were produced by conditions affecting all countries — shortage of gold was one factor, for instance — and not simply by Britain's adherence to Free Trade. The force of this opinion was largely confirmed by the improvement experienced after 1896. Demand for British iron, steel, coal, and ships began to increase, and though there was no return to the halcyon days of the mid-century no one could doubt that a recovery was taking place.

Chamberlain's hopes of support for his Protectionist campaign were raised a little by the sharp rise in government expenditure at the end of the century. Apart from the cost of the South African War, annual government expenditure rose by 40 per cent between 1895 and 1902. In the 1902 budget this contributed to an increase in income tax from 1s 2d to 1s 3d in the £ and to the imposition of a small duty on imported corn and flour. Any hope that this was a prelude to the full-scale adoption of Protection was swiftly dispelled in the budget of the following year. Ritchie, who succeeded Hicks-Beach as Chancellor of the Exchequer in July 1902, found himself dealing with a surplus. He took fourpence in the £ off income tax and abolished the corn duty; obviously it was extremely difficult to discredit Free Trade when the economy was proving so resilient. The 1903 budget was a severe set-back for Chamberlain, for whom the Tariff Reform campaign had now acquired the force of a monomania. He resigned and continued to campaign for Protectionism. Yet in the years which intervened between his resignation and his paralytic stroke in 1906 the trading recovery was broadly maintained.[1] Certainly there seemed no strong economic reason to adopt the drastic remedy which Chamberlain proposed.

The Free Traders for their part had powerful arguments at their command. Protection, they said, would add to the costs of industrial production by making factory plant and raw materials more expensive. Food prices would rise, causing hardship to workers unless wages were adjusted to keep pace with them — but this too would add to the costs of production making it more difficult for Britain to sell at competitive prices in overseas markets. It was unlikely that the colonies would be able to supply a substantial proportion of the food which Britain needed. Besides, if imperial preference were to be established, as Chamberlain wished, food imports from other countries would bear a correspondingly heavier tariff and the cost of food for the home consumer would be disproportionately high. It was hardly surprising that the Liberal poster contrasting the Free Traders' big loaf with the Tariff Reformers' small one was so effective. It pin-pointed the economic weakness of Chamberlain's campaign.

But there is another aspect of this campaign which deserves attention. When Chamberlain resigned from the Cabinet in 1903 the economic merits of Protection had very little to do with it. The motive which actuated him was not national interest — after all, Britain, as has been shown, seemed now to have weathered the trading difficulties of the late nineteenth century — but self-interest. Chamberlain was obsessed with his own grandiose schemes for closer integration of the Empire and also with the ever-present urge of a man of disappointed ambition to impose his will on his colleagues. His personal influence was strong, strong enough to split the Cabinet and the Conservative Party and to ensure as a result a crushing victory for the Liberals in the 1906 election. The Tariff Reform issue was not enough in itself to justify the savage blows which Chamberlain inflicted on his party; inevitably his motives must be suspect.

It is fitting that the career of this man so vigorous in character and so fertile in ideas is remembered primarily for its

[1] See Ensor, *England 1870–1914*, pp. 498–513, for a convenient summary of the position.

negative effects, notably the shattering impact of his career on the two parties which he successively joined. His positive achievements are extraordinarily small in relation to his great capacity. He established a reputation early in his political career as a Radical, and during his service under Gladstone there was some hope that his Radicalism might become a powerful beneficial force both for his party and his country. His legislation improved conditions of service for merchant seamen, he played a leading part in securing the extension of the franchise in 1884, and his unauthorised programme seemed to offer the prospect of extensive social reforms. Then came the break with the Liberals, the alliance with the Conservatives, and a declining interest in the social reforms so greatly needed in Britain, as Chamberlain devoted his energies and ambitions to imperialism in Africa, to the alliance with Germany and, ultimately, to Tariff Reform. In the end he failed to avert war against the Boers, he failed to secure the German alliance, and he failed to secure Tariff Reform. By an odd irony, in view of his radicalism, the major social reform introduced by the Conservatives between 1895 and 1906, namely the 1902 Education Act, was opposed by Chamberlain. He thought that it was too favourable to the Church of England and wanted to give local authorities the right not to accept the Bill. Fortunately for the systematic development of national education in Britain the House of Commons rejected this idea.

One might perhaps blame misfortune for the incompleteness and frustration of Chamberlain's career. To do so is to blind oneself to the nature of the man. Many qualities are needed to achieve a successful political career. In some respects Chamberlain was well endowed, but he lacked patience, he lacked loyalty, he lacked the ability to compromise and to work with others, he lacked a sense of political timing. His disputes with his colleagues suggest at times a perversity which is more concerned with the assertion of dominance than with the merits of the issue concerned. He was, in short, an egotist who failed to learn that the matters of policy for which he was responsible were more important than his own career.

Defence

During the period when Chamberlain's political career was at its prime, from 1880, the year of his first ministerial appointment, until his illness in 1906, none of his contemporaries exercised so decisive and valuable an influence on the nation's affairs. Gladstone had passed his best by 1880 and was increasingly preoccupied with the then delusive hope of giving Ireland Home Rule. Disraeli died in 1881. Lord Salisbury presided over the Conservative Governments of 1886 to 1892, and of 1895 to 1902, but did so with a distaste for the affairs of state more reminiscent of the eighteenth century than the nineteeth. Balfour, his successor, Prime Minister between 1902 and 1905, was too indecisive, too intellectual and detached to make much impact in the hurly-burly of politics. Lord Randolph Churchill, the *enfant terrible* of the Conservative party, had much of the force and imagination which had brought Chamberlain himself to the forefront in public life, but Churchill's premature death in 1895 at the age of forty-five left Chamberlain with no rival. From this stage onwards Chamberlain was without question the dominant force in English politics. His dominance sprang not merely from his strong sense of principle but from the vision which he brought to bear on the leading issues of his time, and which he communicated so vividly to others. He had the capacity, rare in politics, to see beyond the problems of the moment, to put them in their context, and to find solutions which were illumined by his creative intellectual power. That he was too practical for the Liberals and too progressive for the Conservatives is a criticism of them, not of him.

His first interest in politics, naturally enough as a Radical, was in social reform. The merits of his work in Birmingham and as President of the Board of Trade need no further elaboration. What does need to be emphasised, however, is the strength and sincerity of his Radicalism. Institutions and interests grown flabby and complacent on overmuch power and unthinking praise felt the sting of Chamberlain's invective. 'We have been too long a peer-ridden nation', said Chamberlain in 1884 when the House of Lords was doing its best to frustrate the Third Reform Bill, 'and I hope you will say to them that if they will not bow to the mandate of the people, they shall lose for ever the authority they have so long abused.' Landowners and the Church discovered likewise that they were not exempt from public criticism; nor would Chamberlain consent to be muzzled if he believed his own party to be at fault. Even before the break with Gladstone over Ireland he had sharply criticised the slowness of his party to protect the interests of the agricultural labourer, and its failure to secure that the poor rather than the rich should benefit from the properties administered by the Charity Commissioners. His ideas on social reform had been taking shape for many years and were crystallised in the unauthorised programme of 1885. That it was unauthorised was not the fault of Chamberlain. Gladstone's mind by this stage was living in a rarefied atmosphere of its own. His purblind devotion to the impossible ideal of Home Rule for Ireland meant that any interest he showed in the domestic affairs of England itself was purely fortuitous. No minister who shared Chamberlain's knowledge of the appalling living conditions which persisted both in town and country could fail to be exasperated by Gladstone's indifference to common sense. Liberalism under Gladstone was losing its *raison d'être* and becoming an appendage to the Irish Nationalist party.

To correct this suicidal tendency Chamberlain therefore put forward his own programme for the forthcoming election. He advocated that schooling should be free, that the Government should encourage the growth of small holdings to diminish agricultural distress, that taxation should be rationalised by the introduction of a graduated system of payment, and that democratically elected local councils should have their functions widely extended. It was an excellent programme, practical, and adapted to the needs of the time. Its appeal was sufficiently strong for the Liberals to win the election in spite of Gladstone's lethargic leadership. When the programme was first advanced Chamberlain was accused by his opponents of Socialism. 'I have learned not to be afraid of words that are flung in my face instead of arguments,' answered Chamberlain. 'Of course it is Socialism . . . every kindly act of legislation by which the community has sought to discharge its responsibilities and its obligations to the poor is Socialism. But it is none the worse for that.'

The break with Gladstone over Home Rule naturally prevented Chamberlain from giving personal effect to his programme. There then followed ten years of 'sterile eternity', as Garvin calls them, until Chamberlain resumed ministerial office, this time under Salisbury, as Colonial Secretary. Yet Chamberlain's influence, even if only indirectly exercised, was curiously strong during this period. Free education was adopted for England and Wales in 1891; between 1888 and 1894 the whole system of local government was reorganised, enlarging the powers of local councils elected on a wide franchise as Chamberlain had recommended; an Allotments Act in 1887 and an Agricultural Holdings Act in 1892 faithfully put into effect Chamberlain's suggestions for a widening of the basis of land ownership. Only graduated taxation remained to be achieved, and in view of the low rate of taxation at the time, and the small number affected by it, this objective was of less urgency than the others. Chamberlain therefore could well feel that so far as it was practicable his programme had been achieved. In part this explains his acceptance of the post of Colonial Secretary in 1895. He continued to show interest in social reforms in Britain, as his strong support for the Workmen's Compensation Act of 1897 indicates; his interest in the social needs of the colonies stemmed from the same impulse.

Even during the distractions of his last years in politics Chamberlain still contrived to interest himself actively in social reforms. The intensity with which he conducted the Tariff Reform campaign, for instance, can be partly attributed to his desire to gain additional revenue to finance an old age pensions scheme. It is true that at first sight he appears to have played a negative role in the debates on the 1902 Education Act, but the nature of the dilemma which confronted him needs to be appreciated before judgment is made. His wish to secure the widest possible extension of national free education is well known and formed part of the unauthorised programme. On the other hand as a lifelong Nonconformist he was strongly antagonistic to the influence of the Church of England over education. Along with many other Nonconformists he bitterly resented the continuance of the 'dual system' in the 1902 Act by which Church of England schools, supported by ratepayers' money, remained in existence alongside the council schools. These church schools were still numerous and in many 'single school' areas there was no alternative schooling for Nonconformist children. Chamberlain felt that the principle of public financial support for Church schools was wrong, and made doubly wrong by the special educational difficulties in which Nonconformists were so often placed. There were therefore special circumstances which justified Chamberlain's opposition to the reorganisation of elementary education in the 1902 Act. Nevertheless, even the briefest conspectus of his activities and speeches shows the depth and value of his views on social reform. Had the Liberals concentrated on domestic reforms, as Chamberlain wished, instead of on Ireland, Socialism might well have become an ally of Liberalism, not a rival, and the forces of Radicalism in Britain would have been immeasurably strengthened.

One of the most frequent charges made against Chamberlain is his abandonment of the Liberal Party, and, so it is asserted, an equivalent disloyalty to Balfour over Tariff Reform leading to the heavy Conservative defeat in the 1906 election. The break with Gladstone requires very little justification. His leader's devotion to Home Rule was farcical but also extremely galling to a man possessed of Chamberlain's zeal for domestic reforms. It was certain that the House of Lords would reject Home Rule and, even if by some constitutional miracle their opposition could be overcome, or by-passed, the terms of the Home Rule Bills of 1886 and 1893 were too naïve to be workable. The problem of Ulster, which was to rouse such fury in 1912, was ignored by Gladstone though not by Chamberlain. The latter was strongly influenced too by the violence of the Irish. When Parnell asserted that the Irish had an absolute right to self-government Chamberlain, with the recent activities of the Irish in mind, denied this. 'It is a right,' he sensibly remarked, 'which must be considered in relation to the security and welfare of the other countries in juxtaposition to which Ireland is placed.' It would be quite wrong to infer from this, however, that Chamberlain had no positive measures to propose on the Irish Question. He believed that agrarian reform and the establishment of local self-government for Ireland were practical measures. When it became clear that Gladstone's almost hypnotic influence on the leading members of the party ruled out of consideration any solution to the Irish problem except Home Rule, Chamberlain naturally enough had to re-assess his own position. He had made his views clearly known, and he rightly felt in 1886 that he could no longer hold ministerial office under a man with whom he so profoundly disagreed. The absurdity of Gladstone's secretiveness over his conversion to Home Rule in the months before the election had already brought home sharply to Chamberlain the almost insurmountable difficulty of working with a man who had so little respect for the opinions of his colleagues.

There were powerful reasons therefore for Chamberlain's resignation, but the point which needs to be grasped beyond this is that the reasons which justified his resignation were also those which justified his alliance with the Conservatives. There are artificialities in party politics which make unthinking loyalty absurd for a man of Chamberlain's force and vision. He believed that Gladstone's fixation over Home Rule was pointless in itself, and a tragic diversion of the energies which the Liberals ought to be devoting to the pressing reforms needed at home. If he tamely followed Gladstone's lead it would be a betrayal of the ideals of Radicalism — of Radicalism, it should be noted, rather than of Liberalism. There had always been a cleavage between Chamberlain and the old guard of Liberalism, whose political approach was inherited from the Whigs, and Chamberlain never professed or owed any loyalty to Liberalism of that kind. They expected the kind of unanimous loyalty shown by the Gadarene swine, but Chamberlain could see no reason why the progressive movement which he so ably represented should commit political suicide.

Even so, Chamberlain made a last effort to bring the party to its senses. In a speech to his constituents in West Birmingham, on 23 December 1886, he broached the idea of a 'round table conference' to be attended by himself and by leading representatives of the Liberal Party. He pointed out that there were many points upon which the Liberals were agreed, and that even on Ireland there was some hope of agreement. The Conference was duly held in 1887. Gladstone himself did not attend; Harcourt, Herschell, and John Morley acted as spokesmen for Gladstone's views. The meetings were a failure. Home Rule had become a cuckoo in the nest and there was no room for anything else. Furthermore, the vindictive attacks launched against Chamberlain at this time and later, some of them from very mixed motives, diminished the hope of agreement. Yet no one could fairly accuse Chamberlain of having acted impulsively or in a fit of pique. Once reconciliation became hopeless, Chamberlain and the Liberal Unionists moved steadily towards an alliance with the Conservatives. That Chamberlain took with him almost a hundred supporters is of some significance in itself, giving a strong indication that Chamberlain's views on the follies of Gladstone's leadership at this stage were widely shared. The alliance of Radicalism and Conservatism was less bizarre than it may seem at first sight. Disraeli had steered Conservatism on a new course and the process was continued under Salisbury. So long as Gladstone was alive there was much more likelihood of constructive and imaginative policies emanating from Conservative than from Liberal Governments. The reforms put into effect by the Conservatives between 1886 and 1905 make impressive reading and are in themselves a justification for Chamberlain's decision to change sides.

The second occasion upon which Chamberlain differed profoundly from his ministerial colleagues was on the matter of tariff reform. The arguments on the relative merits of Free Trade and Protection are very evenly balanced. Those in favour of the continuance of Free Trade have already been put,[1] and the specific arguments for Protection will also shortly be given. Quite apart from support for this or that view, however, it needs to be established at the outset that the decision was of crucial importance for Britain's economy. Chamberlain was justified in forcing the issue into the forefront of public attention and in resigning when it was plain that he differed substantially from many of his colleagues in the Cabinet. Again, as over Home Rule, he might have allowed himself to be muzzled and earned a cheap reputation for party loyalty, but it was never Chamberlain's practice to curry favour in this contemptible way. There is another parallel with the 1886 situation in that once more Chamberlain found himself serving under a leader with whom it was impossible to make effective contact. Gladstone was mentally

[1] See p. 173.

isolated from his colleagues: Balfour's fault was the opposite one. He drifted and wavered, always at the mercy of the latest opinion given to him, giving hope to all factions and leadership to none.

Although it is true that the adoption of Tariff Reform would make possible the introduction of Chamberlain's plan of imperial preference, this was only of incidental importance in the arguments which he advanced. There was a very strong case for Tariff Reform at the turn of the century on purely economic grounds, irrespective of its effect in leading to a closer integration of the Empire. It is significant, for instance, that Chamberlain during the Protectionist campaign received strong support from many leading industrialists, and they had no vested interests in securing the adoption of imperial preference. These industrialists felt, as did Chamberlain, a business man himself, that it was folly to cling on unthinkingly to Free Trade in the rapidly changing economic circumstances of the time. Free Trade had been a sound policy in the mid-nineteenth century when Britain still enjoyed the easy supremacy given by the early onset of her Industrial Revolution. Exports had expanded at a remarkable rate between 1842 and 1873, but in the next phase, 1873–98, the rate of growth slowed down considerably. The average rate of growth of exports in terms of volume had been 11 per cent between 1842 and 1873; between 1873 and 1898 it was reduced to $2\frac{1}{2}$ per cent,[1] and a sharp fall in export prices added to the difficulties of many industrialists. It was too much to expect them to believe that it was purely coincidental that during this period all the leading European powers and the United States had adopted high tariff policies. After 1898 there was a limited recovery. A price rise and an increase in some exports masked the true situation. The demand for British coal, machinery, ships, increased substantially. On the other hand it was disquieting that these were precisely the commodities which would enable foreign countries to expand their own production and commerce at a rate which was bound to have repercussions on Britain's trade in the world. The continued decline in demand for British textile

[1] These figures are taken from Imlah, *Economic Elements in the Pax Britannica*.

goods was equally disturbing; so too was the fact that the
United States and Germany by 1900 had far outstripped
Britain in steel production and that even in the coal industry
the United States was producing more tons than Britain.
Chamberlain's view was that the revival Britain was experiencing at the beginning of the century was partial and
misleading. He was equally concerned at the growing evidence after 1900 of German 'dumping' of iron and steel in
Britain at artificially low prices calculated to undercut the
British iron and steel industry. This was the penalty of the
unimaginative adherence to Free Trade when our most powerful trading rivals were shielded by tariffs against counter-
measures. Chamberlain, with characteristic vision, saw far
more clearly than his colleagues the needs of the situation.
His mind was already moving towards a 'managed economy',
an idea with which Britain has flirted but which she has never
attained. Eventually, imperial preference was adopted at the
Ottawa Conference in 1932 long after Chamberlain's death.
The First World War had intervened between Chamberlain's
first advocacy of Tariff Reform and its acceptance in 1932, but
most modern economists would probably agree that the deficiencies of the Free Trade policy were as evident before the
war as they were after it; Britain's adoption of Protection
was almost incredibly tardy.

The details of Balfour's indecisive leadership are not of
great significance here except that they justify Chamberlain's
resignation from the Government. The import duty on corn
and flour imposed in the 1902 budget was a symbol of the
struggle between the Protectionists and the Free Traders.
Its abandonment in the 1903 budget, introduced while
Chamberlain was away in South Africa, was a set-back to his
cause. If Balfour had now committed himself fully to Free
Trade at least the position would have been clear. Instead,
Balfour in September 1903 produced a memorandum for his
ministers called *Economic Notes on Insular Free Trade*. It
was intended as a compromise. Britain would be prepared,
said Balfour, to impose retaliatory tariffs if necessary on
foreign countries, but would not impose any duties which
would raise the price of food. How successful this compromise
was can reasonably be deduced from the fact that it was followed by Balfour's dismissal from the Cabinet of two Free

Traders, Ritchie and Lord Balfour, the resignation of two more, Lord George Hamilton and the Duke of Devonshire and then, to complete the muddle, the resignation of Chamberlain himself.[1] The question of Tariff Reform was too important for Chamberlain to wait on indefinitely while Balfour blundered on from one half policy to the next. It was this kind of leadership rather than Chamberlain's conduct which led to the Conservative defeat in 1906. Moreover, Chamberlain was very conscious of the fact that this was a time when the interests of the nation would be better served by strong advocacy of an honestly held opinion than by the devising of some inoffensive compromise.

Two other matters remain to be examined — Chamberlain's conduct of colonial affairs, particularly in South Africa, and the attempted Anglo-German alliance in which he took so prominent a part. When he became Colonial Secretary in 1895 there was no immediate crisis to occupy his attention and he devoted his energies to the much-needed work of improving communications and living conditions in West Africa. Railways and harbours were constructed, and encouragement was given to methodical research into the medical problems of this area, where feverish diseases had long produced an alarmingly high death rate. At the end of 1895, however, the Jameson Raid was launched; this episode and its consequences demanded Chamberlain's closest attention and provided a searching test of his diplomatic skill. There is no question that the Boer Government in the Transvaal was treating the Uitlanders in a manner which was intolerably provocative. The Boers owed much to the technical mining skills of these Europeans, but were giving them an inferior status in the State. The Uitlanders were denied ordinary civic rights and subjected to heavy taxation. The imposition of these hardships was thoroughly discreditable. There was no satisfactory reason for depriving the Uitlanders of their full rights as citizens; the discrimination practised by the Boers was an unpleasant mixture of prejudice and greed. These facts do not justify the raid which Jameson launched on the Transvaal, but they do much to explain it. The official inquiry by a House of Commons committee cleared Chamberlain of any com-

[1] See Ensor, *England 1870–1914*, p. 374, for an account of Balfour's mishandling of the situation.

plicity. As soon as Chamberlain was notified of the raid he had telegraphed the British High Commissioner in South Africa with instructions to order Jameson to withdraw from Boer territory. Though this had proved impossible in practice Chamberlain's total opposition to the raid was abundantly plain.

At the same time Chamberlain saw clearly that, though the raid itself was reprehensible, the root cause for it lay in the stubbornly unreasonable attitude of the Boers; not surprisingly the attitude of the Boers towards the Uitlanders hardened after the raid, making a solution of the problem even more difficult. It was almost impossible to have any rational dealings with Kruger. He denied that the Uitlanders had any grievances, and he regarded all attempts to negotiate with him on this subject as an infringement of the independence of the Transvaal. He was obsessed with his irritation over Britain's right of suzerainty over the Transvaal's affairs, and though there were practical and possibly legal grounds for a review of this position this was no justification for ignoring the elementary human rights of the Uitlanders. The shooting of Thomas Edgar, an Englishman living in Johannesburg, by Boer police on 24 December 1898, illustrated the dangers. Edgar had knocked down a Boer with whom he had had an argument. Four armed police burst into Edgar's house to arrest him. So far as one can tell from reports, he was not armed and offered no violence, but he was shot and killed in the presence of his wife by one of the Boer police. The subsequent acquittal of the policeman by a jury of Boers, and his commendation by the judge, justifiably inflamed Uitlander opinion. Meetings of protest by the Uitlanders were broken up by the Boers, though in the end they succeeded in sending a petition to the Queen complaining of their treatment. A dispatch from Milner, the High Commisioner in South Africa, gave official confirmation of the harshness of treatment to which British subjects in the Transvaal were exposed.

Kruger meanwhile showed not the slightest sign of moderation. At the Bloemfontein Conference in 1899 with Milner Kruger refused to make any concession on the extension of the franchise to the Uitlanders, or on any other matter, unless Britain immediately dropped any claim to intervene in the internal affairs of the Transvaal. In view of the large number of British subjects there, and the recent incidents which had taken place, this was an impossible demand. It was totally unrealistic, in Chamberlain's words, 'that we should promise never to interfere again to protect our subjects in a foreign country from injustice'. Nor was it satisfactory, when the abuses were so flagrant, to refer the issues in dispute to arbitration, as Kruger wished; it would have been discreditable to the British Government to shelve its responsibilities in this way. There can be little doubt that Kruger had no intention of dealing with the situation by negotiation. He had an alliance with the Orange Free State, he had received arms and encouragement from Germany, and the victory over the British at Majuba Hill in 1881 had given the Boers military confidence, so that by the autumn of 1899 the Boers were merely waiting for the right tactical moment to launch a war against the British. The presence of many Dutch people in Cape Colony gave them the added hope of expelling the British altogether from South Africa. It is difficult to see any other policy which Chamberlain could have adopted in the years which preceded the war, except to have abandoned the Uitlanders abjectly to the mismanagement of the Boers. The small number of British troops in South Africa in 1899 and the striking Boer successes in the early months of the war make it only too plain which country set most store by violence as a solution to the dispute. Between 1899 and 1902 the war and the operations which followed it naturally became matters for decision by the military leaders rather than by Chamberlain. He was able to exercise his influence strongly, however, over the peace settlement, the Treaty of Vereeniging, one of the most moderate and statesmanlike treaties ever made at the conclusion of a war. Conspicuous among its very generous terms was the promise of self-government to the Boers and a grant of £3 million to compensate for the damage done to Boer farms during the fighting.

By the end of the nineteenth century it was plain in foreign affairs that Britain's policy of isolationism had become a source of weakness, not strength. Salisbury made approaches to Russia but disputes over Russian aggression in the Far East prevented any agreement. Relations with France were bad and became worse in the autumn of 1898 when the two

G

countries disputed the possession of Fashoda on the upper waters of the Nile. There was much to be said, therefore, for an agreement with Germany. It would moderate the tensions created by economic, naval, and colonial rivalries, and strengthen the international position of both countries. Chamberlain took the lead in pressing for this alliance, which might have been extended also by the addition of the United States; Salisbury fully supported the move. Had they been dealing with men as far-sighted as themselves an alliance might well have been made, with incalculable effects on the history of the twentieth century. Unfortunately the Kaiser and his ministers were small-minded nationalists wedded to the corrupting doctrine that war is a cleansing creative force. The negotiations therefore failed, but it was plain enough where the fault lay. There was nothing in the concept of the alliance, nor in Chamberlain's handling of the negotiations, which would have prevented success had the Germans been capable of goodwill.

Chamberlain's career was brought to a premature conclusion in 1906 by a paralytic stroke from which he never recovered. He has been described as the ablest politician who was never Prime Minister; certainly the range of his abilities was extraordinarily wide. He was an ardent social reformer; a beneficent imperialist. His grasp of the more important issues of his time was unmatched. The development of Socialism, the adoption of Protection, the closer integration of the territories of the Empire, and the abandonment of isolationism; all these are foreshadowed in the career of this remarkable man. Most of his objectives were frustrated in his own lifetime by colleagues less gifted than he was, but the course of events since 1914 has shown how right he was in every major aspect of policy; the pity of it is, both for himself and for Britain, that the soundness of his ideas was not recognised in his own time. Certainly it was not because they lacked practicality. In none of the issues in which he found himself in conflict with his colleagues or his opponents can he be accused of lack of realism. It was his robust common sense which made him react so strongly, for instance, against the foolishness of Gladstone's Irish policy. His insight into affairs and his strongly marked individuality made him unpopular at times. 'Joseph dreamed a dream, and he told it to his brethren; and they hated him yet the more.' Yet had he allowed his great gifts to be submerged by the mediocrity around him he would have robbed the nation of one of the most creative minds ever devoted to its service.

8. THE CONDITION OF THE PEOPLE 1846–1900 PROGRESS OR POVERTY?

Prelude

The impact of the Industrial Revolution upon the lives of the people both in their homes and in their places of work has been given close attention by economists and by social historians. The focus of interest has been primarily the period about which there is the least reliable evidence, that is from about 1760 to the early 1840s. Statistical information is clearly one of the considerations to be taken into account, though by no means the only one. But throughout the early period of the Industrial Revolution historians are hampered partly by a shortage of statistical information, and partly by the existence of information which is inaccurate and misleading if the historian is not fully aware of the intentions and limitations of those who compiled the original statistics. Census returns of the first half of the nineteenth century, attempts to deduce meat consumption from the Smithfield market returns,[1] the unreliability of Board of Trade returns on exports and imports before the 1840s,[2] these spring to mind as examples of the pitfalls for those who place blind faith in the value of statistics. The difficulties of assessing conditions during the Industrial Revolution have been further bedevilled at times by the political attitudes of historians themselves, who consciously or unconsciously use the Industrial Revolution as a sermon on the virtues of private enterprise and self-reliance, or on the vices of capitalism and materialism, in accordance with their own preferences in these matters. The controversy over the influence of industrial change upon the community has thus raged long and hard.

[1] See A. J. Taylor, 'Progress and Poverty in Britain 1780–1850', *Essays in Economic History*, vol. 3 (London: Arnold, 1962).
[2] See Imlah, *Economic Elements in the Pax Britannica*.

The 'Optimist' and 'Pessimist' schools of thought on the Industrial Revolution belabour each other resoundingly, and if at times the dust of conflict seems to conceal more than it reveals this is largely because the dearth of reliable evidence on living and working conditions prevents either side from being entirely convincing. What does emerge, however, is that so far as the available evidence goes the argument has been squeezed dry. Total agreement on the standard of living before 1850 seems even less likely than it is on most historical problems, and it would be impossible in a short chapter of this kind to present the issues without a degree of simplification which would do more harm than good. These earlier phases of the Industrial Revolution have been given a wealth of expert attention to which the reader seeking detail is referred.[1] Since improvement or decline in the standard of living is best judged in relation to the period which has gone before there will be frequent references in the following pages to conditions in the first half of the nineteenth century, but the central theme will be the years from 1846.

In turning to an examination of the condition of the people in the second half of the nineteenth century many of the difficulties which hamper the historian of the earlier period are removed, but by no means all. Statistics become more reliable, markedly so after the 1880s, but interpretation of their significance still presents problems. A study of these problems provides, incidentally, a useful introduction to any attempt to assess the greater complexities of the earlier period. Students of economic and social history know what a profusion

[1] The following books and articles provide a useful conspectus of evidence and opinions on the Industrial Revolution up to the middle of the nineteenth century:

T. S. Ashton, *The Industrial Revolution* (London: Oxford University Press, 1948);

A. J. Taylor, 'Progress and Poverty in Britain', *Essays in Economic History*, vol. 3 (London: Arnold, 1962);

The Industrial Revolution in Britain — Triumph or Disaster, ed. Philip A. M. Taylor (London: Harrap, 1958);

R. M. Hartwell, *The Industrial Revolution in England* (Historical Association, 1958);

E. J. Hobsbawm and R. M. Hartwell, 'The Standard of Living during the Industrial Revolution: a discussion', *Economic History Review*, 2nd series, vol. xvi, no. 1 (August 1963).

of reservations have to be made in any comments on living standards. Wage statistics, for instance, are unrevealing unless one also knows the price of food-stuffs and of household equipment, and the level of rents. Nor is this an end of the difficulties. The prices of food do not show how much was consumed; assessments of food consumption *per capita* do not show how much more sugar or butter, for instance, would be consumed in a rich family than in a poor one. Dietary habits change and need to be judged by the standards of the time and not by those of the present day. Occupational differences and regional variations make generalisations about living conditions enormously difficult. An agricultural labourer in the second half of the century earned a relatively small wage, but he might be living in a rent-free cottage, he might have his main meals at the farm, and he gained the sundry benefits of living in the countryside, a small garden, abundant wood for fuel and home repairs, and a diet enriched by occasional poaching. He had long hours of work, the advantages and disadvantages of an open-air life, and a social existence not far removed from the feudal system. His counterpart in the factory or town shared none of his advantages but had the compensation of a higher wage. He had escaped from the dominance of the squire, but was just as vulnerable to his new master, a business man who might be a Robert Owen, perhaps, but who might bear a closer resemblance to Josiah Bounderby, Dickens's villain in *Hard Times*.

Moreover, within the same occupation there were great variations in standards. The factory worker might be a prosperous skilled artisan or an unskilled machine hand. He might be in a declining industry like Cornish tin- and copper-mining at the end of the century, or in an expanding one like the coal industry where production and exports were bounding up as the century progressed. But if profits were being made to what extent did the factory worker or miner share them? If he worked in the country would he be equally prosperous in the industrial north where alternative occupations could easily be found, and in the south where the only effective alternative to farm work was probably emigration? Even Cobbett in his gloomy comments on the state of English agriculture in 1830 found that there were exceptions. Later in the century these variations became more pronounced in proportion to the willingness of farmers to show enterprise over drainage, new fertilisers, and machinery.

Yet when all these qualifications have been made there remains obvious evidence that living and working conditions have changed, sometimes for better, sometimes for worse, over the centuries. There are always counter-tendencies to the particular trends at work; by using exceptions for evidence it is possible to distort the picture and to suggest that conditions were better or worse for the generality of people than they actually were. The point still remains that there is enough evidence available, particularly from the middle of the nineteenth century onwards, to form a broad picture of living conditions which does not diverge very far from the truth for most people. The views which can be balanced against each other now remain to be considered.

Attack

If no other evidence were considered except statistics the second half of the nineteenth century might well seem to be the golden age which it is sometimes claimed to be. Real wages were virtually the same in 1850 as they had been in 1800, yet between 1850 and 1900 they almost doubled.[1] A 4 lb loaf of bread cost 6¾d in 1850 but only 5¼d in 1900. Sugar consumption *per capita*, a significant guide to living standards, rose from 25·26 lb in 1850 to 85·53 lb in 1900. Reservations need to be made about the value of some of this evidence — the statistics for sugar, for instance, give no indication that some of the increase in its consumption was a result of commercial developments in sweet- and cake-making — but the general trend is undeniably in favour of the view that the people were becoming better paid and better fed as the century progressed. The interesting point about these figures, however, is the extent to which statistics can lie. The standard of living depends on other things besides a man's purchasing power. His environment, his security, his health, his opportunities for leisure and self-improvement, his wife's ability to manage his money and his household effici-

[1] See the statistical table on p. 204.

ently, all these are relevant considerations in talking about standards of living. Statistics can give information about standards of earning and standards of spending, though they do not always do these things very well, but on the other matters mentioned, less tangible but certainly no less important, statistics give very little help. Frustrated in this direction the historian has two other lines of approach. He can make use of contemporary comment, and he can make inferences from his knowledge of social legislation and of general economic trends.

There is at least one point, however, on which all the sources, statistical and others, agree, namely that there was a steady and substantial migration from the countryside to the towns. Up to 1851 agriculture held its own as an occupation; the census of that year shows that about one person in five of the working population was engaged in agriculture in spite of the Industrial Revolution. Yet by 1901 agriculture had sharply declined both in relative importance and in the absolute numbers employed. Between 1851 and 1901 the number of workers in agriculture shrank by about one-third. Some of these workers emigrated but the great majority merely made their way from the villages into the towns. Examination of conditions of life in the towns is therefore of crucial importance since in the nineteenth century the town takes over from the country as the normal background for the lives of many thousands of people.

That these conditions were appalling is conspicuously obvious from a wealth of evidence. Engels' book, *The Condition of the Working Classes in England* in 1844, had drawn attention to the disgraceful conditions experienced in the squalid alleys and cellars of Manchester; these criticisms were no less relevant as the century progressed. For instance, the report which preceded Mr Chamberlain's improvement scheme for Birmingham in 1876 notes that: 'It is not easy to describe or imagine the dreary desolation which acre after acre of the town presents to anyone who will take the trouble to visit it. . . . In one case a filthy drain from a neighbouring court oozed into a little back yard; in another the sitting-room windows could not be opened owing to the horrible effluvia from a yawning midden just under it.' Conditions indeed were worse in the latter half of the century than they had been earlier. House building had not kept pace with the growth of population in the towns. It was desirable in the days before local train and bus services were properly organised, and this did not come about until the end of the century, that workers should live within sound of the factory hooter summoning them to work. Moreover, the residential areas of the middle classes were sedulously protected by the local councils so that the scope for housing expansion was limited. Even in those towns where slum clearance schemes were put into effect the problem was worsened for a long period by the delays in building new houses to replace those which had been condemned and destroyed. The inevitable consequence of these factors was gross overcrowding in buildings whose condition worsened year by year through lack of repairs and totally inadequate drainage. Tenants were not likely to spend money themselves on repairs, and even landlords of goodwill wearied of providing fittings which were damaged or sold by tenants within a few weeks for what they could fetch. Many landlords employed agents to deal with tenants. These agents collected the rents, gave a fixed proportion to the landlord, and made their own earnings from the rest; it was hardly surprising that there was little interest in house repair. It is a relevant consideration also that even when builders were called in, to deal with drainage work for instance, the work was often very shoddily done, frustrating the intentions of the reformers.

Contemporaries were thoroughly aware of the scandalous state of housing. The sense of outrage against conditions which were an affront to human dignity rings through Chamberlain's speeches on housing in Birmingham; it finds vivid expression in George Sims's pamphlet *The Bitter Cry of Outcast London* (1883), and it was given governmental support, though not very much action, in the report of the Royal Commission on Housing which sat during 1884 and 1885.

One result of this overcrowding in such foul conditions was the outbreak of epidemics which struck with cruel frequency. Cholera was one of the by-products of the Industrial Revolution. It is usually caused by a micro-organism absorbed into the body through drinking infected water. The reliance in towns on water from wells and pumps, the practice of leaving water exposed in tubs in the home to save journeys to a pump,

*

and the ease with which water could be contaminated through leakage from inexpertly assembled sewer pipes, make it surprising that cholera was not even more of a killer disease than it was. Nevertheless the havoc and distress which it created were bad enough. The first epidemic in 1831 caused 31,000 deaths and, though Dr Snow established the connection between the disease and water-pollution in 1849, national and local lethargy over remedial action enabled cholera to strike time after time. There were major epidemics in 1848, 1849, 1854, and between 1863 and 1866, while there were smaller outbreaks in 1872 and as late as 1894. The scathing comments made by the Board of Health on the inertia and selfishness of parochial authorities in the report in July 1849 make abundantly clear the scant degree of help which the poorer classes could expect from those theoretically responsible for them. When cholera broke out in Dumfries, for instance, in 1848, the parochial board allowed twenty days to pass without taking any effective precautions. 'On the first outbreak of the epidemic, indeed, a system of medical relief, apparently well adapted for meeting it, was agreed to; but this was broken up on the following day, by order of the parochial Board, on the alleged ground of expense.'[1] Apart from cholera the other great scourge which owed its deadly effectiveness to urban conditions was typhus. Shortage of water, the wearing of dirty cast-off clothing, and indifference to personal cleanliness provided exactly the conditions in which lice multiplied, and they carried the virus which produced typhus. Medical science lagged woefully behind the demands made upon it. It was not until 1880 that Pasteur's germ theory of infectious disease gained widespread support, and it was some years before the significance of his discovery percolated down to the general practitioner and to local medical officers of health. Consequently typhus continued to be a recurrent menace until the end of the century. Individual occupations also had their own specific dangers for health when official control was either imperfectly organised or else non-existent. The lung diseases of miners, cutlery workers, and of potters, the consumption of textile workers and of the unfortunate women working in the tailoring 'sweat-shops',

---

[1] Quoted in *English Historical Documents*, ed. D. C. Douglas (London: Eyre & Spottiswoode, 1956), vol. xii (ii), p. 797.

the facial disfigurement of those whose work in the match industry brought them into close contact with phosphorus, all combine to make a depressing but just commentary on the cost of Britain's trading supremacy.

Much of the suffering could have been obviated if the politicians and administrators had shown more foresight and humanity. It has been shrewdly pointed out that the Industrial Revolution was an impersonal agent, neither good nor bad in itself.[1] Wisely controlled it could have been a blessing; slackly controlled it could be a curse. It was virtually useless to pin any faith on the parochial authorities and the Improvement Commissions. The purpose of their existence in practice was to make life more comfortable for the middle classes. Since germs are not class-conscious this meant that the local authorities were spasmodically goaded into action by the onset of disease but then relapsed into selfish somnolence. Some cities, notably Leeds, Manchester, Birmingham, and Liverpool appointed medical officers, but this worked no miracles. It was plain beyond question that if conditions were to be brought under proper control everything would depend on the degree of urgency and efficiency shown by the central government.

A review of governmental social legislation between 1850 and 1900 gives not the slightest suggestion of urgency and very little of efficiency. An outbreak of cholera in 1847 spurred Russell's Government into appointing a Public Health Board in 1848. At the same time the Board was so hedged about with restrictions that it was robbed of much of its possible effectiveness from the start. It was only allowed to create local boards of health if there was a petition to this effect from one-tenth of the inhabitants of the district concerned, though it could set up a local board by order in any district where the death rate exceeded 23 per 1,000. This figure was above the national average for the time so that the Board was frustrated of any hope of grappling with health problems with the help of a nation-wide organisation. Nevertheless Chadwick, one of the three Commissioners chosen by the Government to form the Board, showed the same single-minded devotion to his work as he had done as a Poor Law

[1] G. Kitson Clark, *The Making of Victorian England* (London: Methuen, 1962).

Commissioner. There was an important difference, however; his work in reorganising the relief of the poor had led to a reduction in the Poor Rate and was therefore popular with the vested interests which were as strongly entrenched in local as they were in national government; the improvements in medical relief for which he pressed in his new capacity would infallibly lead to greater local expenditure. Besides this, the Board's blunt criticisms of the inadequacy of the health measures adopted by local authorities roused strong resentment. Thus Chadwick and his fellow commissioners had probed at two tender spots of the local officials — their money and their self-esteem — and could expect to be disliked. It was easy in an age which glorified self-help to rouse antagonism against the Board. Chadwick became the first victim when he was dismissed in 1854. 'We prefer to take our chance of cholera and the rest than to be bullied into health,' said *The Times*; had the editor or his readers lived in an industrial slum the wording might have been different, but those who were most influential in society had thoroughly mastered the art of turning a blind eye to any aspect of life which was likely to be inconvenient. In 1858 the Board was dissolved with its functions indifferently divided among indifferent government departments.

Epidemics, however, could not be so easily disposed of, and their frequent recurrence stimulated a certain amount of administrative action by governments in the 1860s and 1870s. The measures adopted lacked coherence and urgency.[1] Like so much of Victorian social legislation the Acts were so badly phrased that each measure spawned off a series of further Acts devised in order to make the original Act workable. By 1869 there was such a chaos of authorities and functions that a Royal Commission was appointed to suggest how order could be re-established. This led to the passing of a Local Government Act in 1871 combining public health and Poor Law functions in a single board. It proved to be a muddled arrangement. A Public Health Act in 1875 pre-

[1] This was not the case when M.P.s' own interests were affected. Their sensitivity to the smells coming from the nearby Thames stimulated their acceptance of the Metropolitan Water Board's plans for a general sewage system for London in 1858. See Sir L. Woodward, *The Age of Reform* (Oxford: Clarendon Press, 1962), p. 464.

scribed the duties of the sanitary authorities, which had
been made responsible for sanitary organisation at local level
in 1872, but the small size and lack of funds of these authorities prevented them from making much impact on a problem
which naturally magnified as the population increased. It was
not until the reorganisation of local government between
1888 and 1894 that Britain had even the basis of the framework needed to deal with the health problem on the scale
required.

Whatever aspect of social organisation one inspects which
was likely to affect the living and working conditions of the
people, the same pattern of muddle, inertia, and obstructionism emerges. In 1847 after a long campaign punctuated by
many set-backs, Fielden's Ten Hour Bill, the product of his
own efforts and those of Ashley, became law. The work of
women and young persons, though not of men, was to be
limited to ten hours a day, shortly extended to ten-and-a-
half hours. The wording of the Act was so ambiguous, and the
continuance of the shift system made evasion of its terms by
factory owners so easy, that Ashley felt that the cause of
factory reform was no further forward after the Bill had
become law than it had been before. It was not until Disraeli's Factory Act of 1874 that the ten-hour day for women
and young persons was effectively secured; men had to wait
until the twentieth century for any comprehensive attempt
to reduce hours by means of legislation.

Exploitation of loopholes in parliamentary legislation likewise enabled many of the smaller manufacturers to evade
regulations designed to improve working conditions. For
many years they traded on the fact that factory legislation
did not apply to the smaller establishments, though these
were precisely the places where through lack of funds the
workers' conditions were likely to be the worst. An Act of
1867 brought these workshops, as they were called, within the
scope of factory law. The Act was so loosely worded and so
laxly applied that its effect was slight. Many employers, too,
were enabled to exploit their workers by the almost incredible
slowness of governments to extend to other industries the
restrictions imposed on the use of labour in the textile and coal
industries. Conditions in calico print works were regulated in
1845, but otherwise it was not until the 1860s that there was a

general extension of controls to other industries employing women and children. Even the most devoted supporter of *laissez-faire* might become uncertain about his philosophy if he were to study the series of reports issued by the Children's Employment Commission from 1863 onwards. The disclosure of the way in which children's labour was exploited and their health abused in the pottery industry, in lace-making, and a whole crop of other industries was eventually sufficient to stimulate the House of Commons into tardy reform.

The inadequacy of factory reform so far had been the result quite as much of active opposition within the House of Commons as of inertia. The protective legislation of the 1860s might easily have taken place in the 1850s, but the rejection by the House of Commons of a Bill to control working conditions in the bleaching and dyeing industries in 1854 had given no encouragement to hopes of early reform. It was ironical that this same Bill had been introduced and passed in the House of Lords, supposedly one of the bastions of reaction, but, until the 1867 Reform Act enabled the workers in towns to remind M.P.s of their existence by the use of the vote, the latter showed very little interest in reforms which might endanger their business profits and those of the predominantly middle-class voters. The 1878 Factory Act eventually brought some coherence into the miscellany of preceding legislation and made it workable, but the process had been a very long one and still remained incomplete for tailoring, cardboard-box making, and other 'sweated' industries which were not effectively controlled until the Trade Boards Act of 1909.

The vulnerability of the worker was increased by his helplessness if he became the victim of unemployment, of sickness, or of wage disputes. It was not until the 1890s that trade unionism gained the numerical support and bargaining strength to make it a useful representative of the workers' interests; even then the legal position of trade unions was ambiguous as the Taff Vale strike in 1900 showed. There was no compulsory unemployment or sickness insurance until 1911, no old age pensions until 1908, no adequate system of workmen's compensation for accidents until 1897, though in Germany all these hazards of a working life, except unemployment, had been provided for in the legislation of the

1880s. In education likewise Britain lagged behind Germany, France, and even smaller countries like Switzerland, in the money allocated *per capita* in education, and in the quality of secondary education. If, as a result of changes in demand or supply, workers lost their jobs, as many in Lancashire did during the cotton famine produced by the American Civil War, the only hope of eking out an existence for them and their families was by applying for Poor Relief or for support by charities. Workhouse conditions were so harsh and the tasks imposed so degrading that many preferred to take their chance of being relieved by charitable action. The scale of workhouse relief was the minimum possible to keep the applicants alive, but not enough to give men the strength to do manual work. Charitable organisations in pre-Welfare State days were numerous and well supported by private sub-scriptions, but the kind of help they could give was haphazard and inadequate to meet large-scale demands over a long period of time. Clearly a State system would have been more efficient, though not if it was administered in the spirit of the iniquitous 1834 Poor Law, which cast a threatening shadow over the lives of workers throughout the period under review.

Nor was it only through changes in world trading con-ditions that workers were brought face to face with the harsh administration of the Poor Law. Winter was a time to be dreaded. A severe winter such as that of 1860–1 increased the number of those in need of poor relief in London by a little over 40 per cent. In the report of the Parliamentary Select Committee on the Administration of Relief of the Poor, 1864, Mr Knox, a police magistrate, described the condition of some of the houses during that winter: 'Their articles of furniture were gone from the house; the frame of a bedstead would be remaining and the sacking gone; there were a man and his wife and six children lying upon shavings in the room; they would show you a bundle of pawn-tickets, with nothing remaining in the room; and I beheld sights such as you would not suppose it possible to witness in London.'[1] Thirty years later, during the hard winters of 1891, 1892, and 1895, the difficulties of the poor remained just as great. Pro-cessions of unemployed men paraded the streets and poverty

[1] Quoted in *English Historical Documents*, ed. Douglas, vol. xii (i), p. 737.

was still treated as if it were virtually a crime, as indeed it was, though not committed by the poor but against them.

There is one final consideration to be taken into account in analysing the condition of the people in the second half of the nineteenth century, and that is the state of mind, the emotional reaction, of those who had moved into the towns from the countryside. At first sight it might be tempting to discount this approach altogether. Discontent cannot be measured statistically, facts can be verified but not feelings, and even if historians accept the validity of some contemporary comment they can balance against it opinions of a contrary nature, they can stress that discontent was exceptional, that the misfits in society are apt to be more vocal than the contented masses, and that ultimately evidence on feelings is so controversial that it would be as well to ignore it altogether. To approach the issue in this way is wrong. The feelings and attitudes of the urban worker of the nineteenth century cannot be reconstructed purely as a matter of fact, but contemporary comment and deductions from known facts give a reasonable basis for forming an opinion on a matter quite as important as statistics on the daily consumption of bread and cheese.

There is no shortage of contemporary evidence on the widespread distress of the period. Reports of Royal Commissions on sanitary conditions, on housing, on the employment of children, reports by the Board of Health and by the Poor Law authorities, Charles Booth's survey of living conditions in London and Seebohm Rowntree's similar survey of York, Mayhew's *London Labour and the London Poor*, Sim's *Bitter Cry of Outcast London*, these and many other contemporary sources show how depressing conditions were. Comments by slum-dwellers themselves show that they had no illusions about the conditions in which they had to live nor about the effect of those conditions on their outlook. When the Birmingham councillors were collecting evidence on conditions there in the 1870s they were given pointed answers by the people concerned. 'What have people got to do but drink here? It is about their only comfort. There is nothing but dirt and nastiness to live in, and stinks and smells.' 'Young 'uns die off pretty quickly, that's certain — there's more bugs than babies.' 'The parsons tell us to be good; nobody can't be good

in such places as these.'[1] Drink was a cheap form of escapism
and posed a social problem on a scale difficult to envisage
now. It demoralised the worker and impoverished his family.
Often it meant that the worker, though not badly paid, preferred to live in bad housing so that the lower rent would
give him more drinking money. The energetic effort made by
the temperance societies and by the Salvation Army to combat
this menace had very limited success in terms of parliamentary
legislation, but the vigour of their campaign shows how urgent
and widespread the problem was.

At a deeper level drink provided a temporary escape from
an existence where men had ceased to have any significance or
self-respect as individual human beings. Work had become
mechanical, not only in the literal sense of the greatly extended use of machinery in industry, and to some extent in
agriculture, but also in the pace and pressure of work in
occupations such as tailoring where there was little or no
reliance on machines. The harshness of the rules imposed in
factories by which, for instance, workers in cotton factories
might be fined for opening a window, exemplifies the subordi-
nation of men to machinery in the nineteenth century. Often,
of course, women were subjected to much the same pressures
at work as men. To make home life pleasant for a family in
these circumstances would have required the stamina of an
athlete and the patience of a saint. A factory inspector,
reporting on conditions in the Potteries in 1865, noted that:
'The women, from going early to work, have had but few
opportunities afforded them of becoming acquainted with
home duties before they marry; and in consequence their
homes are deserted by the men for the public house.'[2] Often
they could not sew and were so ignorant in household management that families enjoyed meat, fish, spirits, and beer at the
beginning of the week, but by the end of it were living on
bread and water. This deficiency in the running of homes by
women was partly a consequence of the stubborn refusal of
the Victorians to take any trouble over the education of
women, but it also stemmed of course from the impossible

[1] Quoted in N. Murrell Marris, *Joseph Chamberlain, The Man and the
Statesman* (London: Hutchinson, 1900), p. 121.

[2] Quoted in *English Historical Documents*, ed. Douglas, vol. xii (i),
p. 995.

conditions imposed by the largely unrestricted operations of industrial enterprise.

It might reasonably be asked why it was that if conditions were so bad the worker and his family did not move to the countryside, from which many of them had come. One reason is plain in the report of the Royal Commission on Agriculture in 1882, which speaks of 'the great extent and intensity of the distress which has fallen upon the agricultural community . . . all without distinction have been involved in a general calamity.' Since the depression of the 1870s agriculture has never been able to stand firmly on its own feet and no worker who returned from the town to the country could be sure of employment. Besides, the growing mechanisation of farming equipment led to a diminishing demand for unskilled labour. Towns therefore became prisons with the occupants sometimes additionally restrained from movement by the difficulty of securing credit in a new area, an important consideration since workers and their wives were notoriously bad managers of their wages. The town dwellers' nostalgia for the blessings, real and imagined, of country life is tellingly described in Mrs Gaskell's book *Mary Barton* — a story based on the writer's first-hand observation of life in nineteenth-century Manchester.

Little needs to be added in conclusion. If the Industrial Revolution had merely disfigured the landscape then it might be justified; but it also disfigured men's minds. It created opportunities for making unparalleled wealth, but it exacted a price which is still being paid. Disraeli in *Sybil* put it best: 'Christianity teaches us to love our neighbour as ourself; modern society acknowledges no neighbour.'

Defence

Demonstration of improvement or decline in the standard of living of the people at any period is obviously beset with great difficulties; and if one tries to take into account matters such as the efficiency of household management, which cannot be measured objectively, the difficulties become almost insuperable. Yet it is plain enough that living and working condi-

tions do change and that, for the most part, they improve.
Even the most obstinate reactionary would be hard put to it
to deny that living and working conditions are far pleasanter
in the mid twentieth century than they were in the early
nineteenth century. It is true that the advances made have
been achieved in spurts rather than in a methodical sequence,
but these advances are not the monopoly of the twentieth
century; it is easy to show, for instance, that the origins of the
Welfare State are to be found in the social theories and legislation of the nineteenth century.[1] Two further considerations
merit special attention in judging the standard of living in the
nineteenth century. One is to judge the standard in relation
to what has gone before, and by reference to what the people
of the time conceived to be reasonable conditions, rather than
to falsify the issue by approaching it from the standpoint of
the twentieth century. As a simple instance the fact that the
drainage system of Buckingham Palace was described as a
menace to public health in 1849, and was not much improved thirty years later, suggests that the rich as well as the
poor were far more indifferent to health risks than is the habit
today. The second point to bear in mind is that absolute
statements about living conditions are bound to be littered
with exceptions. The most which can be achieved is a broad
picture of conditions, and the balance of objective evidence
on the second half of the nineteenth century is very much
more in favour of improvement than of decline. Obviously if
one relies for evidence on reports of conditions in condemned
areas, on investigations into sub-standard building and other
similar matters, it is not difficult to make conditions seem
worse in general than they actually were.

The evidence to which most weight ought to be attached,
therefore, is that which applies to the whole nation, not particular groups within it. Statistics are in some respects vulnerable to attack as evidence, but they do have the virtue that
to a greater extent than any other evidence they show the
broad national situation in objective terms. Moreover, their
limitations are not so great that they can be discounted altogether. It is quite true that the *per capita* consumption of
butter or sugar does not indicate how much would be consumed in a rich household and how much in a poor one.

[1] See p. 39.

Nevertheless, if the *per capita* consumption of foodstuffs rises to a very marked extent, common sense suggests that there is a limit to the intake and digestive capacities of the rich, and that therefore the poor are receiving a greater share of food than they did before. If the following statistics (Table I) on various aspects of the standard of living are approached in this way, being neither swallowed nor ejected whole, they have a value not shared by other evidence, and the impression they create of widespread progress is very striking indeed.

TABLE I

Real Wages and the Standard of Comfort since 1850

1850 = 100

YEAR[1]	AVERAGE REAL WAGES[2]
1850	100
1855	94
1860	105
1865	120
1870	118
1875	138
1880	132
1885	140
1890	169
1895	170
1900	184

Source: G. H. Wood in *The Journal of the Royal Statistical Society,* 1909.

The statistics which follow on individual items of food and drink confirm in detail how conditions were improving. Tea, coffee, sugar, and tobacco consumption is a reasonably good indicator of the standard of living since purchase of these goods represents to some extent the amount of surplus money available for these 'luxury' goods after the staple food-stuffs have been bought. Qualifications have to be made about the value of the figures since the amounts imported varied with the efficiency of shipping services, which were much more vulnerable then to delay and disaster than they are now, and they varied, too, with changes in dietary habits. Coffee, for instance, was a less popular drink in the late nineteenth cen-

[1] Figures have been extracted to show changes at five-yearly intervals.
[2] Real wages show the relationship between money wages and price levels.

tury than it had been earlier.[1] Changing rates in customs duties also affect demand. Nevertheless, the increase in consumption of these goods is so strongly marked, except for coffee, that it must be a reasonable assumption that the extreme poverty found in some areas was the exception not the rule.

TABLE II

Consumption in lb per capita of coffee, tea, sugar, and tobacco 1820–1900

	COFFEE	TEA	SUGAR	TOBACCO
1820	0·34	1·22	17·74	0·76
1830	0·95	1·26	19·08	0·81
1840	1·08	1·22	15·20	0·87
1850	1·13	1·86	25·26	1·00
1860	1·23	2·67	34·14	1·22
1870	0·97	3·76	47·11	1·32
1880	0·92	4·57	60·28	1·42
1890	0·75	5·17	71·09	1·55
1900	0·71	6·07	85·53	1·95

Source: P. Deane and W. A. Cole, *British Economic Growth 1688–1955* (London: Cambridge University Press, 1962).

The downward plunge of the prices of staple food-stuffs between 1850 and 1900 (see Tables III and IV) likewise suggests that, since wages were more than holding their own with prices, families were far more likely to have money to spare in the second half of the nineteenth century than they were earlier in the century.

TABLE III

Prices in pence of a 4-lb loaf in London

1850	6·75
1860	8·75
1870	8·00
1880	6·98
1890	6·00
1900	5·23

Source: *Sessional Papers* (1904), lxxix.

The significance of this trend is increased if one takes into account the fact that the price of a 4-lb loaf between 1820 and 1840 varied between 10d and 10½d. Beef, mutton, butter, bacon, potatoes (these last two being of particular importance

[1] See B. R. Mitchell and Phyllis Deane, *Abstract of British Historical Statistics* (London: Cambridge University Press, 1962), p. 342.

for the poorer classes), and a wide range of other food-stuffs were also tending to fall in price towards the end of the century. The figures below show the movement.

TABLE IV

Wholesale prices of animal and vegetable foods between 1850 and 1900

1866–7 = 100

	A[1]	B[2]
1850	67	74
1860	91	99
1870	98	88
1880	101	89
1890	82	65
1900	85	62

Source: Sauerbeck, *Statist Price Indices 1846–1938.*

The lists could be extended to include other items. Coal prices, for instance, were lower in the 1890s than they had been in the 1850s, but enough evidence has been given to make the general improvement in the variety and cheapness of food, drink, and other items plain beyond dispute. It only remains to emphasise that while the interpretation of statistics needs to be carried out judiciously it would be absurd to approach the question of the standard of living in the second half of the nineteenth century as if statistics did not exist.[3]

Statistical information taken from the censuses from 1851 to 1901 shows some marked changes in the occupations followed. Some of these changes are of obvious relevance to the matters which have been raised. It is usual, for instance, in attacking the effects of industrialisation to draw attention to the horrors of bad housing, bad sanitation, and overcrowding in the towns. There is clearly something to be said for this in some places and at some times. Yet if conditions were so bad in the towns why were workers so anxious to leave the countryside for the towns? Statistics represent the movement faithfully. In 1851 agriculture gave employment to 20·9 per

[1] A — animal, viz. prime and middling beef and mutton, pork, bacon, and butter.

[2] B — vegetable, viz. English and American wheat, flour, barley, oats, maize, potatoes, rice.

[3] The statistical tables on pp. 204–6 have been compiled from Mitchell and Deane, *Abstract of British Historical Statistics.*

cent of the population; by 1901 this number had shrunk to
8·7 per cent. Some had emigrated, some remained in the
country to work on the railways instead of the land. The
great majority, however, had voluntarily sought work in the
towns, partly because wages there were better for those in
regular employment, partly because town life had attractions
which, as will be seen later, outweighed the overrated charms
of country life. Naturally among those who moved into the
towns there were irresponsible drifters, like those who used
the Embankment as a down-and-outs' dormitory, but these
were scarcely typical. Moving house for a family man in those
days was not a change to be lightly undertaken; unless there
was reasonable certainty of securing employment he would not
take the risk. Nor was it a matter of agriculture being in such
a parlous condition that workers moved out of sheer desperation. The years from the early 1850s to about 1873 have been
described as 'the golden age of agriculture', and though the
description is a little too flattering there is no doubt that
conditions in agriculture were vastly better than they had
been between 1815 and 1850. Even in the last quarter of the
century, often described as a period of depression, agricultural wages tended to be lowest and to fall most sharply
in areas furthest away from industrial towns, in south-west
England and in East Anglia for instance; yet these were
precisely the areas from which movement into the towns was
least likely. When workers did move into towns there was a
strong tendency for the move to be a short one in terms of
distance and into a town with which the worker was already
familiar. This was particularly apt to occur in the north and
midlands, where the close proximity of industrial employment
was a constant inducement to the farmer to pay high wages to
keep his labourers, who nevertheless continued to move
steadily into the towns. The inference is clear that for the
majority of workers it was not a matter of going into the
towns to escape from poverty; they were exchanging a good
wage for a better one and were gaining a little too in reduced
hours of work, especially towards the end of the century. The
bogy of bad urban living conditions, which is apt to receive
excessive attention, seems to have acted as no deterrent at all
to movement into the towns. The worker, from his own experience, probably had fewer illusions about the idyllic condi-

tions of life in a country cottage than some of those who have written on the subject since.

As manufacturing, trading, and financial services became more complex the incentives to move to the towns became still more powerful. It was not only that the general level of wages tended to be higher and employment more regular but also that prospects of advancement were so much greater in the towns. By the end of the nineteenth century the dividing line between the working and the middle classes was becoming much more blurred than it had been earlier, largely because of the increase in the number of men with specialist industrial skills, well rewarded by increased wage differentials. Engineers, ship-building workers, and printers were more numerous and better paid than they had been in the middle of the century, and their pride in their skills sharpened their desire for improved status in society. The greater complexity of mercantile and of financial organisation stimulated the growth in numbers of white-collar workers, and the establishment of a free national system of elementary education between 1870 and 1891 reinforced this strongly marked change in occupational habits. For a small minority of capable men, with thorough practical knowledge of business, the opportunities for self-improvement became greater still with the extension of the limited liability principle between 1858 and 1862. The owner-manager gradually became a less frequent phenomenon. Instead, control of the business was nominally vested in a board of directors elected by the shareholders, but the real power of business decision generally lay with men who had worked their way from the factory floor to the manager's office. Their knowledge and energy were part of the 'living capital' of the firm, and they were rewarded with responsibility and good pay. For men of this kind, as well as for men with specialist industrial skills and, to a lesser extent, for white-collar workers, town life provided a challenge and the hope not only of better pay but also of a higher status in society. The Victorian ideal of respectability is sometimes derided, but there can be no doubt of the sense of achievement experienced by workers and their families when they succeeded in imitating the virtues of the middle class. After all, 'respectability' as the Victorians knew it was a creditable aim; in times when self-help was still more in vogue than

State support the effort required to succeed was great, and
satisfaction with success correspondingly great too.

The great increase in the number of those engaged in occupations where there were good prospects of bettering pay
and status is clear from the following census figures for 1851,
1881, and 1901. The figures for 1851 were calculated on a
different basis from the other two dates given, since, until
1881, it was the practice to include within the various occupational groups men who had retired as well as those currently
working in the occupation concerned. For purposes of comparison the 1851 figures would therefore be lower in practice
than those actually given. However, the figures show quite
clearly which occupations had become attractive by 1901.
The labour force was much more evenly divided by 1901
than it had been in 1851, and the movement naturally enough
had been to occupations such as metal manufacture where
pay and prospects were greater. The occupations cited in
Table V are merely a selection to show the nature of the
change taking place in the major occupations. These occupations have been placed in order so that those with the greatest
proportionate increase in workers have been placed at the head
of the list. The figures are in thousands, and relate to male
workers.

TABLE V

OCCUPATION[1]	1851	1881	1901
Commercial occupations	91	352	597
Transport	433	870	1409
Public administration	64	109	191
Metal manufacture	536	977	1485
Building	496	875	1216
Mining	383	604	931
Professional occupations	162	254	348
Food, drink, tobacco	348	494	701
Domestic offices	193	238	341
Textiles	661	554	557
Agriculture	1788	1517	1339

The main occupations for women in employment changed
less strikingly. The number of women in domestic service in

[1] These occupational descriptions are taken from those adopted in
the 1911 classification. See Mitchell and Deane, *Abstract of British Historical Statistics*, p. 60.

1901, however, was two million, nearly double the number of those similarly employed in 1851. In days when domestic service was plentiful the work was likely to be less arduous than it was in factories, so that women benefited from that, and also of course from the fact that domestic service was a good preparation for home-making for those who married. The increase in the number of women engaged in public administration — there were 326,000 in 1901 compared with 103,000 in 1851 — was another sign that working lives were becoming more varied and responsible than they had been earlier in the century.

Another source of evidence with a firm factual basis is the social legislation of the period. To dismiss this legislation as if it were negligible is nonsensical. *Laissez-faire*, as a social policy, had been given a mortal blow by the legislation of the 1830s, and though it can be argued that the corpse took an uncommonly long time to lie still, to argue in this way shows very little knowledge of politics, history, or of human nature. It is neither possible nor desirable to attempt to cure the country's social ills by instant legislation. Obviously it takes time to prepare the administrative framework for social change, to educate public opinion, to persuade or to outwit opponents inside and outside Parliament. After all, when one considers the extraordinary slowness and inadequacy of twentieth-century legislation on the social and economic problems created by the great increase in motor transport — and this is only one instance — it does not suggest that one can afford to be too condescending about the achievements of the nineteenth-century legislators who were facing problems of a greater magnitude still.

If these achievements are seen in perspective it is astonishing that so much progress was made in so short a time. 'We have been living, as it were, the life of three hundred years in thirty,' wrote Thomas Arnold. As an expression of what was involved for the community in the vast upheaval known as the Industrial Revolution his remark is worth pondering; so too is the tremendous response which was made to the challenge. The social and administrative theories of the Benthamites gave the impetus,[1] and the Civil Service, with its system of recruitment substantially reformed following the North-

[1] See pp. 31 and 39.

cote–Trevelyan report of 1854 and changes in the entry system in 1870, steadily developed more expertise in social administration. It is true that after the outburst of legislation by the Whigs in the 1830s and by Peel in his ministry of 1841–6 the pace of reform slackened. To some extent this was the result of the Crimean War which doubled the rate of taxation; it was also, in part, a result of Palmerston's undue preoccupation with foreign policy. But, more fundamentally, the slackening in the flow of social reform was the result of a phenomenon perfectly familiar to students of British history. There seems to be an almost natural rhythm in which a spurt of social reforms is followed by a lull during which the country adapts itself to the changes which have been made. Common sense rather than coincidence is the heart of the matter and one can see the process at work just as readily in the twentieth century as in the nineteenth.

There is no intention of course of suggesting that social reform came to a standstill between 1846 and the establishment of Gladstone's first Government in 1868. The Ten Hour Bill of 1847, still a landmark in spite of its imperfections, the wide extension of factory regulations in the 1860s, a much greater provision of public baths and wash-houses, reform of hospital conditions, and measures to prevent adulteration of food, were all put into effect within these twenty-two years. Within this period, too, the Act of 1848 set up the Public Health Board. The Board, largely as a result of Chadwick's ebullient personality, had a brief but lively existence. In some ways his pugnacious approach towards inefficiency by local authorities on health matters was an asset. It stirred consciences and produced greater activity than might otherwise have been secured. The Board's report of 1849 points out that where local authorities had taken the precautions suggested, as they did generally in London, the mortality rate in the 1848 cholera epidemic was proportionately much lower than in St Petersburg or Paris. At the same time Chadwick's dedication to his task was of a kind to produce hostility. He was dismissed in 1854 and the Board dissolved in 1858. This did not mean that the attempts to improve public health dried up altogether. After Chadwick's dismissal John Simon exercised powerful and valuable influence on public health reform for over twenty years. He became chief medical officer

to the Public Health Board in 1854 and during the reorganisation of 1858 he was placed in charge of the medical department of the Privy Council. His persuasiveness was of a gentler
kind than Chadwick's, but he was no less determined. By
1875 he had the satisfaction of seeing the first and most vital
phase of his work completed when the local sanitary authorities, established on a national basis in 1872, had their exact
duties prescribed on drainage and other matters relating to
public health. Of course there had been difficulties and delays.
One cannot abolish self-interest and apathy at the stroke of a
pen. Administrative change, without which social reform
would be too haphazard to be effective, is even more difficult
to secure at local level, where the voluntary element is so
strong, than it is in central government. Nevertheless, by
1875 the battle had been won. Was it worth winning? The
statistics on death rates give the best answer to that question.
Between 1861 and 1871 the average death rate was 22·5 per
1,000. It then shrank steadily. Between 1891 and 1901 the
rate was 18·2 per 1,000.

It has been shown that even in the 'lull' period between
1846 and 1868 the reforming principle was so strongly
established that it continued to be influential. Between 1868
and 1888 the pace of reform quickened again. There is no question that by this stage both parties had fully accepted their
responsibility for the conditions of living experienced by the
people. Apart from the organisation of public health functions,
Governments within these twenty years created a national
system of elementary education, tackled bad housing by the
Artisans' Dwelling Act of 1875, strengthened the bargaining
position of the worker by the Conspiracy and Protection of
Property Act and the Employers and Workmen Act, also in
1875, and in 1888 created the county councils and county
borough councils, which have acted as the essential basis for
the administration of social policies ever since. There were of
course many other reforms too which can be found in detail
in the sections on Gladstone, Disraeli, and Joseph Chamberlain. There were blemishes in this legislation at times, and
there were omissions and delays, but these are familiar weaknesses in legislation at any time, particularly when there is
such a flurry of activity. Even in the twentieth century we feel
a little short of Utopia in our social policies, and in the nine-

teenth century they had rather further to go. Comparison with social progress in other countries in the nineteenth century is also misleading. In legislation to protect the worker against the hazards of illness, accident, and old age, Germany was ahead of Britain; on the other hand Germany did not acquire a fully effective code of factory law until 1891, thirteen years after Disraeli's Act of 1878.

There remains to be considered the more speculative matters of the mood and feelings of the thousands of people whose work obliged them to live in the towns. To paint a doleful picture of a working man's life as an eternal triangle made up of the factory, the public house, and the pawn-shop, grossly underestimates his wage packet and his initiative. Materially he was better off than he was before and this has already been demonstrated. But he was better off in other respects too. He had more leisure and greater social freedom than his counterpart in agriculture. The town offered greater variety of enjoyment and developed an ethos of its own. The Londoner in the last quarter of the nineteenth century could take his family by train for an outing to Margate or Brighton, he could play billiards or read at a Working Men's Club, he might watch W. G. Grace play cricket against the Australians, or the home countries playing against each other at football and rugby, he could join, untunefully perhaps, in choruses at the music-hall, or, if he was differently inclined, could take his children by bus or tram to give them instruction at art galleries and museums. Other towns had similar attractions and different ones — one should not, for instance, forget the brass bands of the northern industrial towns and the widespread interest and activity in choral music.

Beyond all these facilities for self-improvement and entertainment there lay also the satisfaction of belonging to a bustling, thriving community. In immediate terms this communal feeling found characteristic expression in the tremendous growth of Friendly Societies whose funds, collected from members' subscriptions, were helpful in tiding workers over the difficulties created by illness and other hazards of a working life. At national level there was a keen awareness of Britain's industrial and naval strength and the satisfaction of belonging to an imperial power for whom all possible rivals entertained a healthy respect. Self-satisfaction may not be an endearing characteristic but it does no harm to morale. Obviously there were some who through misfortunes of character or circumstances did not share in the general well-being, but it would be an extraordinarily ill-balanced view to regard them as typical. For the majority the situation was very different. The evils of industrialism had been largely surmounted, but the benefits survived.

9. WAS THERE A VICTORIAN AGE?

Prelude

It was the best of times, it was the worst of times, it was the age of wisdom, it was the age of foolishness, it was the epoch of belief, it was the epoch of incredulity, it was the season of Light, it was the season of Darkness, it was the spring of hope, it was the winter of despair, we had everything before us, we had nothing before us, we were all going direct to Heaven, we were all going direct the other way — in short, the period was so far like the present period that some of its noisiest authorities insisted on its being received, for good or for evil, in the superlative degree of comparison only.

So Charles Dickens, never a model of conciseness, described the year 1775 in the opening words of *A Tale of Two Cities*, and at the same time makes clear his own belief that in fundamental matters one age is very like another. If he was right, then the habit of christening ages with the names of monarchs — the Georgian Age, the Victorian Age, the Edwardian period, and so on, has no significance except to mark off periods of time.

Even the critics of period labels might be willing to accept, however, that there are clearly marked differences between the ages in externals, in architecture, furniture, dress, and all the other paraphernalia of living. The Victorian Age in this sense creates a readily identified mental picture of Albert watch-chains, imperial beards, bustles, Landseer, gas-lamps, horse-buses, Osborne House, Euston Station, and rooms furnished like souvenir-shops. Whether one moves forward to the bleaker functionalism of modern times or back to the elegant veneer of eighteenth-century society, the external differences between one age and another are sufficiently striking to justify the use of period labels without much risk of contradiction. Argument on external differences of this kind accordingly forms no part of the intention in this chapter. The

main focus of the controversy will be the belief, often advanced, that there were characteristic mental and emotional attitudes which were as unique to the Victorian Age
as its battlemented terrace houses.

Dickens would clearly not have accepted this belief.
Among the general public, however, the word 'Victorian'
means something more than bad taste in furniture; it rouses
associations which are quite clearly defined. For them the
Victorian age is a blend of piety and prejudice, of patriotism
and hypocrisy, of self-reliance and snobbery. Historians are
less positive in their opinions. It is commonplace to assert that
all ages are ages of transition. One age merges imperceptibly
into the next, nineteenth-century intellectualism owes much
to the eighteenth century, and it also looks ahead to the
twentieth century. It would be absurd from this viewpoint
to look on the Victorian period as a Procrustean bed with
strongly defined mental and moral characteristics neatly
chopped off at 1837 and 1901. On the other hand historians are
frequently willing to group together a period of years and to
name it the Age of this or that, according to their inclinations;
the titles of many history books make the tendency plain
enough. It may be historically sound, therefore, to accept that
there was a Victorian Age if it can be established that it had
strongly marked characteristics of its own which differentiate
it clearly from earlier and later ages. The popular view of
Victorianism, after certain reservations have been made, may
still contain a sufficient nucleus of truth to be acceptable;
alternatively Victorianism may be a myth.

Attack

Perhaps the commonest assumption about the Victorian Age
is that it was a religious age, a contrast with the laxity of the
eighteenth century and the spiritual nihilism of the twentieth.
Family prayers, grace before meals, regular church-going,
cross-questioning of children on the content of sermons and
lesson-readings, the study on Sunday afternoons of Foxe's
Book of Martyrs — these and other exercises in spiritual
discipline gave the nation a certainty in its standards of

moral judgment unique since the Reformation; or so it is believed. 'Surely it is possible', says G. M. Young, writing about Gladstone in *Victorian England: Portrait of an Age*, 'to be a religious man and an intelligent man, and yet not deem it necessary to enter into the chamber of the soul, the recesses of the heart, yea, the presence of Almighty God, when the question at issue is whether in the last Irish tussle, the policeman or the Ribbonman hit the other first.' Few would disagree with G. M. Young's logic, but many would accept that in acting in this way Gladstone typified the outlook of his age; one cannot imagine Walpole or any of Britain's modern Prime Ministers assigning quite so much importance to spiritual introspection. Yet if life in the nineteenth century is examined more closely the belief that it was an age of simple faith becomes quite untenable.

Religion in the nineteenth century was a Noah's Ark which had sprung many leaks. There was no reason why they should prove fatal, but it was useless and dangerous to pretend that they did not exist; nor could they be repaired by unintelligent botching. It was understandable that those who believed in an after-life should view the damage with dismay. Geology, archaeology, and biology, all leagued with historical criticism, had been the wreckers. The Victorian period, far from being the age of simple confident faith it is sometimes represented to be, was rent with religious crisis and doubt. In the latter respect at least it is very little different from other ages in modern history, and this strongly suggests the improbability of the idea that the Victorian age had any precisely marked mental characteristics of its own. The first scientific challenge to unthinking orthodoxy was made by Sir Charles Lyell shortly before Victoria's reign began. In his *Principles of Geology* published in three volumes between 1830 and 1833 he exposed the naïveté of Old Testament chronology of the creation of the world. Study of fossils and of remains of Stone Age man gave further evidence that literal acceptance of the Biblical explanation of the creation simply did not tally with visible facts. As soon as it became possible to assign dates to the fossilised remains of prehistoric monsters it also became evident that the order of creation of living things could not have been precisely as the Book of Genesis suggests.

These scientific investigations became the basis of the

H

theory of Natural Selection towards which Chambers, Wallace, and Darwin were all working, though it was the latter who in his *Origin of Species* (1859) first expressed the theory in clear and unmistakable terms. If Darwin's theories were accepted, then evolution had occurred over a far longer period of time than had been visualised in the Book of Genesis, and the references to the creation of fish, whales, fowl, and cattle were merely the kind of hazy approximation to the truth to be found in any folk-lore; more importantly still the Bible gave no indication of Man's own evolution from the animal world. Darwin's theory also raised further doubts. If natural selection was the basis of life was it still reasonable to assume a divine purpose behind the working of the universe or had life evolved simply in accordance with the workings of chance? Only those immune to reason could ignore these questionings. Unfortunately the Church was neither authoritative enough to shake off the challenge nor intelligent enough to come to terms with it, as it could have done quite easily without any abandonment of the central tenets of the Christian faith. It was this inability to distinguish between essentials and dogma which produced the kind of pompous inadequacy displayed by Bishop Wilberforce in the famous discussion at Oxford in 1860 with T. H. Huxley. 'Was it through his grandfather or his grandmother that he claimed his descent from a monkey?' asked the bishop. Religion was under too serious a challenge to be rescued by adolescent witticisms or by ostrich-like evasion. It was one of the ironies of the situation that the scientists who had brought these controversies into the forefront of public attention were far from being enemies of religion, though that fact gave no comfort to those churchmen whose faith owed more to habit than to thought.

The lamentable inability of the leading churchmen to reconcile the discoveries of the scientists with the teachings of Christ was bound to produce spiritual uncertainty. Nor were these doubts the monopoly of a few intellectuals. One of the benefits of the Industrial Revolution was that it had given the middle classes and the more intelligent of the working classes some incentive to use their brains. Mechanics Institutes, providing education after working hours, helped workmen and clerks to become more proficient at their work, but though attempts were made to confine the education given there to this practical purpose, minds once awakened are not easily lulled. It has been estimated that over half a million people were attending these Institutes by 1850; among them there must have been many whose minds had been sufficiently trained to recognise a good argument from a bad one. The Church could no longer bank on unthinking deference from the masses. In addition, even before the crisis precipitated by Darwin's book, the Church had to contend with a dead weight of inertia among large numbers of the population, particularly in the cities. It would have needed more saintliness than the average person is endowed with to keep alive any sense of faith in the squalor in which so many of them had to live. At a census on church attendance held on one Sunday in 1851, 5,288,294 people who were not debarred by age, illness, or occupation from attending a church service failed to attend either morning, afternoon, or evening service. The number of absentees was a little greater than the number of those who attended. Long before the doubts of the scientists and of intellectuals such as George Eliot percolated down to the masses, the Church was ceasing to be a decisive force in the lives of a majority of the population. When one takes into account, too, the fact that outward conformity to religious observance was still expected from those who wished to stand well in the eyes of authority, whether in universities or factories, the notion of the Victorian period as a markedly religious age loses much of its force. No doubt, as it is asserted, it had its share of hypocrisy, but does this distinguish it particularly from any other age before or since?

Even if Lyell, Darwin, and the rest had never existed it is unlikely that the Church would ever have had the influence which is sometimes ascribed to it. It had all the disadvantages which wealth and lack of persecution can bring to a spiritual movement. In rural England particularly the alliance between the clergy and the squirearchy continued to be too close to give the Church the free hand it needs if its views are to be of any consequence. There was every temptation for a clergy-man in a rich country benefice to share the habits and the prejudices of the landowners. Christianity and the *status quo* cannot always be reconciled and these squires in surplices had a preference for the latter. The workings of patronage and of vested interest were no less influential upon those poorer priests so deftly described by Trollope. Conformity was more profitable than criticism and in this the Victorian period was not unique.

The lower classes in the country districts, still relatively thickly populated, found it expedient to attend church. Whether they were impressed with what they heard there is another matter. The marathon three-hour harangues to be heard from eighteenth-century pulpits were no longer in vogue, but sermons were still long enough to be a strain on concentration; in content there was an emphasis on sobriety, thrift, and hard work. These were safe social virtues strongly supported but not extensively practised by the upper classes, a fact unlikely to be overlooked among congregations; cynicism, after all, is at least as likely to be found in the servants' hall as in the master's dining-room. Quite apart from the large numbers of non-attenders at Church disclosed by the 1851 census it would be naïve to believe therefore that the conduct of those who did attend was greatly influenced by their regular attendance. It is unlikely as a matter of common sense that the Victorian period was any more religious, or for that matter any more hypocritical, than the ages which had preceded it or the ages to come. On the contrary the slight hold of religion upon the people of the time is clearly illustrated by the unrest so strongly present throughout the period; that this unrest was not confined to the intellectuals is amply demonstrated by the extensive indications of social disorder, the protest marches, demonstrations, strikes, and riots. The notion that the Victorian period was characterised by a generally accepted standard of values producing social solidarity is odd, even by the standards of historical mythology.

The Church was as much troubled by divisions within as by attacks from without, and this contributed to the mental and spiritual uncertainties of the age. Nonconformist beliefs, particularly Methodism, gathered strength during the century, and this in itself was an indication of the inept leadership provided by the Church of England. In many ways, however, this was merely exchanging one form of blinkered outlook for another. The bitterness of the wrangles between Nonconformity and the Church of England over the control of elementary education is a distasteful reminder of the pettiness of which churchmen were capable, in spite of the central faith which both supposedly shared. The same propensity for straining at gnats and swallowing camels is evident in the tedious controversies over ritualism, and the disproportionate importance attached to Cardinal Newman's lengthy and well-publicised wrestling with his conscience before he joined the Roman Catholic Church. It does not need much perception to recognise that sectarian squabbles and internal divisions do not serve to distinguish the Victorian Age sharply from any other.

The doubts with which the period was riven were not confined to religious controversy. 'The function of the nineteenth century,' wrote G. M. Young, 'was to disengage the disinterested intelligence, to release it from the entanglements of party and sect . . . and to set it operating over the whole range of human life and circumstance.'[1] His penetrating comment can be abundantly justified in detail. Disinterested intelligence is a rare faculty but recognisable. Its possessor is not the prisoner of his age since he has a standard of objective judgment relevant to any period of time. The foremost writers of the Victorian Age were plainly not mere echoes of their age: they had a universality which makes the label 'Victorian' irrelevant except as an indication of the time when these writers were active. Matthew Arnold pillored stupidity, greed, and prejudice with an irony made sharper by his vision of what society might be at its best. Dickens, less constructive, pounded away with his heavy artillery at materialism and ignorance. Respect for independence of mind lies at the heart of the writing of Browning and George Eliot. Tennyson's *In Memoriam* is beset with spiritual uncertainty, J. S. Mill's *Essay on Liberty* with the growing inequality of the struggle between society and the individual. The irony, insight, and essential humanity of Bagehot's writings illuminate the Victorian political scene. Ruskin's *Unto This Last* is the foundation stone of the Labour movement to a much greater extent than Marxism. The list is not exhaustive but the point is perhaps plain. These writers have an objectivity and talent which make them one with Plato, Erasmus, Locke, Swift, Dr Johnson, Shaw, and many others who by a

[1] G. M. Young, *Victorian England: Portrait of an Age*, 2nd ed. (London: Oxford University Press, 1953).

happy blend of common sense and idealism have shaken free
of the transitory prejudices of their own times; their writings
are always relevant. If Arnold and the rest are set in the
balance against those writers and writings considered to be
typically Victorian, Samuel Smiles, or Dickens and Words-
worth at their worst, then a truer view of the age can be
formed. It needs to be remembered, too, that this matter is
not merely of literary significance. Collectively the great Victorian writers, like others before and since, were shaping
ideas not for their own sake, but as a basis for individual and
social conduct.

The Victorian period was plainly far less distinctive than it
is sometimes claimed to be. This is no less true of material
advancement than it is of its religious outlook or of its
philosophy. Close analysis of the nineteenth century makes
one more conscious of its resemblances to the twentieth century than of its differences. Benthamism put *laissez-faire* to
flight and laid the foundation of the Welfare State. The
structure of local government created by the Acts of 1888,
1894, and 1899 remained virtually unchanged until the
London Government Act of 1963, and it seems certain that it
will continue to provide the basic administrative framework
for many years to come in the provinces. Political parties in
the nineteenth century were already beginning to lose some
of their distinctive character. Governmental responsibility
sobered radical zeal while, at the other extreme, Disraeli and
his successors saw the wisdom of making Conservatism a
national rather than a class movement. 'The Conservatives,'
said Alexander Macdonald in 1880, 'have done more for the
working classes in five years than the Liberals in fifty.' The
extensions of the franchise in 1832, and particularly in 1867
and 1884, ensured by an unobtrusive revolution, more glorious
than 1688, that sovereign power passed from the politicians
to the people, or, more accurately, to adult male voters. In
this, too, the twentieth century is foreshadowed, as it is in the
fears of State authoritarianism which prompted Mill and
others to write in defence of individual freedoms. The parallels
between the two centuries become almost innumerable. Are
there not close similarities between the heated disputes over
defence expenditure in the twentieth century, and those on
the same subject in the late nineteenth century which helped

to produce Gladstone's resignation in 1894? Was not Britain's
nervousness of Germany closely akin to its modern fears of
Russia and China? Was there not the same strange compound of guilt and paternalism in the nineteenth-century
attitude towards Empire as there has been in the twentieth?
Has the twentieth century a greater monopoly of pleasure-
loving decadence than Britain had in the 1890s? Are Oscar
Wilde and Aubrey Beardsley without their modern parallels?
Did the exploration of the African continent stir the imagination any less than the modern voyages into space? Had not
trade unionism left far behind it the stage when it was piti-
fully defenceless against employers? Had not the political
influence of the Queen been reduced to a shadow? Was there
not persistent criticism of British industrial techniques and
training at least from the time of the 1851 Exhibition onwards? Did not the possibility of speedy travel by rail have
at least as much impact on social, economic, and military
development as speedy travel by air in the twentieth century?
In short, the background to the lives of our Victorian fore-
fathers, and the issues which troubled them, were remarkably
similar to those of modern times: in writing about the Victorians we are writing about ourselves; the period label is
an irrelevance.

To speak of the Victorian Age as if it were a single entity is
a quite untenable position. The monarch who gave her name
to the age ruled for over sixty years. The artificiality of re-
garding this period of time as being in some way self-contained
is plain if, by a parallel process, one takes a period of some
sixty years in the twentieth century and expects the intellectual and moral outlook to be the same at the end as at the
beginning. The changes in the Victorian period were no less
great. It is only necessary to think of a few of the contrasts,
Lord Melbourne and Joseph Chamberlain, the Duke of
Wellington and Disraeli, Carlyle and Kipling, Macaulay and
H. G. Wells, or, in other terms, the vast changes in attitude
towards trade unionism, voting rights, the conduct of elections, and national responsibilities for matters of health and
education, to realise the impossibility of considering the
Victorian Age as a unity. At the beginning of the period there
are traces of eighteenth-century selfishness and complacency
in the business of government. In the middle years of the

century there is a transitional period of uncertainty, represented, for instance, in the writings of Dickens and even of
Macaulay, when there was a revulsion against privilege and
prejudice but no clear vision of the precise role of the State in
society; the uncertainty on this matter is curiously parallel
both in time and nature to the crisis in religious thought pro-
voked by Lyell, Darwin, and the rest. Finally, from about
1870 onwards, there emerged a broad measure of agreement
among both Liberals and Conservatives that the State had an
active duty to promote the welfare of all the people. If it is
necessary to think in terms of ages at all there are thus at
least three Victorian Ages, and it would not be difficult to
create still further sub-divisions.

Naturally these changes, like earth-tremors, produced
ripples of movement throughout the whole structure of
society. At the beginning of the period the privileges of the
Establishment, the great landowners, the county gentry, the
Church, seemed timeless and immovable. The only hope of
progress for the working man was to accept society as he
found it and to strive, by means of the thrifty, sober, hard-
working behaviour so often advocated by his betters, to attain
the ideal of respectability. By the end of the century his
power of social manœuvre was by no means so restricted.
It was not respectability which earned the dockers their
'tanner an hour' in 1889; and it was the votes of the working
classes not their virtues which stimulated the spate of social
legislation from 1868 onwards.

One aspect of the Victorian legend remains to be demolished
and this centres on the person and influence of the Queen herself. A long reign supposedly gives greater influence to the
monarch. Constant contact with public affairs and with
leading statesmen is assumed to build up a store of experience
and political judgment, so that the monarch's advice on public
affairs becomes of real significance instead of a meaningless
formality. In Victoria's reign the reverse is true. As a self-
willed girl she was able to prevent the Conservatives from
taking office in 1839, when she refused to take Peel's advice
on the appointment of her Bedchamber attendants. Her dislike of Palmerston was instrumental in securing his dismissal
by Lord John Russell in 1851. Yet by the end of the period
her tetchy opposition to Gladstone's policies had become

WAS THERE A VICTORIAN AGE? 225

wholly ineffectual. It was said that at Cabinet meetings Gladstone would read to ministers the views of the Queen on
political issues. The Cabinet would listen in respectful but
unimpressed silence, then pass on to the business of the
day.

It might be argued perhaps that the Queen gained in her
personal influence upon the community in proportion as her
political influence diminished. Certainly as she grew older
there was some sympathy for her of a general kind. The
misfortune of Prince Albert's early death, the Prince of
Wales's serious illness in 1871, and the sense of pathos in the
jubilee celebrations in 1887 and 1897 springing from the contrast between the colourful splendour of the ceremonies and
the small, rotund, and aged lady at their centre, all contributed for brief periods of time to give the Queen some popularity among her subjects. Newspapers, particularly *The
Times*, became excessively sentimental about the monarchy
during the Queen's last years. Few people, however, would
subscribe to the view that *The Times* was particularly representative of public opinion. In forming an impression of Queen
Victoria's influence one needs to take into account both the
feeling of dislike which she roused at times and the more permanent feeling that monarchy was now merely a convenient
anachronism. The Queen's adoration of her husband roused no
answering sentiment among her countrymen. Prince Albert's
Teutonic virtues won him no support in spite of the valuable
contributions he made to scientific progress, to the success of
the 1851 Exhibition, and to a more rational foreign policy
than Palmerston favoured. He remained an alien. Nor was
the Queen herself blessed with the charm and intelligence
which might have reconciled the country to the marriage. The
pettiness of her interventions in politics, her childlike partiality for Disraeli, and her rudeness to Gladstone were the
marks of an immature mind. Her views on political matters
were clouded by a compound of prejudice and personal
antagonisms which made them irrelevant, particularly in a
period which witnessed such a ferment of change. When
Prince Albert died in 1861 Victoria's mind, never very constructive, died with him. Far from being influential her
attitude to her responsibilities roused strong antagonism. 'A
retired widow and an unemployed youth' was Bagehot's
*

succinct description of the Queen and the Prince of Wales. Republicanism, stemming from the Queen's neglect of her public duties, became a more powerful force than it had been since the seventeenth century. Republican clubs existed in some of the large cities. Sir Charles Dilke and Henry Labouchère, prominent members of the Liberal Party, were strongly critical of the monarchical system, in spite of the Queen's grave displeasure. Beyond all these criticisms of the Queen there lies too the general consideration that the mass of the community is far too preoccupied with personal matters to care very much about what takes place in palaces. For most people the Queen was merely a symbol of government, a distant recluse of no consequence in everyday life.

Historians are rightly sceptical about the use of 'label' terms in history. Terms which are invented as a kind of convenient historical shorthand can take on an absolute significance out of all proportion to their worth, if they are unthinkingly used. The phrase 'Industrial Revolution' is a notorious instance of the way in which a 'label' term can lead to wholly misleading conclusions. The stereotyped descriptions of the Industrial Revolution as if it were some national disaster have long since been superseded by the efforts of scholars who have shown the unevenness of its effects, and who have furthermore made some important reservations about the wisdom of using the term 'Industrial Revolution' at all. Precisely the same disciplined thinking needs to be applied to the term 'the Victorian Age'. Except for the trivial connection to be made with the years of Queen Victoria's accession and death the term 'Victorian Age' has no significance. It has no beginning and no end. It looks back to the eighteenth century and to the Regency — 'there was Victorianism before Victoria', comments Asa Briggs,[1] and it equally looks forward to Edwardian England and to modern times. 'I read constantly', writes G. M. Young, 'that the Victorians did this and the Victorians believed that; as if they had lived within the sound of the town-crier's bell, and at all times behaved, and thought, and worshipped with the disciplined unanimity of a city state on a holy day.'[2] It sounds, as he implies, inherently improbable. The Victorian Age, in

---

[1] Briggs, *The Age of Improvement*, p. 452.
[2] Young, *Victorian England: Portrait of an Age*, p. 150.

short, differs little if at all in fundamental matters from any other age; within it is found all the confusion of purpose and outlook commonly found in human affairs at any period in history: the term is a myth.

Defence

There is no doubt that some periods of history, to a greater extent than others, have the faculty of stirring the interest of later generations. The excitements of the Tudor period make more impact on the minds of most people than the dreary struggles of Lancaster and York in the fifteenth century. There are arid reaches in eighteenth- and twentieth-century history when, in spite of great wars and political crises, there is a somnolence of the spirit which conveys itself to the student. It needs to be stated at the outset, therefore, that to view history as if it were a continuous line of uniform development with one age merging imperceptibly into another in a sea of anonymity is a gross misrepresentation. There are crests and troughs in the history of human physical and mental achievement; the Victorian Age, like the Elizabethan Age with which it has much in common, is plainly a crest period and clearly recognisable.

Obviously in a period of some sixty years it is possible to attack generalisations about Victorianism and to draw attention to differences in outlook among the intellectuals and among the mass of the people. Yet much of what passes for historical criticism of label terms, such as 'the Industrial Revolution', 'the Victorian Age', and so on, is merely a matter of minute investigation of the fringe activities of great social movements. Knowledge of deviations from the pattern is valuable, but not if it leads to the topsy-turvy notion that there was no pattern at all. It is as if one were to deny that there was an Italian Renaissance because some obscure Florentine shopkeeper had never heard of the Mona Lisa. Popular descriptions of historical periods may fall short of the high standards of scholarship, but they are based on the common-sense approach that a wood is not the same as a tree — a simple fact which can escape specialist historians.

Life in the nineteenth century had been transmuted by twin revolutions — the French Revolution and the Industrial Revolution. The onset of these two powerful disruptive forces has conditioned the course of all subsequent history. By coincidence Queen Victoria came to the throne almost precisely at the time that Britain was beginning to come to terms, in her own cautious way, with some of the consequences of these political and economic revolutions. The 1832 Reform Act, and the abandonment of *laissez-faire* implicit in the social reforms of Grey's ministry, signalise this new stage. By coincidence, too, Victoria died just when the political and social framework for the development of twentieth-century Britain had been completed. The social legislation of Gladstone and Disraeli, the revolutionary recasting of the administrative structure involved in the reorganisation of local government between 1888 and 1899, and the wide extension of the vote in 1867 and 1884, these were the most important reactions of the politicians to the problems posed originally by the French and Industrial Revolutions. By the end of Victoria's reign it could reasonably be claimed that the foundations on which the Liberals were to build so spectacularly between 1906 and 1914 had been laid. It was clearly a matter of chance that Victoria's reign virtually coincided with such an important phase in Britain's history: her influence upon the developments which took place was negligible, even negative at times, yet by her mere existence she gave a sense of unity to the period.

One of the consequences of the fundamental readjustment of outlook taking place in Victorian times was that values which had been at least nominally accepted previously now began to be strongly challenged. Much can be made of the criticisms of orthodoxy which followed the writings of Darwin and Lyell, and of the proliferation of divisions within religion represented by the Tractarians, the Methodists, the Christian Socialists, the ritualists, and so on. It is easy to overlook the fact that divisions, doubts, and criticisms did not mean that religion had become the inert force which it is for many in the twentieth century. On the contrary the vigour of the disputes was an indication of the vitality of religion. Perfect unanimity is only found in cemeteries. Victorian religion was not dead. It was a powerful living force, worth arguing about, especially at a time when the certainties of faith had been made all the more important by the uncertainty of everything else.

Religion was the backbone of Victorian life. Snug within their Oxford colleges dons might flirt with agnosticism. Exhibitionists like Oscar Wilde capered before the public, eagerly trading a virtue for a paradox, so long as it secured them a little attention. For the mass of the people these posturings were irrelevant. Nor will it do to argue on the basis of statistics on church attendance that religion was not a powerful force in society. The figures taken on Census Sunday 1851 show that about half of those who might theoretically have been expected to attend church on that day failed to do so. Leading churchmen were shocked by the numbers of absentees and this in itself indicates the responsible view they took of their duty of moral leadership of the community; so too does the spate of church-building which followed this revelation, since in industrial areas particularly a shortage of seating contributed to absenteeism. Yet if churches in twentieth-century Britain could muster an attendance of 50 per cent of the population it would be looked upon as evidence of a national spiritual renaissance. It was not until the end of the nineteenth century that there is the kind of decline in church attendance which was to become commonplace in the twentieth century.[1]

Throughout almost all the Victorian period, therefore, there was a strong nucleus of people who regularly attended church. The discipline of church life would have a strong influence on genuine believers, and some influence even on those who attended church merely to secure social standing. It is true that church-going made more appeal to the middle classes than to the working classes, but from the nineteenth century onwards it has been the middle classes who have imposed their moral stamp on society. It was the middle-class notion of respectability, later derided so unfairly by Shaw, which set the pattern of conduct for the more responsible members of the working classes. In this way religious influence reached right down to the roots of Victorian society and made people aware of their moral responsibilities in a manner which clearly differentiates the period from Regency or Edwardian England, for instance. Of course there were deviations. Those

[1] See Ensor, *England 1870–1914*, pp. 305–10.

who wished to lead dissipated lives could do so with very little difficulty in London or other large cities. But when abuses existed they were at least recognised for what they were by an age which had sufficient awareness of religious principles to be able to distinguish between right and wrong. Evangelism, in Ensor's words, 'induced a highly civilised people to put pleasure in the background, and what it conceived to be its duty in the foreground, to a quite exceptional degree.'[1] Religion was then a pervading influence, and it was stimulated not quenched by the controversy which followed the publication of *The Origin of Species*. Darwin's book was not an attack on religion, but it was an attack on slovenly thinking about religion. Obviously there were many church-goers who continued to worship as their ancestors had done, supremely indifferent to the excitements of evolution, and perhaps they were not any the worse for that. On the other hand, for the more thoughtful church-goers Darwin's theory was an incentive to study and perhaps revise their religious beliefs. It was perfectly possible for faith to be strengthened not weakened by this process. 'The reverse side of the respect for honest doubt was the respect for honest faith.'[2]

Family life gained immeasurably from the firm foundation given by regular religious devotions. This not only meant attendance at church two or three times a day on Sunday, but also attendance at a mid-week service and the devotion of most of Sunday to religious self-improvement with a dedication little removed from monasticism. Even among the less devout the Victorian Sunday possessed a special atmosphere of its own which could hardly fail to be influential. The State and the Church, with the willing co-operation of many of the people, made every effort to preserve Sunday as a holy day in a way which is popularly and rightly conceived to be characteristically Victorian. The day was set aside for the recreation of spiritual life, not for recreation in any more general sense. On the contrary, distractions were avoided, by legislation where necessary. In 1856, for instance, on the insistence of Sumner, the Archbishop of Canterbury, military bands were forbidden to play in London parks on Sunday afternoons.

[1] Ensor, *England 1870–1914*, p. 138.
[2] W. L. Burn, *The Age of Equipoise* (London: Allen & Unwin, 1964), p. 276.

It was only after persistent campaigning by the National Sunday League that Sunday opening of museums and art galleries was secured, and the concession only came about in 1896, almost at the end of the Victorian period. Likewise, it was not until late in the nineteenth century that railway excursions began to make possible the outings which were ultimately to revolutionise the nation's Sunday habits. No doubt there was an element of Grundyism in this restrictive attitude to pleasure, however innocent, but there was an element of self-discipline in it too. One of its most valuable by-products was a strong sense of family solidarity founded on a mutual acceptance of clearly defined moral standards. Ensor has pointed out the immense popularity of the song 'Home Sweet Home' which 'became for the seventies and eighties a second National Anthem, simply because of the idea which it expressed'.[1] Cynics may suggest that not every home was sweet but at least there was an intention to make it so among the middle class and among the growing number of working-class people ambitious to achieve social respectability.

The strong religious bias of the period not only influenced individual conduct and family life; it also generated a practical helpfulness towards those in need or distress which welded the community together in a way difficult to imagine in the twentieth century. The Welfare State has made a fundamental contribution to human progress, but inevitably it has pushed into the background the need for acts of personal kindness; yet before the development of modern methods of assisting those in need it was only by acts of personal initiative and kindness that families could be saved from the humiliation of entry into the workhouse, and that others, less hard-pressed, could be given the incentive to save and to plan for the future. The extent to which philanthropy was practised in the Victorian period would be remarkable if it were not the expected consequence of the steady inculcation of a code of moral conduct. Sickness and Friendly Societies tided working people over difficulties. Then, too, Victorian charity, though it may have had a trace of condescension, was on a generous scale. A committee set up to investigate the working of Poor Relief in London during the severe winter of 1860–1 was told by one witness that but for charitable subscriptions 'there would

[1] Ensor, *England 1870–1914*, p. 169.

have been a fearful loss of life from starvation'.[1] There were many funds and clubs to encourage sensible management of money to provide for basic needs. There were Blanket Clubs, Coal Clubs, and Children's Clubs. There were savings banks, insurance societies, and building societies. There were church missions and hospital committees, while in country districts the squire and his family, and the parson and his family, took it as part of their expected duties to visit the villagers and to help them when they were in difficulties. Philanthropy was the everyday accompaniment of Victorian life and was made the more necessary by the social and economic upheaval brought about by the Industrial Revolution. There is nothing to match this great fund of active personal sympathy for distress in the twentieth century, nor in the pre-Victorian period; it is permissible therefore to regard it as a distinctive Victorian characteristic.

The Victorian community shared another identifiable characteristic, and this was its faith in progress. The same self-confidence is found to some degree in the eighteenth century, but only among intellectuals hopeful that rationalism could create a new world. These bookish ideals existed in the nineteenth century — Tennyson's *In Memoriam* shows a similar idealism in places — but the advances being made in the Victorian period were of a kind which could be appreciated by everyone. The sudden upsurge of population in the industrial towns, the enormous social and economic consequences of constructing an extensive network of railway lines, the feeling that Britain was both the workshop of the world and its banker, the changes in food habits made possible by the use of refrigeration on cargo ships, the exploration of the African continent and the acquisition of so much imperial territory, all these were matters which could easily be comprehended by the mass of the community. They were equally aware of their own deep involvement in the consequences of these changes. Voting rights, education, trade unionism, the economic and social responsibilities of government, these were issues which had scarcely arisen in the eighteenth century but they were issues with which the Victorians had to come to terms in a changing world, devising solutions without

[1] Quoted in *English Historical Documents*, ed. Douglas, vol. xii (i), p. 737.

precedents to guide them. In these matters the Victorians were pioneers; politicians and people were buoyed up by the challenge which half-solved problems present. No one can seriously claim that the Victorian Age was static, but it was not fragmentary and unpredictable as modern Britain is. Change was taking place then as now, but it was change being acted out against the unchanging backcloth of moral certainty and optimism to be found in a society upheld by an active faith. In this sense the popular view of the Victorian Age as one of solidarity and stability is founded on truth.

The popular belief that the Victorian Age was uniquely religious is often accompanied by an equally strong belief that it was uniquely hypocritical. Victorian writers themselves were aware of the dichotomy. Dickens provides Mr Murdstone, Mr Squeers, and Uriah Heep as evidence, Matthew Arnold castigates the middle-class Philistines, Charlotte Brontë creates the unpleasant Mr Brocklehurst in *Jane Eyre*. At a lower level there is the intolerable smugness of juvenile know-alls found in *Pleasant Pages for Young People* and other books of that kind. It was, said Grote succinctly, 'the Age of Steam and Cant'. It is too terse a description to trap the truth, but the correlation between Victorianism and hypocrisy is more than a chance association of ideas. The strict discipline which Nonconformity, in particular, imposed on its adherents gave strength where it succeeded, but its intolerance towards human weakness was an incitement to hypocrisy for those incapable of maintaining the high standards set. Even so the faint odour of cant which filters through from the Victorian period is in itself a tribute to the fact that there were widely accepted tenets of moral behaviour; in a society where permissiveness has eroded traditional standards hypocrisy is superfluous.

The woman who gave her name to the age summed up in herself many of its characteristics. Though not a religious devotee, conventional religion moulded her outlook. Metaphysical problems left her indifferent. Yet like so many of her subjects she had acquired, as if through the pores, a settled judgment on moral issues which remained entirely intact, in spite of scientific discoveries and theological disputes. Her attitude to divorce, for instance, made it impossible for Sir Charles Dilke to remain a minister of the Crown in 1886 when a divorce case in that year failed to clear him entirely of responsibility as co-respondent. The Queen's judgment on matters of this kind was harsh but consistent. At times individuals such as Lady Flora Hastings and Dilke suffered, probably unjustly, but there is no doubt that the Queen's stern moral sense purged Court life of laxity. Even as a very young queen the strength of her influence was felt. Lord Melbourne, writes Asa Briggs, 'watched his language — usually "interlarded with damns" — sat bolt upright in his chair, and greatly restricted the range of his anecdotes.'[1]

The Queen's early marriage to Prince Albert reinforced this side of her character. His Teutonic earnestness and devotion to family life mirrored similar qualities in his wife and in many of her subjects. Albert was perhaps a little more intelligent than the British like their rulers to be, but it was an intelligence softened by the almost overpowering domesticity so easily sensed in Osborne House, the Queen's favourite residence. Albert did not live long enough for respect to change into popularity, but while he lived the royal couple were an exemplar to the people of qualities which many of them possessed themselves. Winterhalter's portrait of the Queen and her husband, surrounded by the royal children, uniformly depicted with faces of expressionless innocence, may be bad art, but it represents a sentiment, and a sentimentality, not to be found at other times in history.

The shock of Albert's death put Victoria out of tune with her times for many years, but the sympathetic relationship between the Queen and Disraeli brought that phase to an end long before her death. In the last twenty-five years of her reign she was often the spokesman of her people — their naïve patriotism, their sentimental imperialism are faithfully reflected in her utterances. 'Oh, if the Queen were a man,' she wrote to Disraeli in 1878, 'she would like to go and give those Russians, whose word one cannot believe, such a beating!' Nor did empire-building give her any inhibitions. She took an almost childish delight in the title of 'Empress of India' adopted in 1876 at Disraeli's suggestion and in the teeth of Liberal opposition which infuriated the Queen. The jubilee celebrations of 1887 and 1897 were used to glorify a Kiplingesque view of Empire, with the queen as a mother-

[1] *The Age of Improvement*, p. 454.

figure of Britain and the Empire, her formal clothes a dramatic contrast with the bright garb of the colonial representatives. Enthusiastic crowds revelled in the colour and the symbolism of these occasions. Even Victoria's cantankerous opposition to Gladstone roused an answering feeling among the people. In part it stemmed from personal antipathy, but at a deeper level it represented the deeply embedded conservatism which is one half of the character of the British people. Her outburst against the feminist movement, 'this mad and wicked folly of women's rights' as she described it, and her suspicions that Joseph Chamberlain planned to subvert the Constitution, stem from the same source. Alongside this resistance to hasty change there was a sturdy confidence not only in herself but also in the nation. When the British experienced three separate defeats at the hands of the Boers within six days in December 1899, generals and politicians did not invariably respond with the same steadiness as the Queen. 'Please understand', she said to Balfour, 'that there is no one depressed in *this* house; we are not interested in the possibilities of defeat; they do not exist.' The words matched the spirit of her people. Like her they had a strongly ingrained belief that the Almighty wished to employ Britain as a universal governess and He would not allow temporary set-backs to prejudice her position.

If one wants to find the touchstone of reality in Victorianism perhaps in the end one cannot do better than study the character of the Queen herself. Censorious, insular, impetuous, and sentimental, but confident in her own standard of values and in the greatness of her people, the Queen herself epitomises the weaknesses and the strengths of Victorianism. Her character and long life give the period an underlying theme which makes the variations of little consequence. At all levels of Victorian society one sees reflections of the Queen's qualities. She was as jingoistic as Palmerston, as romantic as Disraeli, as moral, and as self-opinionated, as Gladstone. She was well endowed with that obtuse self-confidence which permeates the *Punch* political cartoons of the period and which is, indeed, omnipresent in Victorian society. When the Queen died an extremely perceptive tribute was paid by Sir John Marriott, in an obituary in *The Times*, to the power of her influence upon her people:

The Queen is dead! The news is benumbing to the heart and brain. The cornerstone of our National and Imperial life, nay, of our individual and family life, is suddenly displaced. We cannot as yet realise what it means; what life in the future will mean bereft of her whose august, beloved, and venerated personality has been for the greater part of the century the centre and mainspring of our national existence.

Victoria was Victorianism; just as individuals have a unique quality so has her age.

SUGGESTIONS FOR FURTHER READING

There are very full bibliographies on the period in *The Age of Reform 1815–70*, 2nd ed. (Oxford: Clarendon Press, 1962) by Sir Llewellyn Woodward and in *England 1870–1914* (Oxford: Clarendon Press, 1936) by R. C. K. Ensor. Both authors give frank and instructive comments on the books mentioned. Younger students, however, may find the scale of these detailed bibliographies a little daunting. If so, they will appreciate the simplicity of the bibliography given in *Nineteenth-Century Britain* (London: Longmans, 1960) by Anthony Wood. There are a few important additions to be made of books published since the bibliography was compiled, but it still remains a valuable and varied source of ideas for further reading. The inclusion by the author of a list of nineteenth-century fiction and non-fiction is of particular interest for those who wish to recapture the atmosphere of nineteenth-century thought.

Documentary sources are listed in the books so far mentioned but by their nature are more appropriate often for the specialist professional historian than for the younger student. However, the latter could profitably gain first-hand experience of the ideas of his nineteenth-century predecessors by studying such excellent books of collected documentary extracts as *English Historical Documents*, General editor D. C. Douglas, vol. xi, 1783–1832 (1959); vol. xii (i), 1833–74 (1956) (London: Eyre & Spottiswoode); *Readings in Economic and Social History* (London: Macmillan, 1964) by M. W. Flinn, and *Human Documents of the Industrial Revolution in Britain* (London: Allen & Unwin, 1966) by E. Royston Pike. Of several books of contemporary memoirs possibly the most valuable and interesting terms of character assessment are *The Greville Memoirs* (London: Batsford, 1963) edited by R. Fulford. They cover the period 1821–60.

Among general histories those already mentioned, *The Age of Reform 1815–70* by Sir Llewellyn Woodward and *England 1870–1914* by R. C. K. Ensor, provide an essential backbone to study of the period. If the reader then proceeds to *History*

238   SUGGESTIONS FOR FURTHER READING

of the English People in the Nineteenth Century by E. Halévy (London: Benn, 1961) vol. i–vi, he will be better fitted to appreciate the differences of interpretation which the French historian skilfully brings to bear on the same material. Volume iv, 1841–95, was not completed at the time of the author's death, but R. B. McCallum has added a supplementary section to take the narrative down to 1895. *The Age of Improvement* (London: Longmans, 1959) by Asa Briggs is a useful addition to the books mentioned, more particularly because of the emphasis he gives to social and economic development. There are many smaller text-books for those requiring a less detailed approach. *Nineteenth-Century Britain* by Anthony Wood, and *Reaction and Reform 1793–1868* (London: Blandford, 1963) by John Derry are excellent examples of this kind.

Social and economic matters are of such paramount importance during the nineteenth century that they deserve particular attention even by the non-specialist reader. *An Economic History of Modern Britain*, vol. i, 1820–50, 2nd ed. (London: Cambridge University Press, 1964) and vol. ii, 1850–86 (1932), by Sir John Clapham, contains very interesting detail and a sense of high scholarship which still makes it authoritative. Of the more recent general social and economic histories T. S. Ashton's *Industrial Revolution 1760–1830* (London: Oxford University Press, 1948), S. G. Checkland's *The Rise of Industrial Society in England 1815–1885* (London: Longmans, 1964), and W. Ashworth's *An Economic History of England 1870–1939* (London: Methuen, 1960) provide between them expert coverage of the periods specified. The emphasis in these books is on economic rather than social change. This approach is reversed in *A Social and Economic History of Britain 1760–1960*, 3rd ed. (London: Harrap, 1962) by Pauline Gregg. The book contains a mass of vivid detail on social habits and living conditions, and its avoidance of the specialist vocabulary sometimes adopted by modern economic historians makes it well within the grasp of young students. Agriculture remained the major occupation of the British people throughout most of the nineteenth century and for an understanding of the conditions and problems of the agricultural population it is doubtful if any other book can match *English Farming, Past and Present*, 6th ed. (London: Heinemann Educational, 1961) by Lord Ernle.

In addition to these books the following are also valuable for consultation on the subjects discussed in the various chapters.

1. Lord Liverpool — Arch-Mediocrity?

There is a useful biography by Sir Charles Petrie *Lord Liverpool and His Times* (London: Barrie, 1954). It is less concerned with the political mechanism of power than is the fashion among some recent historians; this has its advantages. It is perhaps too flattering as an estimate of Lord Liverpool, but in compensation there are many interesting selections from Lord Liverpool's letters and the book has the salient virtue that the central character does emerge credibly as a person. *Waterloo to Peterloo* (London: Mercury, 1963) by R. J. White, is concerned with a very limited period, as its title shows, but the author's understanding and his lively style give an insight into the mood of the times which more ponderous books cannot match. The books mentioned in the general works on social and economic history are particularly relevant to this chapter, since judgment on Lord Liverpool is bound up to a greater extent with internal policies than it is with foreign policy where Castlereagh and Canning made their own strongly individualistic contributions. Those seeking a quick but shrewd assessment of the Congress System and Britain's part in it could usefully consult *From Vienna to Versailles* (London: Methuen, 1955) by L. C. B. Seaman. The last phase of Lord Liverpool's ministry is illuminatingly described by W. R. Brock in *Lord Liverpool and Liberal Toryism* (London: Cambridge University Press, 1941).

2. The Whigs 1830–41 — Reformers or Reactionaries?

The biographies by Sir George Trevelyan, *Lord Grey of the Reform Bill* (London: Longmans, 1929), and by Lord David Cecil, *Lord M.* (London: Constable, 1954) are both products of scholarship and keen observation of human affairs. The extent of Benthamite influence on social reforms, both in the decade described in this chapter and later, is an important issue in nineteenth-century history. *Jeremy Bentham* (London:

Heinemann, 1962) by M. P. Mack, gives the theory of Benthamism and is difficult but rewarding reading. Those who also
wish to see the principles of Benthamism being put into action
by a forthright personality should read *The Life and Times of
Sir Edwin Chadwick* (London: Methuen, 1952) by S. E. Finer.
Two reprints from *Economic History Review* articles in *Essays
in Economic History* (Arnold, 1962) vol. 3, edited by E. M.
Carus-Wilson are particularly relevant to the ideas mentioned
in this chapter. They are 'The New Poor Law' by H. L.
Beales and '*Laissez-faire* and State Intervention in Nineteenth-Century Britain' by J. B. Brebner. The article by
M. E. Rose, 'The Allowance System under the New Poor
Law' *Economic History Review*, 2nd Series, vol. xix, no. 3
(December 1966) has some interesting information on the
continuance of outdoor relief after 1834. For the Reform Act
of 1832 it would be difficult to find a more realistic appraisal
than that given by N. Gash in *Politics in the Age of Peel*
(London: Longmans, 1953).

3. Peel and the Tories — Martyr or Renegade?

Peel's enigmatic character and the almost equally puzzling
changes in party structure and organisation taking place in
his time are described with a great fund of scholarship by N.
Gash in *Politics in the Age of Peel* (London: Longmans, 1953)
and in *Mr Secretary Peel* (London: Longmans, 1961). Most of
the dramatic interest of Peel's career centres on his part in
the repeal of the Corn Laws. For a fuller understanding of the
issues involved, knowledge of the social and economic influences at work is essential. The following books and articles
have proved to be particularly helpful in this respect: *The
Anti-Corn Law League* (London: Allen & Unwin, 1958) by
N. McCord; *The Manchester School of Economics* (London:
Oxford University Press, 1960) by W. D. Grampp; *Economic
Elements in the Pax Britannica* (Cambridge, Mass.: Harvard
University Press, 1958) by A. H. Imlah; 'The Corn Laws and
High Farming,' *Economic History Review*, 2nd Series, vol.
xviii, no. 3 (December 1965) by D. C. Moore; and 'Progress
and Poverty in Britain 1780–1850' by A. J. Taylor in *Essays
in Economic History*, vol. 3 (London: Arnold, 1962) edited by
E. M. Carus-Wilson.

4. Palmerston and Foreign Policy — Ginger Beer or Champagne?

For many years the major biography of Lord Palmerston was that by H. C. F. Bell, *Lord Palmerston*, 2 vols. (London: Longmans, 1936). There is also now a very recent assessment by D. G. Southgate, *The Most English Minister* (London: Macmillan, 1966), which is a very full and well documented study. The European background to Palmerston's activities is described by A. J. P. Taylor in his usual trenchant manner in *The Struggle for Mastery in Europe 1848–1918* (Oxford: Clarendon Press, 1954). There is a brief but masterly sketch of Palmerston's character in *Historical Essays* (New York: Anchor Books, Doubleday, 1965) by W. Bagehot

5. Gladstone — Statesman or Bigot?

Gladstone combined force of character with unpredictability of behaviour to an extent which makes it impossible perhaps to write a biography of him which is wholly convincing. Nevertheless there have been two outstanding attempts to overcome this difficulty in J. Morley's *Life of Gladstone*, 3 vols. (London: Macmillan, 1903) and in Sir Philip Magnus's *Gladstone* (London: Murray, 1954). Again there are some brief but illuminating comments on Gladstone in Bagehot's *Historical Essays*. The interesting issue of Gladstone's contribution to Liberalism is examined by J. L. Hammond and M. R. D. Foot in *Gladstone and Liberalism* (London: English Universities Press, 1952).

6. Disraeli — Statesman or Charlatan?

Disraeli (London: Eyre & Spottiswoode, 1966) by R. Blake appeared after this chapter was written. Its important assessment of Disraeli's influence upon Toryism is the result of lengthy and scholarly research of the highest quality; it is precisely the kind of book to meet the needs of students weighing up the clash of opinion over Disraeli's achievements. The standard biography previously was that by W. F. Monypenny and G. E. Buckle, *The Life of Benjamin Disraeli, Earl of Beaconsfield* (London: Murray, 1910–20). It still retains its importance. Volumes 4–6, dealing with the years 1855–81, are the most relevant to this chapter. There are brief but interesting assessments of Disraeli's work and character in *Victorian People* (London: Odhams, 1954) by A. Briggs, and in Bagehot's *Historical Essays*, though the latter's harsh appraisal is a warning perhaps of the danger of accepting all contemporary estimates as if they were true gold.

7. Joseph Chamberlain — Egotist or Visionary?

The standard biography of Joseph Chamberlain is that by J. L. Garvin, *The Life of Joseph Chamberlain*, vols. 1–3, 1836–1900 (London: Macmillan, 1935), with a continuation by J. Amery, vol. 4, 1901–3 (London: Macmillan, 1951). *Joseph Chamberlain, The Man and the Statesman* (London: Hutchinson, 1900) by N. Murrell Marris is much too flattering to its subject, but it does contain a good store of letters, speeches, and contemporary comment, often of unusual interest. Chamberlain's part in the Protectionist campaign cannot be soundly evaluated unless the economic background in Britain, Europe, and the United States is understood. There are several books which provide this information expertly. Those particularly recommended are the two books by W. Ashworth, *An Economic History of England 1870–1939* (London: Methuen, 1960) and *Short History of the International Economy since 1850*, 2nd ed. (London: Longmans, 1962); A. H. Imlah's *Economic Elements in the Pax Britannica* (Cambridge, Mass.: Harvard University Press, 1958); and Volume 3, *Machines and National Rivalries 1887–1914*, of Sir John Clapham's *An Economic History of Modern Britain* (London: Cambridge University Press, 1938).

8. The Condition of the People 1846–1900 — Progress or Poverty?

'The Condition of the People' is a wide-ranging title and, correspondingly, the general, political, social, and economic histories already mentioned are particularly valuable. The influence of religion and of the Industrial Revolution is skilfully and shrewdly described in *The Making of Victorian England* (London: Methuen, 1962) by G. Kitson Clark; this book, incidentally, also includes an opening chapter on the problems of writing history which should be prescribed reading for all historians, young or old. The statistical approach has considerable relevance to living conditions. *Abstract of British Historical Statistics* (London: Cambridge University Press, 1962) by B. R. Mitchell and P. Deane is an admirable compilation. There are two fascinating studies of urban development, *Victorian Suburb*, a study of the growth of Camberwell (Leicester University Press, 1961) by H. J. Dyos, and *Victorian Cities* (London: Odhams, 1964) by A. Briggs. Trade unionism has furnished subject matter for some bulky volumes. It is an important but not central issue in this chapter and as follow-up reading a lucid, simple, and sound account such as *A History of British Trade Unionism* (London: Macmillan, 1963) by H. Pelling best meets the needs of the situation. It contains a good bibliography of trade union history for those who wish to delve more deeply. Two works of fiction, Charles Dickens's *Hard Times* (1854) and Mrs Gaskell's *Mary Barton* (1848), though perhaps giving undue support to those who take a pessimistic view of the Industrial Revolution, help to bring home vividly the plight of those whose lives were warped by industrial advance.

9. Was There a Victorian Age?

The Victorian period is still new enough to excite emotional reactions; fortunately it has also attracted the interest of several historians of outstanding calibre whose knowledge and objectivity keep the issues in perspective. G. M. Young's *Victorian England: Portrait of an Age*, 2nd ed. (London: Oxford University Press, 1953) is a brilliant assessment. In parts it may flatter the reader with more knowledge than he possesses, but the writer maintains a momentum of interest which makes this occasional difficulty of little consequence. *The Age of Equipoise* (London: Allen & Unwin, 1964) by W. L. Burn is a thoroughly scholarly analysis of the mid-Victorian period. The author's diligent research is strongly in evidence and is a healthy corrective to vague speculations about the nature of Victorianism. A book with a very similar approach is that by O. Chadwick, *The Victorian Church, Part I* (London: Black, 1966), which seems certain to become the standard work on that important subject. G. Kitson Clark's scholarly study, *The Making of Victorian England* (London: Methuen, 1962), skilfully puts religious issues in their social context. The lengthy and absorbing biography by Lady Elizabeth Longford, *Victoria R.I.* (London: Weidenfeld & Nicolson, 1964) is likewise obligatory reading for those seeking a fuller understanding of the period. The Queen was more self-revealing as a letter writer than most. Her characteristic mental attitudes at her most formative stage emerge very clearly from a volume such as *Queen Victoria's Early Letters* (London: Batsford, 1963) edited by J. Raymond. For the reader who likes information to be well spiced with entertainment *The Victorians* (London: Cambridge University Press, 1966) by Joan Evans is a fascinating collection of contemporary comments on the social scene, and it has the further merit of being beautifully illustrated. The books so far mentioned are of course merely a starting-point for a detailed assessment of the Victorian period and others could well be added to the list. Nevertheless, collectively, they represent a powerful nucleus of knowledge. The works of the Victorian writers in prose and poetry provide another most useful source of evidence in assessing whether there was a Victorian Age with distinctive mental attributes of its own. A most useful list of many of these writers, including a note of the period when their literary powers were at their greatest, is to be found in G. M. Young's *Victorian England: Portrait of an Age.* No one, to my knowledge, has yet compiled an anthology of bad writing from the Victorian period; it would be a fascinating study and no less instructive about the nature of the age than orthodox selections of fine writing, but this must be left to the enterprise of the reader.

INDEX

Aberdeen, 4th Earl of, 74, 87
Afghanistan, 110, 125, 134–5, 150–1
Agriculture, in 1815, 15; riots of 1830,
  28–9, 35; Corn Law repeal, 54, 62–3;
  effects on, of Free Trade, 100, 116–
  17, 146; in 1850–1900, 192, 202, 207;
  Royal Commission on (1882), 202
Alabama, the, 80, 91, 109, 124
Albert, Prince, 80, 90, 91, 225, 234
Alsace-Lorraine, 109, 124
America, United States of, 70, 80,
  100, 109
American Civil War, 80, 90, 110, 113,
  119, 124, 199
Anti-Corn Law League, 51, 53, 55, 60,
  99, 100
Arabi Pasha, 110, 111, 125
Armenia, 139, 154
Army reforms, 102, 103, 121
Arnold, Matthew, 221, 222, 233
Artisans' Dwellings Act (1875), 143,
  148, 212
Austria-Hungary, the 1815 settle-
  ment, 22, 66; the Eastern Question,
  68, 71–2, 73, 77, 85, 136, 137, 138,
  152, 153, 154; Schleswig-Holstein,
  69, 81; 1848 Revolutions, 75–6;
  Italy, 76, 79–80, 90

Bagehot, Walter, 93, 129, 144, 221,
  225
Balkan Crisis (1875–8), 112, 136–41,
  152–5
Ballot Act (1872), 41, 102, 105, 120
Belgian rebellion (1830), 70–1, 72, 84
Bentham, Jeremy, 6, 31, 35, 47
Benthamism, 24, 31, 35, 39, 222
Berlin, Congress of (1878), 112, 125,
  138, 140–1, 150, 152
Berlin Memorandum, 137, 152–3
Berlin, Treaty of (1878), 153–5
Birmingham, 156–7, 158, 193, 200
Bismarck, Prince, 81, 92, 109, 112,
  115, 136
'Blanketeers', 9, 18, 19
Boers, 104, 110, 125, 133–4, 151–2,
  165, 166, 167, 168, 183–5
Bosnia, 136, 139, 152, 154
Brandreth, Jeremiah, 9

Bulgaria, 138–9, 140, 154
Bülow, Prince, 169, 181, 182, 183

Canning, George, 1, 13, 21, 22, 48, 67,
  68
Cardwell, Edward (afterwards Viscount), 103, 104, 121
Castlereagh, Viscount, 1, 13, 22
Catholic emancipation, 13, 22, 47, 48–
  50, 53, 58
Chadwick, Edwin, 24, 31, 35, 195,
  211, 212
Chamberlain, Joseph: career to 1880,
  156–9; failures, 159–60; weaknesses, 160–1; social reforms, 161–3;
  175–8; split with Gladstone, 164–5,
  178–80; policy towards the Boer
  states (1895–9), 165–8, 183–5;
  negotiations with Germany, 168–9,
  185–6; advocates imperial federation, 170; Tariff Reform, 171–3,
  180–3; hostile assessment, 173–4;
  political dominance, 175; favourable assessment, 186–7
China, 70, 74, 78, 79, 89
Cholera, 37, 143, 193–4, 195
Church attendance, census (1851),
  219, 220, 229
Civil Service reforms, 102, 104, 210–
  11
Cobbett, William, 18, 29, 42
Cobden–Chevalier Treaty (1860),
  99, 115
Condition of the People (1846–1900):
  statistical evidence, 189–90, 191–2,
  203–7, 209; urban living conditions,
  192–3, 207, 213–14; epidemics, 193–
  5; social legislation, 195–8, 210–13;
  working conditions, 197–8, 208–9;
  social insurance, 198; poverty, 199–
  200; emotional factors, 200–1;
  household management, 201–2;
  agriculture, 192, 202, 207; women
  in employment, 209–10
Congress System, 13, 82
Conservative Party: and Municipal
  Corporations Act, 36–7, 44; under
  Peel's leadership, 50–1, 52, 56, 57–8,
  59–60; under Disraeli's leadership,